GV
709.2
.G34

Galton, Lawrence.

Your child in sports

© THE BAKER & TAYLOR CO.

YOUR
CHILD
IN SPORTS

YOUR CHILD IN SPORTS

A COMPLETE GUIDE

By Lawrence Galton

Franklin Watts
New York/London/Toronto/Sydney
1980

Library of Congress Cataloging in Publication Data

Galton, Lawrence.
   Your child in sports.

   Includes index.
   1.   Sports for children.   I.   Title.
GV709.2.G34   796'.01'922   80-15787
ISBN 0-531-09928-8

CONTENTS

Preface   vii

PART I   Sports and the Child   1

CHAPTER 1   Values, Hazards, and Making the
              Most of Sports   3

CHAPTER 2   Who Should, and Who Should Not
              Participate   20

CHAPTER 3   Are There Any Special
              Values and Hazards for Girls?   33

CHAPTER 4   The Preadolescent Athlete   53

CHAPTER 5   Pluses and Minuses of School and
              Other Organized Athletics   69

CHAPTER 6   Athletes: Born or Made?   87

CHAPTER 7   Conditioning for Sports   93

CHAPTER 8   Nutrition for the Athlete:
              Fables and Facts   108

CHAPTER 9   Making Weight for Sports   129

CHAPTER 10   Drugs as Athletic Aids:
              Fact or Fiction?   141

v

CHAPTER 11   The Emergence of Sports Medicine   151
CHAPTER 12   Common Questions and Answers   161

PART II   Special Notes About Individual
             Sports   173

PART III   Common Athletic Injuries and
             Their Care   223

             Index   261

PREFACE

Sports can have much to offer youngsters—including many who might in the past have been considered physically unable to participate.

They can, provided they are played under suitable auspices, with reasonable safeguards, and are properly prepared for.

Sensitive parents and many children, as well—including some at quite young ages—have questions about many aspects of sports. This book is intended to answer those questions.

I hope that, concisely, clearly, and fully, it will provide information about:

● The benefits of sports in general and of individual sports in particular: baseball, basketball, football, soccer, biking, tennis, and more

● Sports that offer lifetime as well as immediate values

● The possible hazards of each sport

- What can be done to minimize hazards and prevent injuries; how parents can help; and how pre-conditioning and continued conditioning can help

- What constitutes good care for injuries when they do occur; and when medical help may not be needed and the kind of home care which may be suitable.

There is also much valuable, up-to-date and often surprising information on:

- Which children should and should not participate; specific disqualifying conditions (both temporary and permanent) for various sports; what conditions, previously considered disqualifying, have been found not to be

- Girls and sports, with old, unjustified beliefs replaced by facts on how well they really do, how much they benefit, and whether, indeed, they are more prone to injury than boys

- The good points and bad about school and other organized athletics; what concerned parents can do about the bad

- Nutrition for athletes: a hard look, in an area cluttered with myths, fads and fallacies, at what constitutes really good nutrition

- Do's and don'ts when kids have to "make weight"; gaining or losing in order to participate

- So-called "athletic aids"—steroids, stimulants and others: Do they do any real good, can they do harm, and how?

If this book serves its purpose well, it will be due to the invaluable help I have had from many sources. They include research reports appearing in many professional journals such as *The American Journal of Sports Medicine*, *The Physician and Sportsmedicine*, the *New England Journal of Medicine*, the *Journal of the American Medical Association*, *Pediatrics*, and others devoted to sports and the medical aspects of sports.

I am grateful to the many physicians, physiologists and others who have helped through interviews, responses to questionnaires, and correspondence. Space limitations prevent a complete listing here. However, many are named throughout the text.

I must, happily, acknowledge a special debt of gratitude to Dr. William A. Grana of the Department of Orthopaedic Surgery, Division of Sports Medicine, University of Oklahoma Health Sciences Center, Oklahoma City.

Lawrence Galton

PART I

SPORTS AND THE CHILD

CHAPTER 1

VALUES, HAZARDS, AND MAKING THE MOST OF SPORTS

It was a big game. The city sandlot baseball championship was hanging in the balance. Inning after inning, the eleven-year-old pitcher hurled as hard as he could. After the game, his arm was so sore he could scarcely straighten it.

When an orthopedist specializing in athletic injuries examined X rays of the boy's arm, he found what he expected: Excessive pitching in that game and other games, and in practice sessions as well—far too much pitching for an eleven-year-old—had injured one of the bones in his elbow. With treatment, it healed, but it took six months to do so.

The youngster is not alone. He is one of many sub-teen and early-teen youngsters who suffer what often is called "Little League elbow" (a misnomer, since the Little League urges limitations on the amount of pitching its young players do). Some of these kids, putting too much pressure on their immature bones, may, if treatment is delayed or neglected, suffer chronic arm trouble throughout life, or later develop arthritis.

Children *can* be hurt in sports, beyond minor injuries such as cuts, scrapes, and bruises. And probably no intelligent, sensitive, concerned parent doesn't ask the question: Are sports for a youngster worth the risk?

They certainly can be, but not always, and not automatically. It isn't likely that there ever will be a sport that doesn't entail some risk. But risks can be greatly minimized.

Sports have much to offer a child, especially if parents act to help make certain sports with long-lasting value are chosen and any relatively small risks involved are not needlessly exaggerated. We'll come back to this.

First, let's look at the potential values of sports for youngsters.

ON THE POSITIVE SIDE

"Sport," *Time* magazine declared recently in a cover story, "has always been one of the primary means of civilizing the human animal, of inculcating the character traits a society desires."

The magazine went on to note: "Wellington in his famous aphorism insisted that the Battle of Waterloo had been won on the playing fields of Eton. The lessons learned on the playing field are among the most basic: the setting of goals and joining with others to achieve them; an understanding of and respect for rules; the persistence to hone ability into skill, prowess into perfection. In games, children learn that success is possible and that failure can be overcome. Championships may be won; when lost, wait till next year. In practicing such skills as fielding a grounder and hitting a tennis ball, young athletes develop work patterns and attitudes that carry over into college, the marketplace, and all of life."

A little overenthusiastic? Perhaps.

But recently, *World Health*, a World Health Organization publication, stated, "Health and sport are closely linked, and physical exercise is every bit as important to the mind as it is to the body. There can be no doubt about it: sport offers the best antidote to the tensions and stress that are everyday hazards as our lives become ever more competitive. It offers a respite from our daily cares and contributes a vital element of balance and relaxation."

An early start in sports, provided it is the right kind of start, can be highly desirable. Properly approached, sports can help to develop both a healthy body for a youngster and a love for physical activity which will stand him or her in good stead for life.

There can be other dividends: acquisition of self-discipline and a positive attitude toward working hard to achieve one's goals, along with feelings of worthwhileness and self-confidence.

Sports can encourage a respect for meaningful authority and can teach a child the value and joy of cooperating and working with others toward a common goal.

And sports can and should be fun.

CHILDHOOD NEEDS

In recent years, we've been witnessing among American adults an almost incredible growth of appreciation of the values of exercise, sports, and physical fitness. Those values can apply to youngsters, and there is mounting evidence that they are necessary for children.

It has become evident that many adult health problems have their seeds in early life. Elevated blood pressure and elevated levels of blood fats, only very recently looked for in children, are being found in many at early ages.

By high school age, one or more of the conditions associated with heart disease in adults—high cholesterol, high blood pressure, or obesity—can be found in a startlingly high proportion of youngsters.

Studying 400 Michigan high school students, Prof. Thomas B. Gilliam of the University of Michigan department of physical education found close to 50 percent showing one or more of the heart disease risk factors. Prof. Gilliam, now engaged in a long-term study to determine how vigorous physical activity can help these youngsters, has already found significant reductions in blood fats occurring within twelve weeks.

Like adults, children can be subjected to stressful situations. Children, too, can become tense, anxious, and depressed. There is good reason to believe that if sports and efforts to achieve fitness can help overcome such problems in adults (and there has been much more study of adults than of youngsters) they can also be valuable for children.

Children could also benefit from many of the other values being enjoyed by adults.

RECENT RESEARCH FINDINGS

Here are some recent findings of studies concerned with determining the relationship between fitness (and the sports and physical activities that help to achieve it) and various aspects of mental and physical health.

Mental achievement. The President's Council on Physical Fitness and Sports publishes a *Research Digest* which contains results of research studies at many centers. One *Digest* considered the evidence from studies on the relationship between fitness and mental achievement. The conclusion: "More studies produced positive relationships between physical-motor traits and mental achievements than resulted in nil or negative results. It may be contended that a person's general learning potential for a given level of intelligence is increased or decreased in accordance with his or her degree of physical fitness."

To put that in less scientific terminology, it appears that whatever a person's intelligence level, ability to learn may be increased by physical fitness.

Emotional health. Many studies have established that vigorous physical activity is a good antidote, perhaps the best, for mental and emotional tension; that it is difficult, if not impossible, to remain tense during vigorous activity.

At the University of Southern California, Dr. Herbert de Vries compared the effects of exercise with those of tranquilizers. In someone who is tense and emotionally upset, almost invariably muscles become tense; so measuring the tension of muscles provides an effective, objective method of establishing a person's emotional state and changes in it. De Vries found that even as little exercise as a fifteen-minute walk is more relaxing than a tranquilizer.

The finding was not unexpected. Many years ago, Dr. Paul Dudley White, the distinguished heart specialist, observed: "It has been said that a five-mile walk will do more good to an unhappy but otherwise healthy man than all the medicine and psychology in the world. Certainly it is true that, in my own case, nervous stress and strain can be counteracted and even prevented by regular vigorous exercise. It is my strong belief that all healthy persons, male and female, should exercise regularly no matter what their ages."

A few years ago, deciding that he needed regular exercise, Dr. Thaddeus Kostrubala of Mercy Medical Center, San Diego, took up running. Before long, he had some of his psychiatric patients running along with him three times a week, an hour at a time. Changes in the patients, he has reported, were remarkable. Those with depression had fewer symptoms; a schizophrenic patient was taken off medication.

At the University of Wisconsin Medical School, psychiatrists and psychologists have reported finding that 30 to 45 minutes of jogging three times a week is at least as effective as talk therapy for the moderately depressed.

At the University of Arizona Medical School, Dr. William P. Morgan has found exercise to be effective in decreasing anxiety.

Fatigue control. Regular exercise contributes to overcoming excessive fatigue in several ways.

Physically, it helps by increasing coordination and efficiency of body movement and by enhancing muscular strength and endurance.

Fatigue, moreover, often involves psychological elements. According to Dr. Peter Karpovich, Professor of Physiology at Springfield College, the human body has the capacity to generate as much as fourteen horsepower with maximum effort, but generates only one-tenth horsepower at rest. In many of the sedentary, unused horsepower may go into building tension, with the tension then becoming a factor in fatigue, as well as other complaints. By counteracting tension, exercise tends to reduce undue fatigue.

The American Heart Association's Committee on Exercise reports that regular and vigorous activity enhances the quality of life by increasing the physical capacity for both work and play.

Sleep. At the State University of New York Downstate Medical Center in Brooklyn, Dr. Frederick Baekeland studied a group of college students accustomed to regular exercise. Baekeland scientifically monitored their sleep in a sleep laboratory during a period when they were engaging in their customary exercise, and again during a month-long period when all exercise was banned.

The subjects complained that they did not sleep as well during the month without exercise. The monitoring instruments also revealed a basic change in sleep patterns—less deep sleep, indicating anxiety—during the no-exercise month.

Evidence that the more a person exercises, the deeper he or she sleeps has also been demonstrated in studies by Dr. R. B. Zloty of the University of Manitoba, Canada, and Dr. Colin Shapiro of Johannesburg, South Africa.

Weight control. Excess weight is a major problem for a large proportion of American adults—and for many children.

Mounting evidence indicates that obesity in adulthood is closely related to excess weight in childhood and to living habits established in the early years.

What is the most common reason for excess weight? Surprisingly, both the Committee on Exercise and Physical Fitness of the American Medical Association and the President's Council on Physical Fitness and Sports report that lack of physical activity is more often the cause than overeating.

Many studies have compared food intake and activity patterns of obese people with those of normal weight at several age levels. In each instance, the obese were found to consume no more calories than their normal-weighted contemporaries, but were much less active.

Some of the most striking studies were done with schoolgirls by Dr. Jean Mayer and a group of Harvard Medical School investigators. When they compared food intake and activity schedules of obese and normal girls, they found that most of the obese girls actually ate less, not more, than the normal girls, but spent two-thirds less time in physical activity.

Mayer and his colleagues did a thorough analysis of a series of 29,000 short (three-second) motion pictures taken every three minutes of obese and normal girls engaged in various physical activities. They found that the amount of time spent in motion by the obese girls and the caloric cost of these motions were far less than for the nonobese. For example, in volleyball, girls of normal weight were motionless half the time, on the average, but obese girls stood still 85 percent of the time. In tennis, normal girls were motionless less than 15 percent of the time; obese girls, 60 percent.

There have been two widely held misconceptions about exercise and weight control. One is that excessive time and effort are required to use up enough calories to affect weight significantly. The other is that exercise is self-defeating, that it increases appetite and will therefore increase rather than decrease weight. But scientific studies have shown the falsity of both assumptions.

An average person will burn 2,400 to 4,500 calories a day, depending upon the amount and kind of exercise he or she gets. Active persons such as athletes, laborers, and soldiers in the field may consume as many as 6,000 calories a day and not gain weight.

In one study, university students increased daily food intake from 3,000 to 6,000 calories without gaining weight because they also stepped up their exercise each day.

To lose a pound of excess weight requires burning 3,500 calories. But it needn't be done all at once. If exercise is increased enough to use an extra 200 calories a day, that would come to 73,000 in a year, enough to lose twenty pounds.

Actually, some recent studies indicate that the effects of exercise continue beyond the time it is taken. During vigorous activity, body processes are stepped up; afterward, they are gradually lowered. Thus, energy use continues for a time after exercise is stopped.

As for the notion that exercise is useless because it increases appetite, the American Medical Association Committee and the President's Council advise: "It is true that a lean person in good condition may eat more following increased activity, but exercise will burn up the extra calories consumed. But the obese person does not react the same way. Only when an obese person exercises to excess will appetite increase. Because of the large stores of fat, moderate exercise does not stimulate appetite. The difference between the response to exercise of fat and lean people is important."

Exercise and the heart. A considerable body of evidence has accumulated on the value of exercise for the heart; for improving its efficiency and for helping to keep it free of disease which can lead to a heart attack.

Studies which began many years ago in Great Britain

and the United States have found that in various occupational groups almost twice as many heart attacks occur among sedentary office workers as among those whose jobs call for vigorous effort.

A government study which has been following more than 5,000 people in Framingham, Massachusetts, for more than twenty-five years has shown that the most sedentary persons have a death rate from heart disease five times greater than that of the most active.

Certain influences, called "risk factors," are known to make people prone to heart disease and heart attacks. Those factors include high blood pressure, high blood fat levels, sedentary living, stress, obesity, smoking, diabetes, and heredity. The presence of a single factor increases risk; several factors greatly increase the risk.

Physical activity, of course, counteracts the sedentary living factor. It can also help to overcome obesity or avoid it, and in doing that, it contributes to the avoidance or control of diabetes. In many diabetics, weight reduction may be all that is needed to bring blood sugar down to normal.

High blood pressure, which affects some 30 million Americans, including many children, is ranked as perhaps the single most important cause of death. It plays a role not only in heart disease but also in strokes and kidney failure. Physical activity is not a panacea for high blood pressure, but it does help to reduce it.

Activity also contributes significantly to controlling blood fat levels. For some years, studies have demonstrated that exercise helps to bring down high cholesterol levels. At Kent State University, for example, an investigation of the effects of a physical fitness program for sedentary people found that in every case blood cholesterol declined, with the greatest drop occurring in those with highest levels at the outset.

More recently, scientists have discovered the importance, in terms of cholesterol levels, of materials in the blood called *lipoproteins* which transport cholesterol.

Certain of these lipoproteins, called high density lipoproteins (HDLs) appear to have a protective effect. Their opposites, low density lipoproteins (LDLs), carry cholesterol to, and deposit it in the walls of arteries and other tissues. HDLs do the reverse: They remove cholesterol from areas where it is deposited and carry it to the liver for disposal.

According to recent studies at Stanford University and elsewhere, people engaging in vigorous physical activity have much higher levels of protective HDLs than do sedentary people.

Additionally, exercise strengthens the heart itself. The heart is a muscle and, like any other muscle in the body, becomes more efficient when it is exercised.

A trained athlete's heart grows larger because heart muscle fibers gradually enlarge, as those of the biceps in the arms do, when exercised. As the fibers enlarge, the pumping chambers within the heart enlarge and can hold and pump more blood.

As a result, when an athlete is resting, his heart, because of its increased capacity, need not pump as often as the heart of a sedentary person. This means greater rest for the heart through much of the day and night.

During vigorous activity, when more blood is needed throughout the body, an athlete's heart responds easily, contracting more completely with each beat to pump out more blood. The heart beat rate does not have to increase as much as it would have to in a sedentary person. And once the activity is over, the athlete's heart rate slows more rapidly than that of a sedentary individual.

A few years ago, the prowess of the Tarahumara Indians of Mexico became a subject of considerable scientific interest. The tribe has a favorite game of kick ball. Trained from childhood, male and female participants can run continuously for more than 100 miles at a speed of six to seven miles an hour while pursuing and kicking a wooden ball.

Heart specialists studied some of the runners. Their blood pressures—checked in the middle of a long kick ball race—had decreased during the game. Pulse rates rose to a range of 120 to 155. Average weight loss during the race was five pounds. Extensive tests after the race showed no abnormal changes of any kind. None of the tribe could recall a single instance of a runner dropping out of a race because of chest pain or shortness of breath.

One of the physician investigators, a professor of medicine and associate dean of the Universtiy of Oklahoma Medical Center, remarked: "These marathon demonstrations of really phenomenal endurance are convincing evidence that most of us, brought up in our comfortable and sedentary civilization, actually develop and use only a fraction of our potential heart reserve."

SPORT HAZARDS

What of sport hazards? Could they outweight the benefits?

Probably there is no completely safe sport, and if there were, it might not be much fun. Some sports involve more risk, more possibility of injury, than others. We will consider this in more detail later.

Overall, it has been estimated that sports-related injuries of one kind or another, major or minor, are sustained by more than 20 million Americans, young and old, each year.

But many, perhaps even most, of those injuries are not inherent in sports. They are largely needless and can be prevented in many ways. This is especially true in the case of children.

It's important to have some background about what has been happening in sports—and about how what has been happening has influenced the risks and even, sometimes, the values of sports.

Compared to the "good old days" of, say, fifty years ago, the range of scholastic sports is significantly wider today.

Once, school children had relatively few choices in sports. Boys played football in autumn, basketball in winter, and baseball or track in spring. Girls had even fewer opportunities. Youngsters developed their own games on the street, in the playground, or in the backyard.

Today, there are more than two dozen officially recognized interscholastic competitive sports for boys. They include archery, crew, pentathlon, table tennis, and weight lifting. An indication of the growth in sports can be found in Ohio, where, in 1971, there were ten officially recognized interscholastic sports for boys. Only three years later, the number had increased to thirteen. Nationally, the number of competitive sports for boys increased from 26 in 1971 to 32 in 1974, and there were four million participants in the latter year.

Even more striking has been the growth in sports activities for girls. In 1971, nationally, there were fourteen interscholastic sports available to girls, and 287,000 girls participating. Within the next three years, the number of sports increased to twenty-five, and the number of participants to 1,300,000—a 350 percent increase. The newer sports for girls included archery, badminton, baseball, fencing, ice hockey, lacrosse, riflery, and table tennis.

The popularity of the newer sports has been striking. Old favorites still remain: Basketball is number one for boys, followed by track and baseball; while basketball, volleyball, and track and field events still attract large numbers of girls.

But boys are showing more and more interest in cross-country sports, wrestling, swimming, tennis and ice hockey each year; and girls are increasingly keen about tennis and cross country.

These changes have been accompanied by others.

At a recent medical symposium, "The School-Age Athlete," Dr. Thomas E. Shaffer of Ohio State University noted: "Years ago, when organized athletics were limited to a few sports, when league championships were rare, and bowl contests were unheard of, one thing stood out—boys and girls played games to have fun. Competition was a kind of recreation and, if the rules had to be stretched a bit or improvised, it was still fun. As schools assumed more responsibility for supervising athletics, the atmosphere surrounding competitive sports slowly began to change, with the advent of coaches, interschool competition, and intensified community interest. Since the 1950s, pressures, at a low key initially, have been more and more evident and there has been less and less fun in the games."

These pressures have been of increasing concern to physicians and educators, and to parents aware of potential consequences. When organized sports are, in fact, overorganized and overemphasized, they can be far more hazardous than sports need be. With undue emphasis on winning, their values can be distorted or completely negated, while undesirable stress, both emotional and physical, is placed on the youngsters.

We'll deal with this subject in a later chapter.

There are hopeful indications of rebellion against such pressures, against the idea of youngsters going all out for winning.

In a recent poll of 2,000 high school students, 86% rated fun and enjoyment as their major objective in sports. More and more high school athletes have become critical of pressures from coaches and also, from many parents.

Some, like Dr. Shaffer, find it likely that the recent growth in sports options for youngsters may be the result of subtle efforts by the youngsters themselves to escape from traditional team sports in favor of more informal activities. These involve more one-to-one competition and less highly organized teamwork. They are activities which can have an important extra value in that they can be carried over to later life for fun, recreation, and fitness.

We need to take a whole new look at what sports are all about and what, in fact, they should be about.

This could lead to greater safety, as well as greater physical benefits.

SPORTS MEDICINE

The recent rapid growth of sports medicine as a specialty is also significant (Chapter 11). Sports medicine is developing several ways of minimizing the hazards of sports.

It is helping to improve standards for classifying sports according to physical requirements; for determining when children are ready for particular sports; for establishing how children with various handicaps can participate safely in some sports. It is investigating the adequacy of sports equipment and bringing (or beginning to bring) better insights to athletic coaches to help them to work more effectively with youngsters. And, of course, it is developing better methods of treating injuries that do occur.

Dr. John A. Bergfeld, the orthopedic surgeon who heads the sports medicine section of the world-famed Cleveland Clinic, has summed up the attitude of physicians in sports medicine as well as anyone: "My biggest concern is the overemphasis on winning," says Dr. Bergfeld. Such emphasis may be understandable in professional sports, he acknowledges, "but in high school or junior high school, it should be a game; youngsters should enjoy the sport."

Would a physician who has seen battered knees, shattered bones, and tortured muscles let his own children play competitive sports? The father of two young girls, Bergfeld says: "I think I would let my kids play any sport they wanted if I thought the coach was letting them play to enjoy the game, and not making it like a professional sport."

Dr. James A. Nicholas, another sports medicine physician, on the staffs of Cornell and New York Universities and founder of the Institute of Sports Medicine at Lenox Hill Hospital, New York City, is well aware of the hazards of children's sports. He is also aware of what can be done to help minimize those hazards and very much aware of the benefits.

"The dangers," he says, "are outweighed by the benefits. A child who likes sports is diverted from other activities that could be harmful to him, and he's also not wasting time. Sports teach discipline. The child learns to be part of a team, learns to accomplish, and learns the feeling of winning. Sports also create a relationship between youngsters and their parents that can be priceless."

But the most important advantage of sports may be expressed in what Dr. Fred Allman of Atlanta calls the "SAID principle." The initials stand for "specific adaptation to imposed demand." What it means is that when you impose a load on your body, the body responds to that demand. The stronger you become, the more force it takes to hurt you. The more flexible you become, the more your body can do in response to the load placed on it.

"If we don't let our kids play sports in order to train them," says Dr. Allman, "they are going to pay the penalty later in terms of cardiovascular disease, physical misfitness, and inability to tolerate loads and demands."

THE PRESCHOOL CHILD

To emphasize the value of physical activity, the American Academy of Pediatrics' Committee on Pediatric Aspects of Physical Fitness, Recreation, and Sports issued a statement on Fitness in the Preschool Child:

"Achieving fitness is a way of life, not a fad or a brief change in one's way of doing things. And, an early start is imperative. A flaw in our present system of health care is the emphasis on evaluation of anatomic or organic soundness and the presence or absence of disease—with less regard for the quality of physiologic function . . . An infant or child may well be regarded as healthy with the proper immunizations and absence of disease. But, is he or she able to meet daily tasks, recreational activities, and unforeseen emergencies with vigor and enthusiasm and without undue fatigue? Is he or she making adequate use of the musculoskeletal and cardiopulmonary systems?

". . . Two to six-year-old children like to run, jump, climb, and balance themselves. They enjoy dancing, they are fond of rhythmic play, and they can use a cycle. They experiment in using their muscles in constantly growing fields of activity. As children approach elementary school age, their social development leads to increased activity in play with other children.

"But, our present culture makes it difficult to maintain functional fitness. As children grow older, current sedentary life-styles tend to diminish opportunities for attaining physical fitness. Even preschool-age children use the many conveniences which eliminate physical effort.

"Physical education should be a unique opportunity for increasing fitness with all children involved in tasks and activities which challenge their musculoskeletal and cardiopulmonary systems. If activities such as swimming, skiing, skating, cycling, hiking, running, and group competitive games are routinely enjoyed during childhood, there will be a tendency to continue such activities later in life. Inquiry, observation, and discussion about exercise and suitable ways to do it should lead parents to a better understanding of their children's needs. The pediatrician can be an important force by helping to form attitudes and influencing courses of action."

The statement had more to say to pediatricians and, through them, to parents:

"An estimate of physical fitness is an essential component of a health appraisal whether it is a periodic examination of a well child, a preschool or precamp evaluation, or an evaluation to authorize participation in strenuous exercise. It is difficult to apply any of the recommended tests for evaluating fitness to infants and preschool children. However, the pediatrician can arrive at a reasonable estimate of fitness by specific questions about physical activity and by observing the child's strength, agility, coordination, and endurance throughout the interview and health examination.

"For example, asking if the infant pulls up to a standing position is routine in evaluating development. This activity also requires strength; and, if the question includes the length of time the infant can stand, endurance can be determined. Most pediatricians routinely ask if a young child can operate a tricycle or bicycle. But, also ask if he or she actually *does* it, *how often*, and for *how long*. 'Can he or she swim?' could be followed by, 'How often?' Also ask,

'How long does he or she play during waking hours?' Questions about fatigue, response to exercise, and motivation for strenuous activity all rightly belong in the health history."

The statement concludes:

"Pediatricians have an important and obligatory role in advising and motivating parents about fitness aspects of the young child's development. The health benefits and the satisfactions from exercise, strenuous activity, and attainment of physical fitness may be established early in life by encouraging attitudes and behavior which carry over into later childhood and adult life. Thus, getting places 'on your own,' using stairways instead of elevators, and physical play instead of sedentary recreation may lead to activities later which have beneficial effects on preventing obesity, lowering the incidence of coronary heart disease and atherosclerosis, and increasing cardiopulmonary efficiency as well as developing a joie de vivre."

CHAPTER 2

WHO SHOULD, AND WHO SHOULD NOT PARTICIPATE

Among participants in the 1976 Olympics at Montreal was a Russian girl, Tatiana Kazankina, who captured gold medals in both the 800- and 1,500-meter track events. Yet five years earlier, she suffered from heart trouble as the result of a severe influenza attack.

Not long ago, children with heart problems—or a considerable variety of other physical problems—were discouraged from taking part in virtually all vigorous physical activity and sports.

This is no longer the case. For solid scientific reasons, there has been a major change in the medical point of view, although not all parents may be aware of it.

More often than not, children with conditions which only a decade ago would have rendered them negligible for sports activities are now encouraged to participate.

As a report on "The Young Athlete" in the *Journal of School Health* pointed out:

"When there is a wide variety of sports available, with varying requirements of physical capability, it should be possible to recommend some kind of sports activity for almost every young person, regardless of physical condition.

"A medical examination of candidates for athletics," the report emphasized, "must not be the occasion for simply sorting the 'fit' from the 'unfit' and sending only the 'perfect physical specimens' into the sports program.

"Those making decisions about health qualifications for sports participants must be cognizant of the total variety of sports in the athletic program and also be familiar with the physical requirements for participation in each of them.

"If there really are valid reasons for restrictions from physical activity of any kind, they should always be clearly explained to the boy or girl, with enough time for planning to follow through with diagnostic evaluation and treatment for the individual who must stand aside."

There are, to be sure, some conditions that may bar engaging in vigorous sports—in some cases permanently, in others temporarily.

First, let's consider some of the health conditions about which there have been dramatic changes of medical viewpoint regarding sports participation.

HEART DISEASE

In April, 1977, the American Academy of Pediatrics, with the approval of the Academy's Council on Child Health, issued a formal policy statement on children with heart problems and their participation in sports.

Does a child have a heart murmur? A heart murmur, the statement noted, may be audible in any child at some time during youth and some investigators have found that about 85 percent of all children have audible murmurs. So if a murmur is found, an effort should be made to see if it really means anything. There can be insignificant abnormalities associated with even loud murmurs and significant abnormalities with soft murmurs. Yet neither necessarily indicates a real problem.

When an abnormality is suspected, the child should have a chest X ray and an electrocardiogram, and if these are normal, there is little likelihood that a limiting cardiovascular defect exists. But if a physician continues to have doubts, he should request further study by a qualified heart specialist with experience in treating youngsters with heart problems.

The statement adds: "Many youths with congenital and rheumatic heart defects which do not cause hemodynamic (blood flow) impairment are capable of full, active interscholastic competition."

What about the child with high blood pressure? If the elevation is mild, the statement emphasizes, "limitation of sports participation is not warranted . . . As a matter of fact, studies in adults have shown that there is a lowering of blood pressure associated with increased cardiovascular fitness induced by moderate to intense aerobic exercises."

The statement does suggest that certain sports might better be avoided. "The child with mild to moderate hypertension should probably not be allowed to participate in activities which are primarily isometric, such as weight lifting, since sustained isometric exercise produces a marked increase in blood pressure."

And what of the child who has an abnormal heart rhythm? Here again, there should be no automatic proscription of sports. As the statement notes, a large proportion of abnormal rhythms in children are benign. Many disappear with mild exercise, and some that do not disappear then, do vanish with even more intense activity.

The official statement concludes:

"In general, one should allow the young individual to achieve maximum exertion and, whenever possible, allow participation rather than to arbitrarily impose restrictions which might predispose to all of the problems attendant with 'cardiac crippling.'

"It is likely that psychologic harm due to limitation of activities far outweighs the risks from leniency in permitting participation. We, therefore, advise a consultation with a cardiologist familiar with the problems of children and youths prior to (a child) being completely excluded from competition."

ASTHMA

In 1977, the American Medical Association's Committee on the Medical Aspects of Sports, in a publication, *The Asthmatic Athlete*, examined old, needless restrictions on asthmatic youngsters.

"For too long," the Committee reported, "children with asthma have been automatically excluded and discouraged from participating in vigorous physical education, intramural recreation and sports programs.

"Such restrictions have resulted from *erroneous* [the emphasis is the Committee's] fears that the exertion required for physical activity might contribute to the severity of the condition. Because of such limitations, asthmatic children have often developed patterns to suppress physical activity.

"This has deprived them of the initiative and confidence so that their participation in, and contributions to, society have been less than optimal. However, more limiting than asthma itself, have been restrictions imposed on asthmatic children by overindulging and overprotecting parents, insufficient medical management, and misinformed physical educators and coaches.

"Sufficient evidence," the Committee went on, "has been acquired to warrant reexamination of previous positions taken regarding activity of asthmatic children. With proper medical management, the majority of asthmatic children can participate in physical activities.

"Total exclusion should be infrequent, and partial restriction of quantity or type of sports activity used only in severe cases. During physical activity, attacks necessitating total withdrawal are a rare occurrence.

"Asthma need not be a barrier to active participation in school physical education, intramural recreation or sports programs. The athletic accomplishments of asthmatics Rick DeMont, Janet Lynn, and Jim Ryun attest to this fact."

In some asthmatics, exercise can induce increased airway obstruction. This may occur during prolonged activity, or five to twenty minutes after a short period of strenuous exertion.

Yet, in youngsters who do experience exercise-induced asthma, the Committee notes, a period of warm-up can significantly reduce the problem. Various asthma medications are also available to help. Drugs such as theophylline are effective in decreasing exercise bronchospasm thirty to sixty minutes after being taken orally. Combinations of theophylline and ephedrine are also effective when taken thirty to sixty minutes before exertion.

Cromolyn sodium may be especially valuable. If inhaled five to sixty minutes before physical exertion, it diminishes exercise-induced asthma in most cases. The drug is usually well tolerated and easily administered—and it is acceptable in international athletic competition. It has been effective for Olympic athletes. It is useful for patients who do not tolerate theophylline or ephedrine, and may provide added benefits to those receiving theophylline for their asthma.

Asthmatic youngsters, the Committee reports, should be encouraged to participate in a wide range of physical activities with nonasthmatic peers.

There are some asthmatic children and adolescents who avoid physical activities because exercise-induced asthma makes them unable to compete on equal terms with their normal peers. For them, swimming is a sport which provokes less asthma than comparable exertion in running or cycling. But the Committee goes on to emphasize: "Asthmatics can also excel in such sports as track, soccer, or basketball with appropriate pharmacologic (drug) management."

EPILEPSY

This is another affliction which once ruled out participation in sports. But no more. There has been an evolutionary change in medical opinion regarding epilepsy.

It was not until 1968, after long consideration of the mounting evidence in favor of allowing and even encouraging vigorous activity for epileptic patients, that the American Medical Association's Committee on the Medical Aspects of Sports concluded that those whose seizures were under reasonable control "should be encouraged to participate in... any sports of interest with the exception of boxing, tackle football, ice hockey, diving, soccer, rugby, lacrosse and other activities where chronic recurrent head trauma may occur."

Between 1969 and 1974, studies appeared which indicated that these restrictions were needless. In August 1974, the Committee revoked its prohibition against collision sports and stated that "there is ample evidence to show that patients will not be affected adversely by indulging in any sports, including football."

Perhaps one of the physicians most experienced in the field of epilepsy is Dr. Samuel Livingston of Baltimore, a consultant to the American Medical Association. He has had forty-one years of experience with treating epilepsy in many thousands of patients, including children and adults who have participated in competitive athletics.

Recently in a special guest editorial in *American Family Physician*, the official organ of the American Academy of Family Practice, Dr. Livingston had this message for physicians which will be helpful for many parents:

"The athletic privileges of young epileptics," he noted, "are often restricted by parents because of fear that injury 'might make the epilepsy worse,' or that resultant fatigue might precipitate seizures, or both. In many cases, parents of a child who has had only an occasional seizure consider him to be as ill as if he had active tuberculosis or acute rheumatic fever, and compel him to rest and take daily afternoon naps.

"These attitudes should be discouraged since they are medically unsound and often do the patient more harm than good. Parents should be instructed to allow the child to play and conduct himself in the same manner as his nonepileptic associates.

"Contrary to popular belief," Dr. Livingston emphasized, "physical activity favorably affects an epileptic disorder in most instances. It is generally agreed that patients have fewer seizures when they are engaged in normal physical activities than when they are idle or resting . . .

"Many of my patients had been instructed by their previous physicians not to participate in any of the physical activities that are usual for their age groups. Except for patients who have frequent seizures, there is generally no valid reason for such an edict. The vast majority of epileptics can participate in all recreational activities without any significant risk of injury to themselves or to others.

"Sports such as football and lacrosse are not prohibited in most cases. Patients who are still having seizures should not ride horseback or climb to heights. Swimming in pools should be allowed under supervised circumstances, such as the presence of a lifeguard or a competent swimming companion. However, deep diving is not advisable because of the obvious complications associated with the occurrence of a seizure far below the surface of the water."

Dr. Livingston would have parents of epileptic children earnestly consider:

". . . that there is a small, calculated risk of injury when they permit their child to participate freely in all normal childhood activities, including collision and contact sports. However, they must weigh this against the greater risk of instilling attitudes of inferiority and of being 'different,' which could handicap the child more severely and more surely than the convulsions themselves. I emphasize that the most serious hazard of epilepsy is often not the seizures per se but the associated emotional aberrations that are prone to develop in patients with this disorder.

"When restrictions on participation in customary activities are imposed on children, they quickly gain the impression that they are 'not the same' as others. Many patients currently under my care suffered severe emotional disturbances when their personal physician or their parents prohibited them from participating in sports. If the epileptic disorder is so severe that the child cannot compete physically with his peers, parents should encourage (but not force) hobbies such as music, photography or stamp collecting."

SKELETAL ABNORMALITIES

Here is still another major area in which there have been significant changes in medical attitudes.

A few years ago, a Joint Committee on Physical Fitness, Recreation and Sports Medicine of the American Academy of Pediatrics considered the possibilities in sports for children with various skeletal abnormalities.

What, if any, sports activities might be permissible in youngsters with rheumatoid arthritis, histories of congenital subluxation (partial dislocation) of the hip, spondylolisthesis (forward displacement of vertebrae in the spinal column), and such bone disorders as Osgood-Schlatter's disease and Legg-Perthes disease?

The Committee consulted with orthopedic experts. Recommendations were sought for children with the various skeletal conditions in terms of the various types of athletic competition—mild, moderate, vigorous—that might be suitable for them.

Sports were categorized as follows:

Mild: walking, bicycle riding, jogging

Moderate: tennis, roller skating, ice skating, baseball, volleyball, swimming

Vigorous: football, skiing, soccer

These were the recommendations, carefully arrived at:

Osgood-Schlatter's disease: Boys should be allowed to take part in vigorous athletic competition up to their pain tolerance. Generally, if the condition is acute, that means mild competition or none; if chronic, mild or moderate activity.

Spondylolisthesis: If there are no symptoms, moderate or vigorous activity can be permitted. If symptoms are present, the child should be treated, usually with a back support and corrective exercises—and if treatment eliminates symptoms, he may be allowed to play football or basketball while wearing the support.

Congenital subluxation of the hip, Legg-Perthes disease, or slipped femoral epiphysis: For children with any of these conditions, the recommendations are generally the same. With mild deformity of the femoral head (head of the thigh bone): moderate to vigorous, preferably non-contact competition. With moderate deformity: mild to moderate activities. With severe deformity: mild activities or none.

Rheumatoid arthritis: If the disease is quiescent and there has been complete recovery of function: moderate to vigorous activity. If the disease is quiescent, with minimal or moderate crippling: mild to moderate activity (especially ice skating or swimming). If functional recovery is complete but the child is still on aspirin or similar treatment: mild to moderate activity.

The Committee report emphasized, "A child should be allowed to participate in formal and informal athletic activities with children of his own age, according to his abilities and interests.

"Any action that keeps a child from full participation with his peers should be considered carefully because it may affect his physical, social, and emotional development and may decrease his self-esteem and self-confidence.

"If restrictions are necessary, the reason should be explained as clearly and reassuringly as possible. The duration of the restriction should be spelled out whenever possible, and substitute activities should be proposed to keep the child involved with his peers in group activities which offer some competition, excitement, or potential for muscle building or development of coordination."

MENTAL RETARDATION

Children who are mentally retarded need suitable physical activity and too often are not getting it. A few years ago, the American Academy of Pediatrics took official cognizance of the problem. The Academy noted that:

• Very often, mentally retarded children are not physically fit, have poor coordination, and are obese; and these conditions become progressively more severe as the retarded child grows older, partly as a result of limited opportunity for athletic activity.

• There is a tendency for parents and children in most communities to exclude the mentally retarded child, so he completely lacks the type of exercise and personal experiences he needs.

• The majority of mentally retarded children can and should participate safely and productively in athletic activities when appropriate supervision is provided.

• Parents of children who are mentally retarded are often confused and uncertain about what to expect from their child. Some tend to restrict their youngsters from physical activities and others may push them at too rapid a pace.

• Most parents are anxious for guidance and the pediatrician can and should advise them.

• In developing a program for retarded children, it is important to distinguish between individual and team sports and competitive and noncompetitive activities.

• Mentally retarded children usually are more successful in individual and dual sports instead of team sports. Activities that require gross rather than fine motor coordination can be stressed.

• Competition is often highly motivating and may promote self-satisfaction, muscle development, and coordination. The Special Olympics has shown how well retarded children can compete against each other. Regardless of intellectual capacity, there is a wide range of athletic ability; some children are remarkably well and others very poorly coordinated.

• Competition with children who are not retarded may be appropriate for some mildly or moderately retarded children but it will mean repeated failure for most unless all competitors are well-matched. If a child continuously fails, his self-image may be damaged instead of supported by athletic activity. Nevertheless, there are mutual benefits when retarded children engage in noncompetitive sports with children of normal intelligence.

And the Academy goes on to underscore the following:

"Every retarded child needs a continuing program of physical maintenance with regular exercising and supervised athletic activities. If he is not able to participate in basketball, football, or baseball, he may be able to compete in track and field events or in the basic skills such as throwing baskets, kicking, or playing catch. Swimming, hiking, camping, archery, soccer, trampoline jumping, tennis, bicycling, folk dancing, and boating are examples of athletic activities that can give a retarded youngster the satisfaction, the sense of participation, the social contacts, and the physical exercise that can be profitable for him."

The U. S. Department of Health, Education and Welfare Bureau of Education for the Handicapped, Washington, D. C., and the Information and Research Utilization Center in Physical Education and Recreation for the Handicapped (c/o American Alliance for Health, Physical Education & Recreation, 1201-16th St., N.W., Washington, D. C. 20036) have information about planning physical education and recreation programs for the mentally retarded and handicapped. Information about specific model programs, such as the Special Olympics Program, is provided by The Kennedy Foundation, 719-13th St., N. W., Washington, D.C. 20005.

DISQUALIFYING CONDITIONS FOR SPORTS

Under some conditions of illness, it may be unwise to participate in sports; under others, it may be okay to engage in one kind but not in another.

The American Medical Association's Committee on the Medical Aspects of Sports has developed guidelines. The Committee has classified sports in four categories:

Collision: Football, rugby, hockey, lacrosse, etc.

Contact: Baseball, soccer, basketball, wrestling, etc.

Noncontact: Cross-country track, tennis, crew, swimming, etc.

Other: Bowling, golf, archery, field events, etc.

Except for findings by physicians indicating otherwise in individual cases, the Committee has these suggestions:

No sports at all if, and as long as, there is an acute infection (respiratory, genitourinary, infectious mononucleosis, hepatitis, active rheumatic fever, active tuberculosis); inadequately controlled diabetes; jaundice; severe pulmonary insufficiency; kidney disease; severe cardiovascular problems such as mitral or aortic stenosis, aortic insufficiency, coarctation of the aorta, severe heart disease, high blood pressure of the relatively rare kind from a physical cause; symptomatic musculoskeletal abnormalities or inflammations.

On the other hand, no type of sport is necessarily barred—if diabetes is controlled; if, after previous heart surgery, physician and operating surgeon judge the child fit; if epilepsy is controlled.

All but "other" sports are advised against in case of

serious bleeding tendencies such as in hemophilia and purpura; inguinal or femoral hernia; functional inadequacy of the musculoskeletal system; a convulsive disorder not well controlled by medication.

Only noncontact and "other" sports are advised for anyone with: only one functioning eye; an enlarged liver; skin problems such as boils or impetigo; an enlarged spleen; absence of one kidney; previous head surgery.

Collision sports are advised against in case of history or symptoms of previous severe head injury or repeated concussions.

GETTING WORTHWHILE ADVICE

As we have noted, there have been marked changes—and, with good reason, thanks to scientific studies which have replaced old theoretical concepts—in medical attitudes toward the participation in sports of children with many adverse health conditions or handicaps. With further studies, there are likely to be still more changes.

Those studies have been and are being stimulated by the increasing recognition of the value of vigorous activity and sports.

Certainly, if you're the parent of a child with a health problem or handicap, you need medical advice about sports participation. But it should be informed medical advice— from a physician not content with lazily "playing it safe" and consigning a child, almost automatically, to a "no play" category.

If necessary, before barring your child from sports participation that could be valuable to him or her and that might well be safer than once was believed, you may be well advised to seek another medical opinion—possibly from a cardiologist, orthopedist, or other specialist with interest and training in sports medicine.

CHAPTER 3

ARE THERE ANY SPECIAL VALUES AND HAZARDS FOR GIRLS?

"Steve Sweeney paces the sidelines, shoulders hunched against the elements. A steady downpour has turned an Atlanta soccer field into a grassy bog. A few yards away, his team of 8- and 9-year-olds, sporting regulation shirts and shorts, churns after the skittering ball. One minute, all is professional intensity as the players struggle to start a play. The next, there is childhood glee in splashing through a huge puddle that has formed in front of one goal. Sweeney squints at his charges and shouts, "Girls, you gotta pass! *Come on, Heather!*

"At eight, Kim Edwards is in the incubator of the national pastime—tee ball. There are no pitchers in this pre-Little League league. The ball is placed on a waist-high, adjustable tee, and for five innings the kids whack away. Kim is one of the hottest tee ball players in Dayton and a fanatical follower of the Cincinnati Reds. Her position is second base. She pulls a Reds cap down over her hair, punches her glove, drops her red-jacketed arms down to rest on red pants, and waits for the action. Kim

has but a single ambition: to play for her beloved Reds.
When a male onlooker points out that no woman has ever
played big league baseball, Kim's face, a mass of
strawberry freckles, is a study in defiant dismissal: 'So?'"

So, not long ago, one national newsmagazine ran a cover
story called "Comes the Revolution." In that story, *Time*
noted:

> "On athletic fields and playgrounds and in parks and
> gymnasiums across the country, a new player has joined
> the grand game that is sporting competition, and she's a
> girl. As the long summer begins, not only is she learning
> to hit a two-fisted backhand like Chris Evert's and turn a
> back flip like Olga Korbut's, she is also learning to jam a
> hitter with a fastball. Season by season, whether age six,
> sixty or beyond, she is running, jumping, hitting, and
> throwing as U. S. women have never done before. She is
> trying everything from jogging to ice hockey, lacrosse, and
> rugby, and in the process acquiring a new sense of self, and
> of self-confidence in her physical abilities and her potential.
> She is leading a revolution that is one of the most important in
> the history of sport."

from *Time*, June 26, 1978

It is, indeed, a sizable revolution. In just the period from
1971 to 1976, the number of high school girls active in sports
shot up from 294,000 to 1,645,000 and the number of girls'
teams from 15,000 to 70,000.

Since 1971, the number of colleges offering athletics
to women has increased from 280 to 825 and the number
of teams from 1,831 to 4,797. In 1974, only 60 colleges
offered athletic scholarships to women; more recently, more
than 500 did. It's now estimated that more than 100,000
women are taking part in intercollegiate sports compared
with 170,000 men; and in 1977 about 10,000 girls from 460

schools received scholarships worth more than $7 million.

It was only in 1971–72 that the Association for Intercollegiate Athletics for Women—the female counterpart of the National Collegiate Athletic Association—was formed. It now has 825 member schools, 115 more than the 73-year-old NCAA.

In 1972, the first all-women minimarathon in New York's Central Park attracted only 78 entries. In 1978, 4,360 competitors entered the 6.2-mile (10,000-meter) race.

INFLUENCES

Until quite recently, only when they were very young did girls have a brief period of grace—a time when, even though they were often labeled "tomboys," they were allowed to play second base or whatever. After that, social pressure virtually forced most girls to withdraw from athletics.

Now, spurred by increasing recognition of the importance of fitness for girls as well as boys, helped by the feminist movement and also by legislative mandates and court rulings, girls are moving from the sidelines onto the field. They are playing for themselves, not just cheering for the boys.

Considerable impetus has come from one federal legislative mandate. In 1972, Congress passed the Education Amendments Act containing a section, Title IX, which forbids sex discrimination in any educational institution receiving federal funds. The prohibition applies to the athletic field as well as classroom. Almost all colleges and public schools get federal money of some kind—and, to enforce Title IX, Congress endowed the Department of Health, Education and Welfare with a powerful weapon: the right to deny federal funds to any institution not measuring up.

While Title IX has forced some schools to upgrade their programs for girls, thousands of elementary and secondary schools, acting on their own, have been improving their programs.

Medicine, too, has been making an important contribution to furthering the participation of girls in sports—with safety.

In 1975, the American Academy of Pediatrics noted that "until recently, girls and women have been deprived of their rightful share in physical recreation and sports by traditional concepts about a socially acceptable feminine image, misconceptions about the extent to which females may safely participate in strenuous activity, and, in fact, society's whole previous notion about woman's role and her basic needs and her physical capabilities."

Girls, the Academy observed, should, of course, have the same safeguards for protecting health and safety as boys in sports and competitive athletics. That means competent medical care before, during and after participation, good conditioning, suitable high-quality equipment, good playing facilities and competent coaching.

To help physicians involved in deciding about participation by girls and young women, the Academy offered a series of simple guidelines:

• There is no reason, before puberty, to separate children by sex in sports, physical education, and recreational activities.

• Girls can compete against boys in any sport if suitably matched for size, weight, degree of physical maturation, and skill.

• Not only can girls achieve high levels of physical fitness through strenuous conditioning, improving their agility, strength, endurance, appearance and sense of psychic well-being; it is also a fact that such activity has no unfavorable influence on menstruation, future pregnancy, and childbirth.

• After puberty, girls should not participate against boys in heavy collision sports because of the serious risk of significant injury due to their lesser muscle mass per unit of body weight.

●   The talented female athlete may participate on a team with boys in an appropriate sport provided that the school or community offers opportunities for all girls to participate in comparable activities.

The Academy went on to emphasize this point: "The best interests of girls and women in sports activities are served by opportunities to experience the thrill of sports competition when they are able to qualify for girls' programs sponsored just for them. Ultimate benefits are greater when efforts are directed to developing girls' programs and the athletes within them, rather than emphasizing the exceptional female athlete who may wish to participate with boys on their teams."

GIRLS' ABILITIES VS. BOYS'

When it comes to athletics, are girls genetically inferior to boys? Are their physical and physiological characteristics so different that there must be a marked difference in athletic ability?

If you examine older record books, you might think so. They suggest that in almost all athletic events, females perform at much lower levels than their male counterparts.

Even as recently as 1974, world records showed that males were 11.1 percent faster in the 100-yard dash; they jumped almost 20 percent higher in the high jump; they ran 14 percent faster in the mile; and they swam 7.3 percent faster in the 400-meter freestyle. But consider what has been happening more recently.

Perhaps the most dramatic gains in female performance have been in swimming. Currently, almost all world-class women competitors routinely break records of men set only a few years ago.

The record for the Olympic 400-meter freestyle of 5:04.2 minutes set by Johnny Weissmuller back in 1924 has, of course, been broken since by many men. In 1976, when Petra Thumer of East Germany swam the distance in 4:09.8 minutes, she came close to the men's 1968 record.

In long-distance swimming, women now hold most of the records. When Diana Nyad swam around Manhattan Island, she beat the best men's time by about two hours.

Track record gaps also have been declining. Women's shot put distances have increased faster than men's. In many other athletic events, women's achievements are rapidly approaching those of men.

Clearly, part of the explanation for male domination of most sports lies in the fact that, because of cultural influences, girls and women have been participating for only a relatively short time and have been trained less effectively. Evidence for this comes from a study by Dr. K. F. Dyer of the Department of Genetics of the University of Adelaide, Australia.

Dyer has found that the differences between male and female performances, as measured by world records, have been declining, for example, in all track events—and most rapidly in those events in which differences have been greatest.

Moreover, analyses of national track records for the same events show considerable variation between countries in average male/female differentials. For the 1,500 meter event, for example, the gap in the records ranges from 10.84 percent in the Soviet Union to 22.47 percent in France.

In swimming events, the national women's records in Australia, East Germany and Italy exceed the same-year male records in at least one other of the countries Dyer studied, which included the United States, Canada, and the European nations.

To Dr. Dyer, it seems evident that social factors such as differing degrees of encouragement and differing levels of expectation play an important role in limiting female athletic performance.

There have been suggestions that another reason why males and females perform unequally in various sports may be that the requirements of the sports better suit the build of the male than of the female who, on average, has a wider pelvis, lower center of gravity, shorter stride, and higher fat content. It has also been suggested that the prominent sports have been biased to accommodate male aptitudes.

It may seem ridiculous now, but consider this newspaper article which appeared in the Jacksonville, Florida, *Union Times* on the subject of tennis and the female:

"The first difficulty," it declared, "is found in grasping the racquet. This is due to the fact that in the female hand a layer of adipose tissue makes the palm too rounded to hold the racquet firmly."

The article went on to note that "the female arm differs from the male arm, also, in that the ulna of the female is much shorter proportionately than that of the male. On this account the female cannot hold the racquet on a line with the arm . . . when the ball is returned the action of the arm tends to knock it sidewise."

Moreover, "the articulation of the humerus with the ulna and the radius is imperfect . . . when, therefore, the racquet hits a ball, it tends to knock it high up in the air. Some have said that this defect is the chief one in causing the female to be a poor tennis player. The smallness of her ribs, the thinness of the scapula, and the shortness of the clavicle unite to prevent her from reaching high balls."

Then, in a generous conclusion, the article allowed that the female would surely surpass the male at tennis if it were not for all these anatomical peculiarities—"but the scientific fact remains that tennis is not a game for the human female."

That article appeared in 1883. Thanks to X rays and studies which have provided better knowledge of human anatomy—as well as Billie Jean King, Chris Evert, and others—what was supposed to be "scientific fact" a century ago is hardly held to be so today.

Many old assumptions, long taken for absolute truths about inherent male/female differences related to sports, are being challenged today.

Are women and girls handicapped because they don't

have the strength of males? In one study of several thousand subjects in Tecumseh, Michigan, the average man in his late twenties was found to have more than twice the arm strength of a woman the same age.

But many investigators believe that the difference may be due to no small extent to social influences which have encouraged the average male to be more active than the average female. They are convinced that these influences may be so great that any inherent physiological differences in strength cannot yet be estimated.

Some support for this comes from studies of increased ability with training. In one study, for example, after college men and women were given ten weeks of weight training, the women were found to have increased their leg strength 29.5 percent; the men, 26 percent. There was even a greater difference in the effect of the training on arm and shoulder strength which increased 28.6 percent in the women, 16.5 percent in the men.

As one of the study directors observed, "This is probably due to the fact that, in daily life, most women make relatively little use of their upper bodies, but even the most unathletic woman exercises her lower body almost as frequently as a man: walking, climbing stairs, bicycling."

Such findings have led Dr. Jack H. Wilmore of the University of Arizona Department of Physical Education to theorize that "the female has the same potential for strength development as the male of comparable size."

A LOOK AT SIMILARITIES AND DIFFERENCES

It may be worthwhile here to consider some specific similarities and differences in males and females in various areas influencing athletic performance. These are based on the reports of many investigators and a review paper prepared by Dr. Wilmore for the *Journal of School Health*.

Body build. Up to about the age of twelve to thirteen, average boys and girls differ little in either height or weight. This is due to the earlier maturation of girls. In the eight-to-twelve age group, girls are about two years ahead of boys in physical, bone, and hormonal development. In this age group, the mean height and weight for females is equal to or greater than that of males. Only in the thirteenth or fourteenth year does the average male undergo sexual development with associated growth spurt; and not until this age does the male surpass the female, on the average, in height, weight and muscular development.

With maturity, the average female is five inches shorter than the average male, and thirty to forty pounds lighter in weight. She is also forty to fifty pounds lighter in lean body weight while having 25 percent relative body fat compared to the male's 15 percent.

Girth measurements are much the same for the two sexes at the abdomen, hips and thigh—but, at maturity, the male, as compared to the female, has broader shoulders and greater chest relative to body size.

In both males and females, both types of sex hormones—androgen and estrogen—are secreted. The higher level of androgen in males is responsible for greater lean body weight, and the higher level of estrogen in the female for the greater amount of fat weight.

Yet it is still not clear whether all of these differences are entirely biological or genetic, or whether cultural and environmental factors may have some influence.

Strength. The average male is stronger than the average female. Several studies have found that, on average, men are about thirty to forty percent stronger than women. At younger ages, from seven to seventeen, the differences are far less, but even so, the female does not have the same level of strength as the male—or, at least, does not exhibit it.

Yet many studies have indicated that the female has

the potential to develop much higher levels of strength than those found in typically sedentary females. Such studies show that weight training in both adolescent and college-age women can lead to marked increases in strength. We mentioned one study earlier. In another, a group of female track and field athletes who completed a six-month weight-training program, had bench press strengths ranging up to 187 pounds and leg press strengths as high as 567 pounds—values far higher than for untrained males of similar age.

Cardiovascular endurance. In the early years, the endurance capacity of females is much the same as for males. It falls off rapidly later. But recent studies indicate that female endurance at ages beyond ten need not be reduced nor be markedly below that of males of similar age levels.

A measurement known as maximal oxygen uptake is considered to be the best single index of cardiovascular endurance capacity.

In one study of that capacity in highly trained female athletes, the average maximum oxygen uptake value was 59.1—much higher than the values for average males or females of similar age. And some of the best female athletes averaged 67.4, only 4.1 percent less than the average value for ten nationally ranked male marathon runners of the same age.

Motor skills and athletic ability. Except for a single activity—throwing a softball for distance—boys and girls are much alike in their performance of physical activities up to the age of ten to twelve. Various tests of specific motor skills and of general athletic ability show few differences during those early years.

In tests of running speed, for example, boys and girls do equally well between the ages of six to twelve.

After age twelve, however, boys become more proficient in almost all motor skills.

But is this inevitable?

The softball throw is worth looking into. Interestingly, girls lag behind boys in this activity at all age levels, throwing only half the distance of boys.

But two investigators decided to study possible reasons why. They theorized that girls might not do as well because of insufficient practice and experience. They worked with 200 girls and boys, aged three to twenty, setting them to throwing softballs for distance with both dominant and non-dominant arms.

While boys clearly outdistanced girls when throwing with the dominant arm, there was no difference at all between boys and girls for the nondominant arm up to the age of ten to twelve.

The investigators suggest that when the influence of practice and experience was eliminated by use of the non-dominant arm, throwing capacity was equal between the sexes.

Is the female outperformed by the male in almost all sports? Yes—but.

The difference between the two sexes is obvious when it comes to something like the shot put, which requires a considerable level of upper body strength. Females use a shot which is 55 percent lighter, yet the world record for the female is still about 1.5 feet shorter in distance than for the male.

But, as Dr. Wilmore points out, in distance swimming the gap between the sexes is narrowing, "and there are indications that this is also true for other events and for other sports. Unfortunately, it is difficult to make valid comparisons since the degree to which the sport, activity or event has been emphasized is not constant, and factors such as coaching, facilities, and training techniques have differed considerably between the sexes over the years. While the performance gap appears to be closing, it is far too early to predict whether it will ever close completely for any or all sports."

Other factors. Other factors that can influence athletic ability are more difficult to define and compare than those already mentioned.

Consider balance, for example. If you measure it by skill in standing on one foot, or walking on a narrow beam, girls do better. If you measure it by ability to balance a stick on one finger, there is no difference between the sexes. If you measure it by ability to keep a teeterboard level while straddling its axis, there is no difference to begin with, but girls actually learn faster. Measure it by ability to climb a free-standing ladder and boys do better.

Reaction time is another factor in which sometimes males and sometimes females score higher, depending on how the tests are designed.

When it comes to psychological factors—such as drive for achievement—recent studies by Linda Bunker, director of the motor learning laboratory at the University of Virginia, found no perceptible difference between male and female athletes. Speculation about the origins of male-female differences continues.

One approach to trying to find the answer has been to test abilities at different ages. Many studies have indicated no significant difference in athletic ability between the sexes before age twelve.

For example, Linda Bunker has found that in the 50-yard dash, preteens run at much the same speed; but after age thirteen, boys continue to improve while females seem to regress. In the standing broad jump and in doing sit-ups, girls' ability also tends to level off after puberty, while the boys' keeps rising.

Some investigators believe that the increasing disparity in athletic skills after the age of twelve is due to physiological differences after puberty. But others attribute it to the increased difference in what society expects of teenage girls versus teenage boys.

It should be noted that although the differences exist, there are girls and women who can hit a ball further than many boys and men, and boys and men who cannot swim as fast as most girls and women can.

One thing is certain: Girls and women have just begun to approach their athletic potential. They have some catching up to do since they started later than males, and they are catching up. Men now run the 800 and 1,500 meters only about 10 percent faster than women; in the middle-distance swimming events, the difference is about 7 percent. Top women marathoners now finish about thirty minutes behind the male winners, and their times are improving from year to year.

Even so, there are holdovers of old attitudes. Witness the refusal of the International Olympic Committee to allow women to run more than 1,500 meters in the 1980 Olympics.

In the Sept. 10, 1977 issue, *Science News,* a serious and respected surveyor of the science scene, surveyed recent research on athletic ability, and came to some conclusions worth noting.

It found that the implications of recent research go far beyond predicting new accomplishments for women athletes.

"Physical educators," it noted, "must reflect on the very justification for sports. Is the point really to find out the very fastest any human being can run? If so, perhaps there should be more cross-cultural interest, surveying African tribesmen and mountain villagers. *Ripley's Believe It or Not* reports that a Pawnee Indian in 1876 ran the mile in 3 minutes, 58 seconds, a record not equalled in formal competition until 1954.

"Or are sports supposed to encourage large numbers of people to exercise, strive to reach the limits of their ability, and get satisfaction out of winning a strenuous match? If so, perhaps there should be more classifications, such as the weight divisions in wrestling, to allow more people to compete.

"Whether sex should remain a dividing factor in all sports is unclear. Women athletes themselves vary in attitudes toward competing with men. Some are already doing so; others oppose the whole idea. 'In the Boston marathon, I didn't care about all the sort of anonymous men running around; I only cared where the other women were,' Ullyot (Dr. Joan Ullyot, a sports physician as well as marathon runner) recalls. 'The physical capabilities I think are quite different between the sexes and it makes sense to compete with your peers.' However, Ullyot does note with some satisfaction, 'In competition with my peers it turns out I beat about two-thirds of the men.'

"The implications for physical education," *Science News* reports, "seem to be that children should not be separated by sex, and possibly not even adults should be so separated. Two studies, one of school children and the other of college students, have indicated that females do better in athletic tasks in coed groups than in all-female groups.

"Whatever the eventual outcome, it is clear that athletes need to feel that they can compete and win according to their determination and skill. Introducing different divisions in competition might be one way to encourage both men and women to develop their athletic potential."

INJURIES: ARE GIRLS MORE SUSCEPTIBLE?

That, of course, is a question of concern. Yet many recent studies are reassuring.

One study found that injury rates for high school girls participating in interscholastic sports are no greater than those for boys in the same games (badminton, basketball, cross-country, gymnastics, softball, swimming, tennis, track and field and volleyball) and most of the injuries are minor.

In a two-year study of four high school athletic programs for girls, Dr. James G. Garrick of Phoenix and Ralph K. Requa of the University of Washington Division of Sports Medicine found that about 22 percent of the girls were injured each season as opposed to a usual injury rate of 24 percent among boys.

Nearly two-thirds of the injuries among the girls were sprains and strains, and a majority could return to full athletic activity within a week. One-third of the injuries required a physician's attention. There were only eight broken bones during the entire study and only three girls—two gymnasts and one basketball player—had to be hospitalized for injuries. No injuries involved breasts or genitalia.

The sports with the highest injury rates for girl players were softball, gymnastics, cross-country, and track and field in that order. Those with the lowest rates were badminton, tennis, swimming, volleyball.

"Injuries," reported Dr. Garrick, "occurred at the rate of one every 650 participation hours. It is difficult to imagine any activity that would not result in one injury for every 650 hours."

In another study published in the *Journal of the American Medical Association*, Dr. Christine E. Haycock of the New Jersey Medical School and Joan V. Gillette of the Office of Intercollegiate Athletics of the University of Nevada, Las Vegas, examined the "Susceptibility of Women Athletes to Injury: Myths versus Reality."

In their article, they noted an important need to separate fact from fiction about susceptibility. For a long time there had been countless predictions "of multitudes of injuries to women athletes that would 'scar them for life,' or if they were not injured would produce 'tomboys' with bulging muscles. Neither of these dire forebodings has occurred and all indications to date suggest that they never will."

The two investigators carried out three surveys covering 361 schools and 19 major sports for a whole school year. Their data showed the greatest variety of injuries occurring in basketball, with gymnastics and volleyball following closely.

The most serious injuries, including major fractures,

head injuries, and dislocations, were in basketball, field hockey, softball and gymnastics.

However, the majority of all injuries, especially in basketball, were of a lesser nature. The most common were sprained ankles, knee injuries, and contusions.

Here is how the injuries occurred in each sport:

Fencing: only lacerations

Competition swimming, badminton, snow skiing, cross-country skiing, soccer, squash, golf: only sprains and strains

Basketball: fractures, dislocations, sprains and strains, lacerations, concussions, eye injuries, heat exhaustion

Volleyball: fractures, dislocations, sprains and strains, eye injuries

Field hockey: fractures, dislocations, sprains and strains, lacerations, concussion, dental injuries

Gymnastics: fractures, dislocations, sprains and strains, concussion, neck injury

Track and field: fractures, dislocations, tendon tears

Softball: fractures, dislocations, sprains and strains, lacerations, concussion

Tennis: sprains and strains, eye injuries, tendon tears

Lacrosse: fractures, dislocations, sprains and strains, lacerations

Of 125 trainers surveyed, only four thought that female athletes were more injury prone, and those four could only allude to such vague items as postural planes, biochemical factors, and structural design and muscular development. Many others noted that many injuries were simply due to more women entering sports without the proper conditioning, training or skills required.

Many trainers put heavy emphasis on the need for protective equipment designed especially for women, for evenly matched teams or opponents, and for conditioning to put them in top physical shape in order to avoid injury. They stressed the need for qualified women coaches and trainers in grade and high schools, and also, the need for "parental understanding and cooperation that encourage participation of female students in sports from an early age so that they learn the attitudes and techniques essential for injury prevention."

Even so, Dr. Haycock and Ms. Gillette concluded, "It would appear that, in general, women athletes sustained the same injuries in relatively the same numbers as their male counterparts, with only injuries related to the patella (kneecap) and joints occurring more often in women . . . only a few of the injuries were unique to women."

But what of injuries to female pelvic organs?

"A man's scrotum is much more vulnerable than a woman's ovaries," says Dr. John Marshall, director of sports medicine at Manhattan's Hospital for Special Surgery, and trainer for Billie Jean King. "A woman's ovaries sit inside a great big sac of fluid—beautifully protected." A woman's breasts are also not easily damaged and, scotching an old myth, Dr. Marshall says: "There's no evidence that trauma to the breasts is a precursor of cancer."

Dr. Haycock, too, has looked into pelvic injury risks. "In an extensive search of available literature," she reports, "I could find no specific reference to sports-related injuries (to the pelvic organs) other than those in water skiing where forceful vaginal douches ensued . . . The National Association on Injuries Related to Sports is now gathering national statistics . . . that may show a few injuries, but I do not expect them to find many. The bony pelvis provides excellent protection to the female reproductive organs."

In a report on "The Female Athlete: Gynecological Considerations" published in the *Journal of Health, Physical Education and Recreation*, Dr. A. J. Ryan considered whether females should avoid exercise and competition during the flow phase of the menstrual cycle. All the evidence he found indicates considerable variability among females on the effects of exercise and competition during various phases of the menstrual cycle.

Many have few or no menstrual difficulties under any circumstances, whether they are active or sedentary. A significant number do have painful menstruation or other menstrual difficulties which apparently are neither helped nor intensified by physical activity, including the most vigorous.

It has been noted that in some very active women—long-distance runners, gymnasts, figure skaters, and dancers, for example—menstruation stops. But this may well be due to their very low body weight and very low body fat levels, since other studies have found absence of menstruation in chronically underweight females regardless of athletic activity. Female distance runners, for example, often run 70 to 100 miles a week in training, and their relative body fat typically goes all the way down to 10 percent or even less. Yet menstruation usually returns after a reduction in the intensity of training.

As for when physical performance is best, that generally seems to be in the period immediately after menstruation up to about the fifteenth day of the cycle. But individual variability is great. Some women have actually demonstrated improved performance during the flow phase and have established records in world-class competition. And the overall number who perform poorly during flow is about the same as the number who experience no difference.

There have been other reassuring findings in studies which have followed up former female athletes and have shown that they have normal pregnancies and deliveries. Some have even shorter delivery times and faster return to normal activities than other women.

THE NEW PERSPECTIVE

After considering the many recent studies, Dr. Wilmore had these remarks to make at a recent medical symposium on The School-Age Athlete:

"... There appear to be rather substantial differences between the average female and the average male in almost all aspects of physical performance beyond the age of ten to twelve years. Prior to this time, there are few, if any differences between the sexes.

"What happens to the female once she reaches puberty? Is she physically over the hill, reaching her peak at a relatively early age, or are there other factors or circumstances that might account for her reduced physical capabilities?

"Recent studies on highly trained female athletes suggest that the female is not that much different from her highly trained male counterpart at ages beyond puberty. It appears that the average values used for comparative purposes beyond the age of puberty are comparing relatively active males with relatively sedentary females.

"Somewhere between ten and twelve years of age, the average female substitutes the piano for climbing in the tree and sewing for chasing boys down the street. It is well known that once one assumes a sedentary life style, the basic physiological components of general fitness deteriorate, i.e., strength, muscular endurance, and cardiovascular endurance are lost and body fat tends to accumulate. Similar trends can be noted for the male by the time he reaches thirty to thirty-five years of age, which corresponds to a reduction in his activity patterns.

"So, what appears to be dramatic biological differences between the sexes may be, in fact, more related to cultural and social restrictions placed on the female as she attains puberty."

Dr. Joanna Bunker Rohrbaugh is a psychologist on the faculties of the Department of Psychiatry at Harvard Medical School and Boston's Massachusetts General Hospital.

When she was an undergraduate at Pembroke College in the early 60s, she took part in three varsity sports—tennis, field hockey, and basketball. That distinguished her—or, in those days, set her apart—from most of her female counterparts across the country, who played few if any sports.

"That wasn't unusual for me," she recalls. "I came from a Quaker background, in which both men and women were encouraged to participate in all sports vigorously. But as I look back, it was a time when most women were afraid to participate in competitive athletics. There was a stigma. Now, that stigma is slowly disappearing.

"There aren't," she adds, "any conclusive studies on this, nothing to show that studying classical piano can't be just as effective for building character as participating in competitive sport. But I personally believe from experience with female patients that they definitely have a better sense of themselves by competing in athletics.

"I had one young woman tell me that she felt that she could withstand the rigors of law school after she became an avid jogger and felt pain. When she conquered pain, she felt she could conquer other cultural barriers. It may be a cliche, but for women, sports is becoming a character builder."

CHAPTER 4

THE
PREADOLESCENT
ATHLETE

This is an era of junior champions and overemphasis on early starts for children, rushing them into formal, intensive athletic training and competition.

When a Kansas boy, five years old, was hailed in some quarters for having broken a marathon record for youngsters under six, it was too much for a leading runners' magazine, which announced that it would no longer accept or keep marathon records for runners under twelve and would not encourage them to compete in marathons.

Said *Runner's World*: "We are not trying to discourage children from running; we merely feel that they should not be attempting the marathon distance because of the extreme stresses, mental and physical, it places on a young child."

Recently, too, an advertisement appeared in a New York newspaper promoting tennis lessons for three-year-olds. This prompted an indignant response from Eve F. Kraft, Technical Editor of *Tennis USA*, official publication of the U. S. Lawn Tennis Association (USLTA), national co-chairman of the USLTA Junior Development and Education Committee, and director of the Princeton Community Tennis Program which, for seventeen years, has been researching the question of when youngsters should begin to play tennis.

"Tennis lessons at age three? Ridiculous!" declared Mrs. Kraft. "What an irresponsible, misleading promotion and how lacking in knowledge of when to start youngsters in tennis."

Are we living in a society which tends to overexpose and overprogram children, offering them too much too soon, and often oblivious to the children's problems, talents and needs? Like others who want to see children enjoy and benefit from sports, Mrs. Kraft believes so, and warns of the harm.

"A classic example that comes to mind," she wrote, "was an Orange Bowl Junior tournament I witnessed many years ago in Florida. The age classification was for ten-and-unders (which, fortunately, is now disbanded). As one reporter aptly remarked: 'The event was characterized by tears, cheating and parents!'

"The anxiety to please parents at such a young age is so great that the tears and cheating are an inevitable result of the tremendous inner tension that is created. A child, with his mother and/or father hanging breathlessly on each point, feels obligated to win—at any cost."

If a child is to have tennis lessons, at what age should that be? Third grade is time enough, says Mrs. Kraft.

If concentrated instruction starts too early, the child whose motor ability is not yet advanced enough often becomes frustrated and gives up. Even if a child is well-coordinated, a too early start may lead to boredom.

Out of the long-term Princeton Community research program, have come these other tenets:

● Not to rush the young beginner, even the one who shows exceptional promise. "Let young children master the rather sophisticated skills gradually, in a relaxed manner, enjoying the sociability of their own peer group. It's like the roller skating twins—one begins too soon, the other at an optimum time. Yet, their skating ability eventually reaches the same level," says Mrs. Kraft.

● Not to write off the slow learner nor be overconfident that the early bloomer will go on flourishing. Both groups have surprises in store. "We make every effort to allow time for the late starters to gather steam and confidence, and to pace the eager beavers so they don't burn out too quickly."

● Resistance to undue pressure to "create champions" as a primary function. The Princeton Community has a population of 25,000. Each year the Princeton Community tennis program draws more than 2,000 individuals out of the 25,000. "Ours is a happy tennis town, with the sign of 'belonging' symbolized by a tennis racket protruding from each kid's bike basket," says Mrs. Kraft. But, she adds, while the program is dedicated to quality instruction and to opening up opportunities for advanced training, "proportionately few of our total enrollment are genuinely interested in—or qualified for—intensive tournament play. Only a handful wish to take the inordinate amount of time and effort to try to be a champion. Most youngsters (and adults, too) choose to play primarily for recreation, exercise, and just pure fun and relaxation . . .

"In our Princeton program, we are as proud of the poorly coordinated child who has progressed enough to find one other player of his ability with whom he can enjoy the game as we are of the trophy winner . . . In our championship-oriented society, let's not forget the average guy."

Sports have much to offer the preadolescent child provided they are not foisted upon him or her and there is an effort to take account of how children grow, the differences between individual youngsters in growth and maturation, and their physical and psychological responses to exercise and sports.

CHILD GROWTH AND DEVELOPMENT

Growth for a child is, of course, a continuous process, but *rate* of growth is not necessarily steady. There are spurts, and also differences in the growth rate of different body segments.

At birth, the head is just about half its adult size; it will only double in size by adulthood. On the other hand, the arms will quadruple and the legs increase fivefold.

From birth to age one, the trunk is the fastest growing body segment and accounts for about 60 percent of the total increase in height during the year.

From age one to puberty, it's the legs which do the greatest growing, accounting for two-thirds of the total increase in height. The later puberty comes, the longer the legs.

As children near puberty, it's often said that they are "all arms and legs." From puberty on, however, as the growth centers in the long bones of the arms and legs fuse, and the arms and legs reach adult size, the trunk continues to grow for a time and overall adult proportions are reached.

As you may have noticed, two growth spurts occur normally. The first, which appears in both boys and girls in the age range of five and one-half to seven years, is called the "midgrowth spurt." The second, the "adolescent growth spurt," usually pops up in girls from eleven to thirteen and in boys thirteen to fifteen.

Boy/girl growth differences. Although boys tend to be a little heavier and taller than girls at birth, the difference generally disappears quickly, and during the childhood years, boys and girls do not differ significantly in height and weight.

But girls do mature earlier. Well before puberty, a girl may be as much as a year nearer to biological maturity—

and by age fourteen, as much as two years ahead biolog-
ically.

During girls' adolescent growth spurt, they grow faster
and larger before slowing down, except for pelvic width,
which continues to increase under the influence of the female growth hormone. Because of the delayed onset of
adolescent growth spurt, boys have an extended growing
time, allowing the legs to become longer. And the influence
of sex hormones causes boys' shoulder width to increase.

Although differences between the sexes in muscle,
bone and fat are small at birth, boys do have greater body
density because of somewhat greater muscle mass, while
girls have larger amounts of fatty tissue. The differences
become pronounced during adolescence. In boys, under
the influence of the male sex hormone, testosterone, muscle
tissue increases; in girls, the hormone estrogen favors fatty
tissue accumulation about hips, breasts and buttocks.

Individual variations.   These can be quite marked. Whether
girls are being compared with girls of the same age or boys
with boys, there can be great variation in physique and
physical skills. It's possible for one thirteen-year-old boy to
resemble an almost fully mature man, while another of the
same age appears to be a child still years away from maturity.

In any representative group of boys or girls at, say, age
twelve, there will usually be some who, despite their age,
are at the maturation level of an average nine- or ten-year-
old and others at the level of an average fifteen-year-old.

The rates at which children mature tend to be related
to physique types. There are three basic types. The ecto-
morph has a thin, linear body structure; the mesomorph has
a heavier, harder, rectangular physique, with heavier muscles and large prominent bones; and the endomorph has
a soft roundness predominating throughout the body.

At any age throughout childhood, mesomorphs and

endomorphs tend to be tallest and heaviest, and because they often mature earlier, they are often shorter and have stockier adult bodies. Ectomorphs mature later and tend to continue to have linear builds.

Differences in rate of maturity can be significant when it comes to sports. For example, in a study of fifty-five Little League Baseball World Series participants, 71 percent of the boys were advanced in maturational development, with 45 percent of them ahead of the norm for their ages by more than a year. Another study of 112 boys participating in a Little League World Series found that the majority were postpubescent and so were mature for their age. Most of the starting pitchers, first basemen and left fielders were postpubescent, and the batting order reflected the maturity of the players; all who batted in fourth "cleanup" position were postpubescent.

YOUTHFUL BODY RESPONSES TO EXERCISE

The human body—the child's as well as adult's—has the capacity to respond well and benefit from vigorous activity. That capacity is not as great in a preadolescent child as in the adolescent or adult. Still, it is greater than many people realize.

The breathing/heart-pumping response. Muscular activity creates an increased demand for energy. The more intense and prolonged the activity, the greater the demand.

The demand is met by the burning of fuel by the muscle cells. For the burning, oxygen is required and must come in large amounts from the bloodstream.

To supply that oxygen, breathing increases in frequency and depth so that more oxygen is absorbed by the lungs and placed in the bloodstream. The heart responds by increasing its beat or rate of pumping so that more oxygen-rich blood arrives at the muscles.

If the activity is intense or prolonged enough, there comes a point of panting and then even of breathlessness. This means that the oxygen requirements of the hard-working muscles no longer can be met. Thereafter, the activity can be continued only briefly.

This whole process is a normal one. The breathlessness which accompanies strenuous exertion, although uncomfortable, is not a medical symptom like pain or nausea. Rather, it is evidence that the body is efficiently recognizing and satisfying its needs. The process takes place in both child and adult.

But, as you might expect, considering the size of a young child, exercise capacity is less than that of the adolescent; according to some authorities, it may be about 80 percent that of the adolescent in the late teens.

The body heat response.   When there is muscular activity, heat develops and the body must dissipate it. It does this in more than one way.

Some heat is removed with breathing. Much is dissipated through the skin. During vigorous activity, the flow of blood to the skin increases. There, conduction and radiation get rid of much excess heat.

Sweating, too, plays a vital role in heat dissipation. While sweating, water is lost and must be replaced during exercise to avoid a decrease in the volume of blood as well as an excessive elevation of body temperature.

Because the temperature control mechanism in young children may not be as adaptable as in adults, some authorities urge that they not engage in very vigorous activity during hot, humid weather.

The heart response.   The heart is essentially a muscle. Like other muscles of the body, it is influenced by physical activity. When called upon to respond to vigorous exercise, the healthy heart increases in size and strength much like the biceps muscles of the arm. It can hold more blood and pump out more with each beat or contraction. Endurance increases.

But is the heart of a preadolescent more vulnerable? There is no evidence that this is the case. If the heart of a child is healthy, the evidence indicates, it responds well to exercise.

The muscle system response. Other muscles also become stronger and more responsive when called upon to do more than the usual amount of work.

This is true in preadolescents.

But during adolescence, marked gains in strength occur in both girls and boys as the result of sexual maturation and its effects on muscle tissue growth. The gains are especially pronounced in boys at and after puberty because of the known influence of the male hormone on muscular development.

While boys tend to be somewhat stronger than girls before adolescence, the difference is not great and may be more a matter of greater physical activity by boys rather than any intrinsic sex difference. With adolescence, however, the strength of girls may be only about 80 percent of that of boys of the same size. This may or may not be unchangeably fixed and it will be interesting to see what findings are made with further studies now that girls are increasingly active.

Motor skills. Motor skills involve movement patterns. During the preadolescent years, crude motor skills are refined.

The refining process involves modifying and combining various movement patterns to accomplish new tasks. In addition to the muscles, the nervous system plays a critical role, picking up cues from the environment and from sensors within the muscles, learning from errors in movement, building upon correct movements.

Sports provide an excellent way of developing motor skills since they have a built-in interest and motivation missing in many other forms of physical activity.

PSYCHOLOGICAL RESPONSES

Given their freedom, uninfluenced by adult direction, healthy children naturally and normally gravitate to play. They love and enjoy games.

Given their freedom, kids' play is guided only by their own desires and abilities. In spontaneous sports, they can compete, but without intensive pressures. They can play many positions and many sports. They can remain in the competition without prolonged practice that may exclude many other worthwhile activities and without super talent. With this kind of competition, they can continue to develop social skills.

"For the eight- and nine-year-olds who are just beginning to venture independently from the close supervision and restriction of the maternal domination of childhood," observes Dr. Joseph Torg of Temple University School of Medicine, a distinguished sports physician, "games and sports with peers serve as a vehicle for exploration of the world . . .

"Another extremely important function of athletics is to provide the preadolescent with a means for learning the art of entertaining himself . . .

"Most important, athletics for the preadolescent must provide the means for simple recreation and enjoyment."

But what bothers Dr. Torg and many others concerned with child development is the too frequent overorganization of sports for youngsters by adults, with "repetitious and demanding practice, unwarranted pressures to win, and the tendency to treat physically and emotionally immature youngsters as adults.

In a report in *The Physician and Sportsmedicine*, Dr. Torg has noted that "There exists today among developmental pediatricians a consensus that the personality of the preadolescent should be guarded from excessive demands and responsibilities. To do otherwise is to invite antisocial behavior in later years. Therefore, to subject the preadolescent to the demands inherent in highly structured competitive athletic programs is to rob him of the essence of a carefree childhood."

Says Dr. William A. Grana, Associate Director of the Division of Sports Medicine at the University of Oklahoma Health Sciences Center and College of Medicine, Oklahoma City: "The emotional impact of organized sports when improperly supervised may lead to one-sidedness in the participants. At a time in emotional and intellectual development when the child should be involved in many activities, his participation in an organized sport may preclude the development of these other sides to a healthy personality. In order to maintain a high level of performance, the practice time will effect his exclusion from other activities. If he wants to continue in the program he must 'pay the price'—the narrowing of his personality . . . Spontaneous sports offer the young child the chance for competition without this one-sidedness."

Some children are pushed into sports by overzealous parents, others by parents who worry that their child may be "left out." But too much overorganized competition too soon and the wrong kind of coaching may destroy interest in sports. It may have devastating psychological consequences as well. "It's bad enough," says child psychologist N. Archer Moore of Macon, Georgia, "to be a bench warmer in high school; think how it feels to be one in kindergarten. At that age, getting cut from the team or failing in a father's eyes can be disastrous."

We will be looking further into organized athletics in the next chapter.

INJURIES

Experts are not in full agreement on the extent of physical hazards in children's sports. Much remains to be learned and undoubtedly will be learned before long, thanks to greatly increased interest in physical fitness, and the emergence of sports medicine. Let us look at what is known.

Certainly, accidental injuries—and not just from sports—

are an important problem in school age children. According to some authoritative estimates, each year 15 million children—about one in three—require medical attention for some sort of injury.

Most of these injuries occur in or near the home. Studies in the U. S. and Canada indicate that only 6 percent and possibly less are related to organized sports. So, considered in terms of the overall statistics, the injury problem from sports does not seem to be of tremendous magnitude. But it is certainly not to be dismissed.

Are younger children—preadolescents—more likely to be injured than older athletes?

Dr. Robert L. Larson of the University of Oregon Medical School, Portland, has reported a study of 1,338 athletic injuries seen by four orthopedists. Twenty percent of the injuries occurred in children fourteen years old and younger, and 40 percent in the group fifteen to eighteen years old.

As Dr. Larson noted, the school population of the area broke down as follows: 60 percent in elementary and junior high schools; 15 percent in high school; and 25 percent in the university. It was the high school students, with 40 percent of the athletic injuries in the smallest numerical group, who appeared to be the most vulnerable to athletic injury.

One of the greatest concerns has been the possibility of permanent damage to bones and joints by early athletic participation. The growing ends of the long bones—the epiphyses, or growth plates—are particularly vulnerable to blows, sudden wrenchings, and other severe stresses. Yet, in Dr. Larson's study, only 6 percent of the injuries in the preadolescent group were epiphyseal.

While epiphyseal injury is a hazard in sports participation, it is in all activities of children, and, as Dr. Larson noted, such injury does not mean permanent deformity. While growth disturbances can result from epiphyseal damage, they are the exception rather than the rule. Most are epiphyseal displacements which can be reduced easily with gentle pressure and traction.

Some children tend to be more susceptible to epiphyseal injury than others. They are the tall, uncoordinated, lanky youngsters with poor muscle development; and others with what is known as Froehlich's syndrome, which is marked by obesity and sexual retardation associated with pituitary gland deficiency. Such children, Dr. Larson advises, should be encouraged to forego contact sports until their body development reaches the stage where they can participate more safely. Similarly, after injury or illness, children should not be okayed for competitive athletics until muscle strength in the injured area is redeveloped to help protect that area.

The risk of epiphyseal injury can be minimized by good supervision in children's athletic activities. Little League baseball, for example, limits pitchers to no more than six innings of pitching per week and if a boy or girl pitches more than three innings in a day there must be three days' rest before pitching again. Some studies have suggested that it might be wise to eliminate curve-ball throwing for youngsters under fourteen.

Dr. Grana of the University of Oklahoma, using his own studies as well as those of others, has concluded that serious musculoskeletal injuries in preadolescents are rare and the most common injuries are abrasions, contusions, and sprains and strains.

INJURIES IN SPECIFIC SPORTS

Looking into injuries in various sports for preadolescents, Dr. Grana has gathered information from reports in medical literature and from the injury statistics of the greater Oklahoma City YMCA, Oklahoma City Amateur Hockey Association, and the Edmond Oklahoma All Sports Program. Here are some of his findings:

Baseball. Although there has been considerable concern in the past about injuries to shoulders and elbows, initial fears have been quieted. The problem appears to be small in preadolescents.

One study found that 1 percent of 595 Little League pitchers had elbow symptoms that excluded them from pitching. In a survey of all physicians in Ohio, only one Little Leaguer was reported to have symptoms. A sensible approach to the amount of pitching done not only in games but also in practice may do much to prevent injury.

Football. In a study of 2,079 players in a Little League program, only forty-eight participants were injured. Sprains and strains accounted for a significant proportion of the injuries. Six percent of injuries were epiphyseal and four percent were head injuries, but serious head and epiphyseal injuries were rare. Such injuries can be minimized by good protective equipment, conditioning, and coaching.

Basketball. In the age group under thirteen in the Oklahoma City Y basketball programs, there were approximately 600 participants during two winter seasons. One injury was reported, a laceration of the face caused by a blow from an opponent's elbow.

Swimming. In this sport the Y reported that among about 400 participants during a two-year period, there were only two injuries and neither was related to the sport itself. Both were lacerations from falls at poolside.

Hockey. In Little League play, the most common injuries were those from stick and puck to face and neck. In Minnesota, in 1975, there were forty-eight eye injuries, seven of which led to blindness. In that same year throughout the country, there were 25,000 facial injuries among 300,000 participants and those alarming statistics led to a ruling by the American Amateur Hockey Association that all players wear protective face masks as well as head gear.

Wrestling. Over a two-year period, the Y had some 350 participants of thirteen years old and under. There were four injuries: three of the shoulder, and one a facial laceration.

Soccer. Only recently organized by the Y for Little League age groups of thirteen and under, there were 125 participants in the first season with no reported injuries.

Gymnastics. The YMCA considered this program a

high-risk one for preadolescents. Over a two-year period, there were nineteen reported injuries among 300 participants. Five of the injuries were associated with the equipment (bars, horses and rings) used for competition and occurred primarily because the children were too small to manage the apparatus well. The remaining fourteen injuries occurred in competition and included one foot fracture and thirteen sprains of mild and moderate severity.

Overall, Dr. Grana indicates, "It seems clear that the risk of physical injury to preadolescents is small if appropriate precautions are taken."

Like many other physicians, Dr. Grana advocates avoiding body contact sports, not just in terms of possible injury, but because he believes that emphasis should be on the development in children of as many physical activity interests as possible that can continue to be used as a means of achieving and maintaining fitness in adulthood.

Indeed, a poll of American physicians indicates that 43.5 percent are opposed to organized contact sports for preadolescents. Moreover, in a questionnaire I submitted to many sports physicians during the course of research for this book, I found virtually all emphasizing that preadolescents should not participate in contact sports such as football. Some also deemed unsuitable sports such as hockey and boxing, and some opposed sports such as power weight lifting, which requires excessive strenth, and the trampoline, as presenting unnecessary risks.

WHICH SPORTS?

In answer to my questionnaire, sports physicians listed sports they considered suitable for preadolescents and also those they considered especially suitable for girls.

Dr. Jack Andrish of the Cleveland Clinic's Department of Orthopaedics and Sports Medicine, whose response typified many, listed as especially suitable sports such as soccer and swimming. These sports encourage active participation and promote general cardiovascular fitness. Sports especially suitable for girls were those involving endurance and agility, such as track, basketball, gymnastics, swimming, and soccer.

Dr. Alfred Moretz, III, of the University of Oklahoma, would add softball, track and basketball; and as especially suitable for girls, swimming, tennis, gymnastics, karate, basketball, soccer, and ice skating.

Others favored tennis and horseback riding, and one proposed ballet as fine for both boys and girls.

Many emphasized that while team sports have certain values, what will really be important as a child grows into an adult are individual sports such as tennis, golf, and swimming.

Meanwhile, a study made by Dr. Richard B. Chambers, now at the University of Cincinnati College of Medicine, suggests that the best fitness "buys" for preadolescents and even for youngsters up to age seventeen may be soccer and swimming. Both have low injury rates and neither favors one sex over the other, or any particular body type or age.

Dr. Chambers' study was carried out over a year-long period at Fort Leavenworth, Kansas, where data could be collected consistently on the sports activities of military dependents.

"Soccer's emphasis is on dexterity rather than strength, and its constant running develops endurance," Dr. Chambers observed. "Swimming probably provides the most balanced form of exercise. Endurance as well as power can be developed along with agility and coordination."

Examining rates of orthopedic injuries—fractures and dislocations—for various sports, the study found:

• Injury risk in football was twice as high as in basketball and gymnastics, which were next highest on the list.

• The risk in soccer was only one-third and in baseball only about one-sixth the risk in basketball and gymnastics.

● Swimming had a zero rate of risk.

Actually, the study found, of all fractures and dislocations during the year, only one-third occurred in youngsters engaged in supervised athletics. Twice as many came from unsupervised activities such as tree climbing, running, and, especially, skateboarding.

Certainly, organized, supervised sports have much to offer young athletes—preadolescent and adolescent. But by no means is that potential always realized.

We'll consider the pluses and minuses of school and other organized athletics in Chapter 5.

PLUSES AND MINUSES OF SCHOOL AND OTHER ORGANIZED ATHLETICS

Each year, 20 million American kids aged from six up play, or try to play, on organized sports teams. Two million go for little league baseball; one million for organized football; others for hockey, soccer, swimming, track, gymnastics, and other activities.

It would be nice to think that all benefit from these activities.

Some do, and they are not necessarily those on winning teams or those who become local celebrities.

Some learn much about themselves and their capabilities, about their potential for improvement however modest, about the value of teamwork, about the fun of sports, and about the lifelong importance of physical fitness.

But some are hurt, and not necessarily physically. Their pride may be damaged; they may be humiliated. They may be so intimidated that they learn to detest rather than love sports. They may learn just the reverse of sportsmanship and fair play.

Some years ago, Dr. Arthur A. Esslinger, past president of the American Association for Health, Physical Education, and Recreation and a long-time member of the board of directors of Little League Baseball, warned that although most people believe playing baseball is a fine thing for youngsters, "nothing could be further from the truth."

It's not automatically a desirable experience for boys. "It might be," Esslinger noted, "under some circumstances but under other conditions it could be positively detrimental . . .

"We have all seen Little League teams," he emphasized, "where boys learned more undesirable habits and attitudes than desirable ones. Whether or not baseball is good for boys depends upon the total effect of the game upon them. Certainly, all will benefit from the vigorous outdoor exercise. However, they derive more than exercise from baseball. Their minds and emotions are involved in the game as well as their muscles."

While learning the game, Dr. Esslinger went on, kids also learn many habits and attitudes important to their futures. They can learn to win and lose graciously or ungraciously; to be loyal or disloyal; to be cooperative or uncooperative; to be courteous or discourteous to opponents and umpires. They can also learn to be prejudiced or not, considerate or not of those with lesser ability. And they may or may not develop self-discipline and the ability to subjugate their own desires for the good of the team.

"Baseball is a two-edged sword," said Dr. Esslinger. "As a result of his baseball experience a boy may acquire many of the attributes of a gentleman or a thug." This is certainly no less true for many other sports.

Increasingly in recent years organized athletics—in schools and leagues for youngsters—have been attracting criticism.

A major focus of that criticism is on the emphasis, or overemphasis, on winning—on winning virtually at all costs.

"WINNING IS ALL"

"In the modern world of sport, winning is not just good; it is the only thing. Losing is not only bad, it is unforgivable. And sportsmanship? It is a quaint but hapless ethic which seems to be more incompatible with athletics every year."

So wrote Jim Brosnan, former major league baseball pitcher, in an American Medical Association publication.

Brosnan was referring mostly to college and pro sports. But overemphasis on winning has been increasingly affecting sports at all levels for all ages.

Dr. Thomas Tutko, cofounder of the Institute of Athletic Motivation at San Jose State University, has been called the Jeremiah of sports psychologists, a prophet crying in the wilderness about the evils of competitive athletics.

"Most Americans," he says, "truly believe that they're going to walk on water if they win. But winning is like drinking salt water. It's never satiable. I'm trying to save sports from the lunatics who believe that winning is the only reason for playing the game."

After sixteen years of serving as psychological consultant to many pro teams—among them the Los Angeles Rams, the Pittsburgh Steelers, the Dallas Cowboys, and the Miami Dolphins—Tutko has become convinced that sports in America is a "chronically stressful, neurotic environment."

He has become concerned about children exposed to the spread of what he calls "the prevailing competitive ethic: Winning is everything . . . you are nothing until you are Number One. . . . Don't tell us how you played the game; did you win? . . . Are you willing to pay the price to keep winning?"

In a book entitled *Winning Is Everything—And Other American Myths*, written with William Bruns, Tutko worried that the win-at-all-costs mania which long ago seized high-level collegiate sports is, even more unfortunately, steadily engulfing children's sports.

"We organize children's leagues, give them uniforms,

hand out trophies, set up play-offs and all-star teams, send them to 'bowl' games, and encourage them to compete at earlier and earlier ages," he notes.

"Many people would argue that this should be the purpose of sports—to strive for records, championships, Olympic teams, and professional careers. But how many million youngsters are we sacrificing along the way so that ten players can entertain us in a pro basketball game? How many people are we eliminating who love sports, but who never make the team because they're not going to be 'winners'—they're too short, or too slow, or too weak.

"I'm concerned with how many good athletes have been scarred by injury or burned out psychologically by the time they were fifteen because they were unable to meet the insatiable demands of their parents, their coach, their fans, or their own personal obsession, or who are rejected and made to feel ashamed of having limited athletic prowess."

Tutko is not against sports nor against sensibly run leagues for children nor against competition and striving to win, which he notes, can provide excitement and help a youngster probe his capacities and limits.

"It's how we're competing that's all wrong," he says. "Even down at the Pop Warner football and Little League baseball level we play with only one real objective and that is to win.

"If parents," he urges, "are going to allow their children to get involved in high-pressure sports during the preadolescent years, then I feel it is imperative that they oversee what is happening. The coach, the league, the pressure, the push may all be very destructive... The idea should be to encourage physical activity by every child, not to weed out those who are uncoordinated or untalented. Let's compete, play to win, but keep it all in perspective. Young athletes should see the thrill of competing, not simply winning; they should be judged by their effort, not just the end results or lack of results."

WINNING OVEREMPHASIS
AND INJURIES

It's to be expected that there are some risks in sports. But are risks markedly, needlessly, increased by the "winning is all" philosophy?

School-age sports and school-age athletes certainly differ greatly from pro sports and pro athletes.

Professional players can be injured. But they are very skilled, physically fit, mature adults who willingly risk injury and are well paid for doing so. Moreover, they commonly get the best, most expert kind of training, the best equipment, and very close, top-notch medical care. Few if any pro teams are without a team physician who is always present at games, thoroughly familiar with each player, and backed up by an array of specialists on call.

School kids don't have such advantages; and youth and school athletic programs can't hope to match the advantages that pro sports, which are bigtime business, can provide.

Perhaps better equipment and facilities and better supervision—even if not up to the calibre provided for pros—could reduce injuries among youngsters. But many experts are coming to believe that a major cause of injuries among kids is the "must win" mentality.

"If we put less emphasis on building championship teams and more on player safety, the incidence of injuries would be significantly curtailed." So says Dr. William A. Liebler, a sports physician who is consultant to the athletic department of the Dalton School in New York City and team physician for the New York Rangers.

Can safety be increased simply from a less intensely competitive atmosphere? Some evidence for this is reported by Dr. Joseph Torg of Temple University School of Medicine after a study of the effects of pitching on the arms of participants in the Lighthouse Boys' Club Baseball program, comparing them with those previously reported for Little League pitchers.

In earlier studies, X-ray studies of the elbows of 80 Little League pitchers revealed abnormalities in 45. The investigator, Dr. J. E. Adams, concluded that they resulted from a competitive situation subjecting young pitchers' elbows to excessive, repeated injury.

Adams had made a number of suggestions to prevent abusing the arms of skeletally immature youngsters. Among them: Discourage kids from practicing pitching at home before, during, and after the season; abolish curve ball pitching at this age; and restrict young pitchers to two innings a game.

The Lighthouse Boys' Club is an organization supported by United Fund Charities and dedicated to providing recreational activities for youth residing in a densely populated Philadelphia area.

A spring baseball program is conducted for 450 club members ranging in age from nine to eighteen. The program is organized to encourage participation and recreation rather than excite intense competition.

At the beginning of each season, teams are arbitrarily chosen. Each team plays twenty games. And each player must play at least three and one-half innings of every game.

Dr. Torg and his colleagues carried out X-ray examinations of forty-four Lighthouse pitchers. They X-rayed shoulders as well as elbows. There were no abnormalities in any of the shoulders, and only two mild elbow changes.

Compared with the earlier findings in Little Leaguers, the Lighthouse boys had relatively few. This is particularly significant, Dr. Torg notes, because the Lighthouse program does not follow Adams' recommendations. It allows a boy to pitch seven innings rather than two in one game; curve ball pitching is not restricted; most of the Lighthouse boys practice pitching at home during and after the season.

What, then, is the difference between pitching in the Little League and pitching in the Lighthouse program?

Says Dr. Torg: "Having considered all factors, we believe that the major difference is the circumstances under which the two groups participate. Specifically, Little Leaguers must compete to make the team, must compete to play in each game, and are subjected to intense pressures to win by adult coaches and spectators.

"On the other hand, all the Lighthouse Boys' Club members are automatically assigned to a team and must play at least three and one-half innings of each game. The general attitude is one of participation for the sake of recreation rather than competition."

THE NEEDLESS PRESSURES

When winning is all that counts, kids are subjected to many kinds of pressure.

Winning can mean many things. It can mean self-improvement and a sense of accomplishment when anybody does something a little better than he or she has done it before and sometimes when performance edges up toward standards set by others.

But when the meaning of winning is narrowed down to just one thing—beating the other team—kids are under many pressures.

When the Special Joint Committee on The Desirability of Athletic Competition for Children of Elementary School Age in the U.S. met several years ago, it noted that children at this age are not miniature adults; they are boys and girls in the process of maturing into adults, and they seek and can profit from suitable play opportunities.

The Committee went on to note that one of the strongest arguments against varsity-type programs for young children is the tendency to start sports specialization too early.

"The elementary school years should be the time," the experts emphasized, "when the basic skills are learned, when children have opportunity to engage in a broad range of skills. They are not yet ready for specialization."

But when winning is the objective, there is too often an insistence that a child specialize in a sport. There often is also an insistence on practice, practice, practice, which for young children, can lead to "early burnout."

In their excellent booklet, *A Family Approach to Youth Sports*, John Ferrell and Jerry Glashagel of the National YMCA Sports Development Program and Values Education Center, and Professor Mick Johnson of the University of Minnesota stated that kids can get too much of regimented sports.

By the time they are eleven or twelve, they note, many kids are veterans of four or five seasons of such sports, and many lose interest early because they simply want more time for other things, are tired of practicing every day after school and having no time for themselves, and tired "of being organized, pressurized and routinized."

The three commentators pointed out that even some kids who have been star performers and stick it out through grade school get burned out. "By junior high they have been to bowl games, been on all-star teams, their room is filled with trophies, and they have had all the public attention they need for the next few years. What's left?"

Ferrell, Glashagel and Johnson provide a case study of the burnout of a fifteen-year-old high school athlete named Jim who, after playing undefeated football on the freshman team, was a member of the varsity squad as a sophomore, considered one of the best football players the city had ever produced, and expected to help carry the city to a state high school championship.

"With that kind of potential there was no way Jim was going to have his future left to fate! Workouts ran over the summer. 'Two-a-day' practice sessions started before summer was over. Much was expected from fifteen-year-old Jim.

"He was also expected to play in the sophomore games. So on nights when the sophomores had games, Jim was involved in varsity practice first, and then he went straight into a sophomore game. Jim's life was sheer exhaustion, with no time for growing and experiencing anything other than football. Winning had brought him honors. Winning had brought him to the pinnacle of expectations for most adults in his city.

"Only, this perspective of winning had edged out fun and enjoyment. He was scared to death of ever losing, of not being as good as everyone expected him to be. That fear and the feeling that something was missing in his life led Jim to simply toss in the towel. At fifteen, he quit. Many adults were disgusted with him. They figured he must be messed up. Then they got mad at him. If he couldn't live their dreams, he must be a hopeless loser."

It was Alistair Cooke, the distinguished historian, newsman and commentator who, in discussing sports in the U.S., summed it up: "This is the age of the prima donna... The crowd loves a character. But what we're doing today is subsidizing bad behavior. The whole theory of sports has changed. The word itself has gone by the board. Sport and sportsmanship have the same root but sportsmen are a disappearing species."

Cooke, of course, was commenting about big-time sports. But the same comments, unfortunately, can be applied to many children's sports. When all that counts is winning, sportsmanship goes by the boards; is never, in fact, inculcated among young participants. It's hardly unknown for some kids to play to hurt opponents, to consider officials as enemies, to break the rules and get away with what they can. That orientation, to be carried over into later life, is hardly a desirable dividend from sports.

COACHES AND PARENTS

In June, 1979, when the Seattle SuperSonics, coached by Lenny Wilkens, won the National Basketball Association championship, Brother R. E. Pigott was moved to take special note of the occasion.

Pigott, who teaches English and is assistant varsity

basketball coach at Monsignor Farrel High School on Staten Island, New York, wrote in the "Views of Sport" section of *The New York Times* June 10, 1979:

"I have been coaching basketball since 1958. During this time I have had the opportunity of observing the tremendous influence professional basketball has had on the lower strata of the basketball world. There are college, high school and grammar school basketball coaches who at least subconsciously emulate the behavior of some pro coaches.

"We coaches at the lower echelons have been in dire need of someone at the top to restore sanity to the game; someone to make class, grace, and gentlemanliness popular again. Fortunately, that someone has arrived in the person of Lenny Wilkens.

"When Wilkens's Seattle SuperSonics won the National Basketball Association championship nine days ago, they did it with style, class and grace. They did it that way because of Wilkens.

"There has to be a way you can win and still be classy. Treat the players like gentlemen. Treat the referees like human beings. Realize these men are out there trying to do their best."

Brother Pigott went on to note that some pro coaches subtly intimidate their players; their counterparts at lower levels scream more openly not only at referees, but at their players, sometimes subjecting players to public humiliation; and the players then scream at each other and the refs.

"Many coaches, myself included," he observed, "have been guilty at some time of such erratic behavior. It has almost become the American way. The desire to win is so great that many coaches will do anything to 'get an edge.'

"He [Wilkens] does not try to intimidate. He does not rant. He is patient. He communicates. He is a teacher.

"Maybe his style will rub off on more coaches and more players in today's professional sports world of win at any cost. As the 'me only' attitude has permeated sports all the way down to the grammar school level, maybe the low-key, dignified approach will eventually do likewise. I certainly hope. We all need it."

If good coaching is important, it is especially so for young children. Ideally, a good coach at the preadolescent level should have many attributes of a good father. He should be, as Dr. Tutko puts it, "always there, sensitive to emotions. The child's performance is important and he'll push the child to improve, but he cares about the child as a human being first and athlete second. He wants the child to learn fundamentals and enjoy the sport, regardless of team victories or personal triumphs along the way. Instead of emulating hard-nosed big league coaches, he tries to be a nice, lovable, concerned guy while also being firm and well-organized, because that's what youngsters respond to at that age. They're thinking, if he knows who I am, if I know I'm going to play regularly, if I know he's concerned about me and it's fun, I don't really care that much about the final score."

Given a sensibly run youth sports program and sensible parents, Tutko sees no reason why a coach with these qualities should not be heartily encouraged and supported even if he never has a winning season. Far more important than winning can be his contribution to youngsters' growth and development.

Unfortunately, there are too few such coaches. Even with young children, too many ape the behavior of hard-nosed pro coaches—shouting, belittling, administering punishment drills—all supporting the idea that winning is the only thing that counts.

All their fault? Hardly. They, too, are commonly under pressure to win—a kind of general pressure coming down from the big leagues that winning is all, and often, too, parental pressure.

As Joseph Margolis, athletic director and associate professor of physical education at Brooklyn College, has observed: "Many parents live vicariously through their children. When their child succeeds or wins, parents view this as a personal victory. If the child is unsuccessful, parents interpret this as a reflection on their ability as a mother or father. The parent's ego has become involved."

There are also parents who hope their child will turn into a college or pro athlete, earning scholarships and huge salaries, and who push the child, no matter what his desires. For them, winning is important, a way to advance toward the goal, and pressure from them passes on to the coach.

SOUND PARENTAL INFLUENCE

If you're a parent who is less concerned with winning than with the welfare and healthy physical and emotional growth and development of your child, there are a number of things you may wish to consider doing.

You can start by discussing with your child, even at an early age, the real values of sports. Make it a two-way conversation, hearing and responding to the child's viewpoint. It should be a joint discussion, not a lecture.

Let him or her know that you would approve participation in one or more sports. Discuss various sports, the child's likes and dislikes, any indications you may have that the youngster might better enjoy some particular sport or sports. Watch various sports—a school or neighborhood game or even a game on TV—and ask if that might possibly be something he or she would like to do.

Once the child goes out for a sports activity, get interested. Talk with the youngster about what is going on. Attend practice sessions now and then. Make it a point never to criticize the child's performance. Encourage yes; but criticize, browbeat, apply pressure, no.

If you want the child to view sports as fun, one good way to get the message across is to show how this is true. Get other kids in the neighborhood and maybe their parents or other adults together for an occasional evening or weekend sandlot game—and let it be fun.

Talk with the child's coach. Make an effort to find out

what his or her philosophy is. Observe the coach at practice sessions.

How in fact does the coach go about his job? Get information in the course of casual conversation with your child. Get it from your own observation. Is there shouting, swearing, ridiculing, scolding, threatening? How does the coach respond when the child fumbles or makes any kind of error? Is there consideration for the child's emotions?

If you like the coach and what he or she is doing, and your youngster does, too, support the coach.

If the coach's practice is not to concentrate entirely on the best players to the exclusion of the others; if attention is given to trying to develop the less able youngsters; if there is an effort to get as many youngsters as possible participating in games; if there are good words and encouragement when a less able or awkward child shows a little progress; if, in short, the coach is concerned less with winning than with the development of his young charges, support him or her. Come out with firm support if there are objections from other sources that not enough attention is being paid to winning.

If you don't like what the coach is doing—from your own observation or the complaints of your youngster or both—you can talk to the coach and make your philosophy known. If you find that other parents are just as concerned, arrange with them for a meeting with the coach.

It could be that, assured of sufficient support from many parents, the coach might decide to change his or her techniques. If not, an appeal to a league president or other higher authority might help.

Failing all else, if you're deeply concerned and the child is unhappy, you might well allow the child to leave the team and try for another sport, or perhaps the same sport in a different program.

Youth sports programs which even put special emphasis on de-emphasizing the "winning is all" concept are now beginning.

YBA—AN ALTERNATIVE

In 1975, YMCAs in many areas of the country set up a Youth Basketball Association which they hoped would set a new tone for youth sports programs throughout the U.S. and Canada.

YBA is a basketball league for both boys and girls, eight to eighteen. Some Ys have organized co-ed teams and leagues. Teams always play against other teams in the same age or grade category.

The most important part of YBA, its organizers emphasize, is the program philosophy:

● The whole family can get involved as volunteers or as participants in special YBA events.

● The style of YBA is consistent with good YMCA physical education and group work philosophy; it's good for everybody, not just those who excel.

● The emphasis is on the development of basic skills in the sport. Players are urged to develop these skills as far as their individual interests and abilities will allow them to go.

● Values education is central to the program. Coaches are urged to set an environment for helping kids think about personal and life values, and learn the skills needed to make sound value decisions for themselves.

● Fair play is discussed, encouraged, and built in. Respect for the opponent, for the rules of the game, and for the officials are YBA values.

● It's fun. That's what games for kids are all about.

● The players are first, the sport second. What matters most is what happens to the players as people—their personal and social development, their skills, their attitudes, and behavior.

- Winning is placed in proper perspective.

- All players are involved equally in the game, regardless of ability.

How has the YBA been working out in actual practice?
After its first year of operation, the *Wall Street Journal* published a story about YBA:

> Needham, Mass.—Bruce Skinner, age 10, likes his new basketball coach at the local YMCA. "The old coach only cared about winning," Bruce says. "Andy, the new coach, just wants us to have fun."
> What Bruce doesn't know is that his former coach was fired for doing precisely the things Bruce disliked. He "over-emphasized competition and set a bad example," says Steve Fulford, 25, the Y physical education director who ordered the switch.
> Few coaches expect to be replaced for trying too hard to win. Steve's decision, however, jibed perfectly with the unorthodox goals of Bruce's league and 350 other leagues in the Youth Basketball Association. Run by YMCAs nationwide, the YBA encourages boys and girls to concentrate on basketball skills and teamwork, not on winning. The Association's coaches, all volunteers, are trained to stress personal values. Players keep scorecards that measure sportsmanship, as well as skills like shooting and dribbling. One question asks, "How much of a team player am I?" and responses range from "ball hog" to "playmaker."
> YBA coaches sometimes even bend the rules to prevent lopsided victories that would discourage losers. When the halftime score was 30 to 2 in a game at Milwaukee, the coaches decreed that the leading team had to complete five passes before each shot. The second-half scoring was even, so the losing team obviously benefitted from

the five-pass rule. The league director said the winners also benefitted because they got to practice their passing. The Association goes out of its way to involve parents in the program. They meet at workshops with coaches and players four times each season to see films, hear speeches and discuss YBA goals.

Parents even receive a bit of sports advice for themselves. The YBA manual includes a personal scorecard for parents that discourages them from putting too much pressure on their children. The manual cautions that "being a 'support' without being a 'push' is one of the big challenges for parents."

Some coaches and parents fear that downgrading competition hurts the quality of play, but Mr. Stepanek thinks the opposite is true. "Over all, the quality of play improves," he says, "because kids with less ability and more sensitive egos do much better without the high pressure. Only the best players are helped by intense competition."

It was the National Basketball Players Association, the union for players in the National Basketball Association, that first suggested YMCA leagues.

Perhaps it's significant of a growing recognition of the real value of sports for kids that the suggestion and continuing support for YBA has come from the NBA.

Says one of the NBA players, John Havlicek: "We all support this program and its goals. We think it's important for *all* kids to have an opportunity to learn to play basketball, regardless of ability, size, or any other of the physical characteristics which often eliminate kids from playing the game.

"We also believe in the YBA concept of fair play and values education. Good basketball is played by people who respect themselves, the other team, and the officials.

"All of us have to work to live up to this idea and all of us need to re-think our values—what we feel is important in our lives."

OTHER ALTERNATIVES

Only a few sports have been organized—and overorganized—by adults for kids, with heavy emphasis on winning is all.

But these are not the only sports, and in fact, they are not the sports with the greatest lifetime values.

Few adults play baseball, football or basketball unless they are pro players, and there aren't many of those.

What sports are most popular with adults? Here, we're talking about adults who don't sit back and live sedentary existences, getting what enjoyment they can out of sports vicariously, at second hand, as spectators only.

A U. S. Public Health Survey found that America's top participant sport among both men and women is swimming; and, as has been obvious, there has been a great increase of interest in jogging, running, biking, tennis.

You might want to consider introducing your child to any one of those or other sports which can be enjoyed for a lifetime. These include: volleyball, soccer, badminton, handball, racquetball, paddleball, cross-country skiing, skating, squash. Among these sports are many that, in addition to providing fun and relaxation, have excellent physical health values.

When the President's Council on Physical Fitness and Sports asked a group of experts to rate fourteen forms of activity in terms of health from the standpoint of heart and lung endurance, muscular endurance, muscular strength, flexibility, balance, and general well-being (weight control, sleep, digestion, etc.), these were the ratings in descending order of value from most helpful to least:

Jogging
Bicycling
Swimming
Skating
Handball/squash

Skiing, cross-country
Basketball
Skiing, downhill
Tennis
Calisthenics
Walking
Golf (with cart)
Softball
Bowling

CHAPTER 6

ATHLETES: BORN OR MADE?

In 1976, at McGill University in Montreal, Dr. Vassilis Klissouras, a physiologist, carried out an unusual study. Working with 200 sets of twins, Klissouras set out to determine the relative importance of heredity versus environment in building champions.

Identical twins, of course, have the same genetic makeup, so any differences between them in athletic accomplishments could be ascribed to nonhereditary influences. Fraternal twins, on the other hand, have different genetic endowments.

About one-half of the twins in the study were identical; the others, nonidentical.

A basic principle used in the study, one commonly used by investigators, is that the higher a person's oxygen uptake per unit of body weight (kilogram, or 2.2 pounds), the better his or her athletic ability is likely to be. Maximal oxygen uptake is a measure of the amount of oxygen the heart and lungs can distribute to body tissues which always need oxygen and need much more during vigorous activity.

For an average person, the uptake is about 40 milliliters per kilogram of body weight, while top athletes commonly have uptakes of 70, 80 or even more milliliters.

From the beginning, Klissouras assumed that if a pair of identical twins were set to working on a treadmill, there would be little or no difference in their oxygen uptake rates. His assumption proved correct.

The treadmill testing showed a far greater difference between the uptake values for nonidentical twins than for the identical.

Going further, Klissouras looked into the potential of training on athletic ability. He worked with a pair of identical twins for eighteen months during which one of them trained as an athlete while the other did not.

The untrained twin had a maximal oxygen uptake of 35.9 milliliters; his trained brother attained a value of 49.2. Obviously, training helped. Yet the trained twin's improve-ment was not very striking considering the values of 70 or more of top athletes. Klissouras and his colleagues had to conclude that starting level, which is genetically determined, is a vital factor.

Klissouras carried out still other studies with the twin volunteers, involving technical details of the interaction be-tween heredity and training.

The final conclusion: An individual can train all he wants but can only reach a top level or ceiling determined by his genes. Beyond this he will not pass.

So if the study is right and is confirmed by others, it means that it's likely to take the right genes to be a cham-pion. And if genes set limits, that's important for parents and kids to understand.

Many of us know individuals who seem to be, and very likely are, natural, well-endowed athletes. Consider, for ex-ample, Mac Wilkins, Olympic gold medal winner in the dis-cus. One day during a meet in Europe, Wilkins picked up the hammer and, although he had tried throwing the hammer only a few times before, tossed it more than 200 feet, a throw which put him among the top American hammer throwers.

There are people who are naturally superb at sports. But even if we are born with limits to our physical prowess, and most of us couldn't toss the hammer more than 200 feet or run a four-minute mile no matter how much we trained, that doesn't inevitably mean mediocrity.

One does not have to be a champion to thoroughly enjoy and benefit from sports. What could spoil the fun and cancel the benefits, would be a fruitless, wild goose chase in pursuit of championships by a youngster, spurred on by misguided parental and personal ambitions.

Despite a ceiling on a youngster's ultimate capacity, there is almost always room for improvement and potential for achieving it.

Properly encouraged by parents, coaches and others, self-confidence buttressed by them, helped to achieve good conditioning, a youngster can work successfully toward achieving whatever his or her full potential may be, making great improvements in skill, strength, and endurance, and having fun in the process.

THE ROAD TO EXCELLENCE

There is a myth that athletes are born and not made.

Even with the best endowment of genetic influences, it still takes dedication and hard work to achieve excellence.

After a tenth-place finish in the preceding Olympics, Bruce Jenner, the 1976 decathlon champion, decided he would be a champion next time around. "For the next four years," he said, "I trained eight hours every day, took off only one day, Christmas, and felt guilty about that."

There are stories told about George Young, four-time Olympic distance runner who never took a day off, even when he looked out the window and saw a heavy snowstorm, always telling himself, "The Russians are out there running."

Muhammad Ali, according to Angelo Dundee, manager of many champions, was the hardest-working fighter of them all, outworking everybody, always jogging, sparring, punching light and heavy bags, watching fight films, even sneaking out at three in the morning to run. "He either trains or sleeps," Dundee has said. "Behind all that talk and poetry is a very hard-working man who likes preparing for a fight."

Without endorsing such all-out, single-minded dedication for a youngster still maturing or even just beginning to mature, with much else to occupy him or her, a suitable degree of dedication and work is needed for achieving full potential.

Good coaches have learned what is needed to encourage a youngster so that he or she will be well-motivated, dedicated, and happy to work. You may wish to check to see whether your youngster's coaches are providing such encouragement; you may wish to provide at least some of it yourself.

It's possible, of course, for a coach to influence a child—or for that matter, an adult—with criticism and punishment. The aim is to change behavior, and this negative kind of approach may accomplish that. But that same aim can be achieved in a positive fashion, and it works better and is much more fun for everybody.

The positive approach makes use of a reward—not a tangible reward, but something as simple as praise, clapping, a pat on the back, even a friendly smile.

Such rewarding should not be limited to the youngster who has made a great catch, batted a homer, sunk a critical basket, or achieved any other major accomplishment. It should be directed to the kid who tries, even if he doesn't succeed.

Does that spoil? Hardly. As some excellent coaches have noted, a child has complete control over his or her effort, but certainly not over the outcome. Effort should be appreciated in order to help make certain that effort is continued.

Encourage by rewarding effort. That goes a long way toward maintaining a youngster's enthusiasm.

Encourage even after mistakes.

Kids—and even adults—often don't realize something important about mistakes. They happen, of course. Nobody likes to make them. There can be great embarrassment when a mistake is made. But mistakes can help to show what needs to be done to improve performance.

Mistakes can have a valuable positive side if kids understand that and if you encourage them to understand. Without encouragement, chances are many youngsters will only suffer from their bungles.

They will suffer even more if a coach or parent leaps on the mistakes, yells disapprovingly, punishes with sarcasm, or issues corrective instructions in a hostile fashion.

One of the major hazards in the mishandling of mistakes is that it may seriously impair self-confidence and saddle the youngster with a fear of failure.

What applies to adults certainly does to kids: It's one thing to understand—and every kid should certainly understand—that nobody is or can be expected to be perfect, and that mistakes are going to be made. It's another, however, when, having made a mistake, the youngster gets no encouragement but instead is criticized and humiliated. All too often then, a youngster, like an adult, may so fear failure that he becomes afraid to act.

Encourage whenever possible. Encourage even small successes. That can help a child considerably in acquiring skills.

Many things can go into learning a skill.

There may be blind trial and error, which is not the most effective. A youngster may thoughtfully observe someone else perform, mentally put himself through the activity, then try to duplicate the performance physically.

He may be able to analyze how he has performed,

where he has fallen short, and then try again. He may receive advice and try again. He may accidentally discover how to improve some aspect of skill.

With good guidance, of course, the process of learning and skill acquisition often can be speeded, with less waste motion and lost time.

But certainly what may be the most important single ingredient in skill learning is reinforcement.

Reinforcement helps to increase the probability that an improvement will recur. Reinforcement usually is achieved by something pleasant such as awareness of success or being praised. The positive pleasure helps the youngster to remember what it is he did and how he did it.

Encouraging, reinforcing praise can be especially important when a youngster does make a little progress, when he or she does something right, and the improvement, though an important step, does not produce immediate obvious results.

Recognition of any amount of progress, however small, is stimulating. It helps to assure that the progress will be retained.

One of the hallmarks of good coaching is such positive reinforcement of performance.

CHAPTER 7

CONDITIONING
FOR SPORTS

It's often said that sports lead to fitness, and they do. They can help to maintain and increase it. But bringing fitness to sports can be equally important, both for playing well and minimizing risk of injury.

Conditioning for sports, which is to say training, getting into shape, and improving the level of fitness may not need as much emphasis for a normally active preadolescent youngster as for an older child.

As Ronald Byrd of the University of Alabama in Birmingham has pointed out, youngsters learning the basics of sports require a minimal level of fitness to help prevent injuries. It's only when competition becomes more significant that conditioning calls for increased emphasis.

"This is true for two reasons," Byrd advises. "First, with the development of speed and power that naturally accompanies maturation, young athletes are more likely to subject their bodies to levels of stress that cause injuries. Compare the forces in tackling by eight- and fourteen-year-old boys; or the centrifugal forces and likelihood of turning an ankle in rounding first base at full speed by children of widely different ages. Second, conditioning is less important for younger athletes because there are fewer opportunities to take part in sports or events in which conditioning could be decisive. The length of games is shorter, fields are smaller, and races shorter."

FITNESS TESTING

If a child is interested in improving physical fitness either for the sake of fitness alone or for participation in sports, or if you suspect a youngster should improve his or her fitness, the American Alliance for Health, Physical Education, and Recreation (AAHPER) has developed a useful fitness testing program.

Its purpose is to encourage and help youngsters discover their physical capabilities and motivate them to work for maximum development of their individual physical potential.

The AAHPER has been encouraging schools, municipal recreation departments, YMCA groups and other organizations dealing with boys and girls between the ages of six and eighteen to give the tests. The testing program may be available in your community.

It's a relatively simple, inexpensive program requiring a minimum of equipment.

Included are tests (pull-ups, push-ups, sit-ups, flexed-arm hang) for muscular endurance; others (walk/run) for circulo-respiratory endurance, (sprint) for speed, (shuttle run) for agility, and (standing broad jump) for power/coordination.

There are standards for boys and girls at different ages, and a youngster who doesn't measure up to begin with in some test area can go on to improve performance.

This is how the events in the testing program are carried out:

Sit-ups: From the starting position, lying on the back with fingers laced behind neck and knees bent and feet flat on the floor, the youngster sits up and touches elbows to knees, then returns to starting position.

Push-ups: There is a regular form for boys, a modified one for girls. For boys, from prone (face down) position, with elbows bent and hands on floor with thumbs next to chest, the child pushes his body up until arms are straight and body weight rests on hands and toes, and with heels, hips, shoulders and head all in the same straight line. The arms are then relaxed and chin is lowered to floor. For girls, from prone position, but with knees bent and lower legs crossed, the push-ups are carried out with the body straight from knees to head.

Standing broad jump: The jump can be executed with the feet in any position to start with but both feet must leave the ground simultaneously. It's permissible to rock back and forth—lifting first heels and then toes. Distance is measured from the mark of the toe at the starting position to the nearest mark on ground or floor made by any part of the body at the finish of the jump.

Walk and run: The child can alternately walk and run as often and as far as he or she wishes to complete the prescribed distance on a circular running track or over a straight course.

Pull-ups (for boys only): With palms either facing or away from him, the youngster grasps a tree limb or a high horizontal bar and hangs so toes are not touching floor or ground, then pulls the body up until chin is raised above the limb or the bar, after which he relaxes arms and lowers body.

Flexed-arm hang (girls): With horizontal bar at standing height, the girl grasps bar with palms downward. Then, with the assistance of two people to help her raise her body so her chin is above the bar and elbows are fully bent, she holds the position as long as she can. Time is taken with a stopwatch when the position is first assumed and time is stopped when the chin falls below the level of the bar.

Sprints: These can be done from any starting position.

Shuttle run: Starting on command, the child runs to a line thirty feet away, picks up an object such as a block or an eraser, runs back and places the object on the starting line, then runs back and picks up a second object and returns across the starting line.

The AAHPER recommends: a two- to three-minute warm-up period before a test, using arm and trunk movements and running in place; a rest of at least five minutes between tests if more than one is carried out on the same day; and several days of practice so the child can work on those events in which he or she feels improvement is necessary.

As an incentive for a continual program of fitness testing, AAHPER has prepared motivational materials for those participating in the testing procedure. Schools or any organized group that administers the test may receive a certificate of participation from AAHPER headquarters. Boys and girls taking part in the testing may receive awards and emblems indicating their performance level on the AAHPER Youth Fitness Test.

There is an achievement award certificate for boys and girls who attain the 50th percentile on all items in the test. An embossed gold merit seal is available for the certificate of achievement for those boys and girls who attain the 80th percentile on all test items. A progress award is available for physically limited boys and girls who, in their instructor's estimation, show improved performance on the test items.

Boys and girls who score at or above the 85th percentile on all six items of the AAHPER Youth Fitness Test are eligible for the Presidential Physical Fitness Award. The following charts show what the 85th percentile scores are for boys and girls.

AAHPER Youth Fitness Test

Administration of this test should not take place until two primary steps are taken: (See page 99)

TRY OUT FOR THE TEAM!

Can you equal or surpass *all* these marks? If you can, you are eligible to receive a citation signed by the President, a colorful emblem and decal to prove you earned a spot on the All-America Physical Fitness Team.

BOYS

REQUIRED EVENTS	Age 10	11	12	13	14	15	16	17
1. BENT-KNEE SIT-UPS (1 MINUTE TIME LIMIT)	42	43	45	48	50	50	50	49
2. STANDING BROAD JUMP	5'8"	5'10"	6'1"	6'8"	6'11"	7'5"	7'9"	8'0"
3. 600-YARD RUN-WALK	2:11	2:09	2:0	1:54	1:47	1:42	1:40	1:38
4. PULL-UPS	5	5	6	7	9	11	11	12
5. 50-YARD DASH	:7.7	:7.4	:7.1	:6.9	:6.5	:6.3	:6.3	:6.1
6. SHUTTLE RUN	:10.4	:10.1	:10.0	:09.7	:09.3	:09.2	:09.1	:09.0

Reprinted by permission of the American Alliance for Health, Physical Education, and Recreation (AAHPER)

85th PERCENTILE SCORES

GIRLS

REQUIRED EVENTS	Age 10	11	12	13	14	15	16	17
1. BENT-KNEE SIT-UPS (1 MINUTE TIME LIMIT)	38	38	38	40	41	40	38	40
2. STANDING BROAD JUMP	5'5"	5'7"	5'9"	6'0"	6'3"	6'1"	6'0"	6'3"
3. 600-YARD RUN-WALK	2:30	2:25	2:21	2:16	2:11	2:14	2:19	2:14
4. FLEXED-ARM HANG	:24	:24	:23	:21	:26	:25	:20	:22
5. 50-YARD DASH	:7.8	:7.5	:7.4	:7.2	:7.1	:7.1	:7.3	:7.1
6. SHUTTLE RUN	:10.9	:10.5	:10.5	:10.2	:10.1	:10.2	:10.4	:10.1

First—Participants should be given several days to practice so that they may work on those events in which they feel improvement is necessary.
Second—There should be a two- or three-minute warm-up session prior to the adminsistration of a test. Such exercises as arm and trunk movements, and running in place, are suggested.

A local school or other organization can obtain further information about the program and its awards by writing to AAHPER headquarters: AAHPER, 1201 16th St., N.W., Washington, DC 20036.

THE PRINCIPLES OF CONDITIONING

It's important for a youngster to understand a number of basic principles of sound physical training. They don't come automatically. In fact, children—and adults as well—tend to unknowingly violate some of them, not without paying a penalty.

These principles are the result of many studies over the years. They can help to assure better results and, actually, faster results, with less likelihood of injury. Here are the important principles:

Adaptation. The normally healthy human body has a remarkable ability to adjust and adapt to change and the demands made upon it. Left to itself, it functions at relatively low levels. Called upon for some exertion, it will adjust its functioning accordingly.

The adjustment doesn't happen overnight. It takes time. A tennis player at first develops muscle ache and blisters. Gradually, however, with continued playing, muscles grow and blood vessels feeding those muscles increase in number and size; callus develops to protect the skin on the hand; the joints used in playing adjust so they move more easily through a greater range of motion.

Tolerance. There should be no sudden demand on the body for bursts of tremendous effort. Straining hard beyond the level bodily functions can handle is not necessary to develop fitness, and it can retard the development by causing injuries.

Overload. Exercising or working out too easily leads to little or no improvement in fitness. It is necessary to push just a bit, to work a little harder than customary in normal daily activities, and to work beyond the first feeling of tiredness but still within tolerance levels.

Actually, pushing a bit does not overload the body, which has more capacity than it is ordinarily called upon to use. Given a little more load than usual, it can handle it, and, progressively, will be able to handle more and more.

With exercise, the working muscles require more blood, and the heart responds by pumping more. The heart beat rate increases. No less important, with each of its beats, the heart pumps out more blood. This greater volume of blood pumped out with each beat, called stroke volume, eases the burden on the heart. With conditioning, the heart doesn't have to beat as often; it can pump as much blood with fewer beats. All told, with physical fitness, the heart may be able to pump twice as much blood as it did before fitness was achieved.

It isn't enough for the heart to pump more blood. The extra blood must go where it is needed, to the working muscles. Ordinarily, at rest, the muscles receive only about 15 percent of the total blood volume, the remainder going to other organs. But during vigorous activity, as much as 85 percent of the blood flow may be needed by the muscles. That redistribution involves opening wide blood vessels where more blood is needed and closing them where blood is not immediately essential. Without efficient redistribution, muscles can become fatigued. With overload activity, over a period of time redistribution becomes more efficient, and endurance increases.

Progression. With regular exercise, strength and endurance increase and workouts, if unmodified, become easier and easier.

A plateau is reached. Improvement has occurred and, with the same workouts, the improvement will be maintained. To go beyond, workouts must become progressively more strenuous until the desired level of fitness is achieved.

Say a youngster in training runs a seven-minute mile. The first time, it's no easy matter; there may be difficulty in completing the run. But from day to day, with more and more repetitions of the mile, the run becomes less and less strenuous. A mile run is no longer an overload. There must then be progression—training at a faster pace or over longer distances—if a higher level of fitness is to be reached.

Specificity. When the objective is to play a sport well, conditioning must be carried beyond the fitness level and must become specific for the sport.

Muscles must be used in the same manner and at the same speed or faster than they will be used in the sport.

Push-ups and jogging, for example, can contribute to overall fitness. But if a youngster wants to be a runner, he must run; if a swimmer, swim. A pitcher can achieve the necessary specific endurance only by throwing, a soccer player by repeated kicking, and baseball players in general must go beyond jogging laps to repeated short sprints with sharp turns.

Consider tennis, for example, and suitable conditioning for it.

To jog for long distances or do a series of mile or half-mile runs would not be specific for tennis. Tennis involves periods of running and periods of rest.

Good coaches have their own specific regimens but one, for example, advises intervals of up to a minute of fast running broken by intervals of slow jogging. In addition, he suggests short rapid moves in various directions: hop half a dozen times, then move four or five steps quickly to the right, hop again, then to the left, with movements backward and forward as well as side to side.

Other suggestions for the young tennis player include squeezing an old tennis ball to strengthen grip; push-ups and chin-ups and fifteen to twenty flexings of the elbow with a barbell or dumbbell to build up strength of muscles and ligaments in the elbow region; exercises in which the racket is swung, simulating forehand, backhand, smash, and serve.

Similarly, there are specific conditioning activities for other sports which will usually be advised by coaches. Some coaches, for example, teach swimmers to stretch their ankles so they bend back beyond a straight line, achieving this by sitting on the ankles every chance they get. The increased ankle flexibility provides more thrust in the water. Some advocate bending and rotating the trunk while sitting on the ankles. Another specific exercise for swimmers: lying on a cushion with arms and legs extended and, holding two soup cans, doing swimming motions with arms and legs.

Strength is important in many sports. Lifting heavy weights, of course, can develop strong muscles. But a more specific strength-building activity for a baseball player, for example, is to swing a weighted bat.

Because a runner's arms help him run, strong arms are important. But, suggests one sports medicine authority, rather than press heavy weights overhead, he will do better to use pulleys adjusted so the arms pull weights with the same motion they use during running.

Of course, speed is important. To be fast in play, it is necessary to train fast in practice.

It's now known that muscles are made up of two primary types of fibers—fast twitch and slow twitch. Slow twitch muscle fibers appear red under a microscope because of their rich blood supply. They are used for endurance activities such as jogging. The fast twitch fibers, which have a limited blood supply and appear white under the microscope, are for speed and power and do much of the work when it comes to activities such as sprinting, or playing tennis, or racquetball.

Actually, each of us is born with a set ratio of fast to slow twitch fibers and the ratio cannot be changed. It's a fact that outstanding endurance sports athletes tend to have a greater proportion of slow twitch fibers while others such as top sprinters tend to have a greater proportion of fast twitch.

But if the ratio cannot be changed, the performance of the fibers can be greatly improved through training. The performance of slow twitch fibers can be improved by slow running, for example; that of fast twitch by fast running.

Recovery. Intensive workouts day after day are not desirable. This is an important lesson for eager young athletes to learn.

With vigorous activity during an intensive workout, glycogen, a muscle fuel is used up and time is needed for the body to produce more. Muscle cells also tend to release a mineral, potassium, during hard workouts and it may take up to forty-eight hours for it to be replenished.

Moreover, some muscle fiber damage can occur with vigorous activitity. It is not serious, only temporary, but time is needed for healing.

These are reasons why experienced athletes alternate easy workouts with hard ones. The easy, which allow for recovery, are performed with much less intensity and at a relaxed pace.

Training without overtraining. Becoming dedicated, many youngsters train hard, too hard, pushing themselves too much. They reason, if so much activity is good, still more must be better. But there is a limit to what even the best-conditioned body can take. Overtraining has its warning signs and they should be heeded.

The chances are that a youngster who is always tired, experiences persistent soreness and stiffness of muscles and joints, and has a heavy-legged feeling is a victim of overtraining.

Other indications include nervousness, depressed feelings, difficulty in relaxing, fall-off in performance, headache, and loss of real interest in training.

Attaining and regaining vital flexibility. As we've already noted, with vigorous activity, there is some temporary muscle injury. As the muscle heals, it tends to become shorter and tighter.

This muscle shortening and tightening is a major reason for stiffness and soreness—and also for increased susceptibility to pulls, strains and other injuries.

The problem can be markedly reduced and flexibility can be regained with stretching exercises: Many top coaches now recommend such exercises both before and immediately after vigorous activity.

While it's possible to stretch muscles with bouncing or jerking movements, such movements often cause soreness. The preferred way is to use static stretching, achieving a stretched position and then holding it for a few seconds, repeating the exercise a number of times.

It's especially important to stretch those muscles used in a sport activity. Usually, a coach will have specific suggestions.

Among useful stretching procedures are the following:

Toe touch to stretch the hamstring muscles in back of the thighs: With heels together and knees straight, try to touch floor or ground with fingers, without bouncing. Hold for a count of ten; repeat five times or more.

Wall push for stretching calves and Achilles tendons: Stand facing a wall four feet away. With palms on wall and keeping the back straight, bend elbows to bring upper part of the body closer to the wall, keeping heels on ground. Hold for a count of ten, straighten elbows, rest briefly, repeat five or more times.

Foot pull to stretch quadriceps muscle in front of thigh: While holding a chair or table for support, grasp right foot with right hand and pull up toward back until you feel a pull on the quadriceps. Hold for three to five seconds, release, rest, repeat ten times. Do the same with left foot.

Split to stretch inner thighs: Keeping knees straight and using palms on floor for balance, gradually spread the legs as far apart as possible, hold ten seconds, rest, repeat five or more times.

Trunk rotation stretch: With feet about shoulder width apart and hands on hips, twist to the right as far as you can. Hold several seconds. Do the same to the left. Repeat a dozen or more times in each direction.

Side stretch: With feet about thirty-six inches apart and hands behind head, legs straight, lean sideways until you feel muscle pull. Hold for a few seconds, return to starting position, and lean to other side. Repeat ten times.

Hip stretch: Standing about eighteen inches from a wall, lean on wall with hand or forearm and push hips inward toward wall. Hold for fifteen or twenty seconds, relax, repeat. Switch sides and stretch the other hip.

Shin stretch: In kneeling position, with feet placed so tops face the floor, gently sit back on heels until you feel a stretch in your shins. Hold several seconds, rest, repeat several times.

Warming up. All physical workouts should start with warm-up activities.

Warm-up is very important for several reasons. It increases blood supply to muscles, raises their temperature, limbers and makes them more resistant to injury.

Warm-up also prepares the heart and lungs for exercise and tunes up the central nervous system which controls muscle functioning.

Many muscles of the body are paired, one of a pair working in one direction, the other in the opposite direction. One muscle, for example, bends knee or elbow; a second straightens knee or elbow. If one muscle is to move efficiently and safely, the other should relax. Nervous system readiness helps to assure this and minimize risk of injury.

Do your warming-up in two phases, beginning with stretching. Bend, twist and stretch—slowly, without bouncing or jerking. Pay special attention to stretching those muscles that are tight from previous activity.

Then go on to warm-up muscles by working them out in the same fashion as when you engage in the sport. Start slowly, gradually increase intensity. Thus, a tennis player, for example, can rally for ten minutes or so before beginning play; a runner can jog slowly for a few minutes.

Cooling down. Cooling down after a workout is important for two reasons.

First, during vigorous effort, the heart pumps out more than the usual amount of blood to keep muscles supplied. After providing nourishment for the muscles, the blood enters the vein system for return to heart and lungs for freshening.

During exercise, contracting muscles press on nearby veins and produce a pumping action that helps return the blood quickly to heart and lungs. If exercise is stopped suddenly, without cool-down, the heart continues to pump extra blood for a time; but the muscles no longer pump on the veins, blood return is slowed, and blood may pool in the legs, producing temporary shortages elsewhere and leading to faintness.

Second, cramps and stiffness are more likely to develop when exercise is terminated abruptly.

For cooling down, use slow walking and repeat the stretching exercises used in warm-up.

A SPECIAL NOTE:
FOR EVERY CHILD,
A PHYSICAL EXAMINATION

It is common for athletes of high school and college age to have routine physical examinations.

Too often, however, this is not true for younger children.

Yet every child who enters a sports program should have a thorough examination. It should be done by a competent physician who appreciates the importance of athletic activity and also of thorough examination as a means of checking and maintaining health and helping to avoid injuries.

A knowledgeable physician may not only provide information about the state of a child's health but also of his or her physical fitness. He or she may have suggestions for how best to go about improving fitness of the individual child.

If the examination should disclose a health problem, the physician should consider the advisability of checking with a consultant specialist. There should be no rush to bar a child from sports or seriously restrict activities without expert study.

CHAPTER 8

NUTRITION FOR THE ATHLETE: FABLES AND FACTS

Good nutrition is critical for all athletes—and certainly for the young. The kind of food the body gets can make a difference in how well it performs. But nutritional myths, worthless or even potentially dangerous, are almost unbelievably prevalent.

In each of its issues, the official *Journal of the American Medical Association* carries a question and answer section. Its purpose is to allow physicians to seek help from experts on puzzling problems. Not long ago, one physician wanted to know whether young athletes might need protein supplements if they are already eating a well-balanced diet.

The answer was emphatic: Protein supplements not only are useless; they may well have detrimental effects.

Athletes, the experts pointed out, need the same amount of protein foods as nonathletes. Protein does not increase strength. Moreover, it is not a particularly efficient energy fuel. It is not stored in the body. And it often takes greater energy for the body to metabolize (handle and digest) excess protein. Further, excess protein intake in the athlete can induce dehydration, appetite loss, and diarrhea.

The fact that a physician had to ask the question is one indication of the confusion which surrounds sports nutrition.

In 1979, a three-man team of Pennsylvania State University investigators—a physician, a director of dietary services at the University medical center, and a professor of physical education—asked a series of questions of seventy-five coaches and trainers involved in various sports. The questions were designed to assess their nutritional knowledge.

None of the seventy-five believed they were up to date on nutrition. The great majority said they needed more information. Most of the questions were answered incorrectly by 70 percent or more of the group. Overall, the results of the study indicated that 95 percent of the group had obsolete or inaccurate nutritional knowledge.

In a country in which food faddism is very common, it would be surprising if it did not extend to sports.

Even outstanding athletes have their idiosyncrasies. One of the nation's top soccer players steadfastly attributes mysterious virtues to bananas. Another well-known athlete reportedly uses his hands to squeeze blood from several pounds of raw hamburger, adds it to tomato juice, and drinks the mixture as a kind of elixir. On the other hand, another prominent athlete won't touch meat and, wherever he goes, carries along lentil seeds which he grows on a windowsill, plus apples, nuts, bulbs, and plants. Still another regularly fasts before he races.

Teams are bombarded with the claims of health food salespeople, peddling their latest concoctions "virtually guaranteed to assure victory." Indeed, a sizable industry operates to inundate individual athletes and whole teams with all sorts of "remarkable" foods—"energy assurers," "body builders," "fatigue defeaters," and much more.

One well-known sports physician, himself a long-time athlete, recalls that he too fell under the spell of the peddlers and faddists early in his career, looking for any competitive advantage.

"I consumed vitamin pills in large quantities," he writes, "took wheat germ oil by the tablespoon, and popped bone meal tablets. I spent a few weeks avoiding starch, but I became so weak that I couldn't run. Once I became a vegetarian. Another time I drank so much milk the cholesterol level in my blood became abnormally high."

And he adds: "After years of experimenting on myself, I now know what nutritionists have known for decades: Everything your body needs can be supplied by a proper diet. The same rules for eating apply universally to those who exercise and those who don't. The only difference is that people who are physically active require more calories and more fluids."

He was hardly as fanatic during his experimenting years as some. Among the assorted supplements used by sports figures—beyond vitamins and wheat germ—are iodine, magnesium, manganese, selenium, copper, zinc, calcium, potassium, phosporus, kelp, garlic, brewer yeast, bee pollen, lecithin, dessicated liver, ginseng, and pumpkin and sunflower seeds.

More than a dozen years ago, Dr. Donald L. Cooper, Director of the Student Health Service and Team Physician at Oklahoma State University, told a meeting of the American College Health Association:

"For several years we have been fascinated, charmed, confused, upset, and puzzled by so much of what we hear about the various dietary programs proposed in feeding athletes to gain better performance. I am sure if we would go around this room and ask everyone to write down those things he has heard mentioned in the past to be especially beneficial to performance in a particular athletic event, the list would be quite formidable. If this audience were mostly track coaches, there would not be enough paper in the Miami area for them to write down all the various things they know to be 'absolutely true' in regard to dietary regimens to be followed by their athletes."

In 1972, Dr. Jean Mayer, then Professor of Nutrition

at Harvard University and now President of Tufts University, Boston, had some observations to make:

"The Olympic tryouts are just getting under way, but already we're hearing from those masters of hyperbole, the sportswriters, about the magic foods or the secret diet that will bring some team a chestful of gold medals. The team may indeed win the medals. The diet won't be the reason for it.

"As an adviser to high school, college and major-league professional football teams, as well as nutritionist-member of the Olympic Medical Committee, I've been witness to the most amazing and sometimes dangerous foolishness. I have seen swimming teams forbidden to drink pure water— because 'they would be waterlogged.' But they could drink tea, coffee, soft drinks, and so forth. I have seen skiing teams thinned down to the point of emaciation, and wrestlers fattened up, like Strasbourg geese, to just below the allowable level for their class. I have seen football players starved for long periods before a game to the point of weakness— particularly during the second half."

Even more recently, Dr. Robert C. Serfass of the Division of Physical Education of the University of Minnesota had to report:

"In the highly competitive atmosphere of professional and amateur sports, it is understandable that the athlete, coach, trainer, and/or parent often fall victim to what might be termed the 'nutritional magic wand syndrome.' Preoccupation with winning, prestige, social and peer approval makes the sports competitor a prime recipient of nutritional misinformation.

"It matters little that there is no conclusive evidence that supplementing a well-balanced diet will improve performance; the search for something to provide the 'competitive edge' continues to be perpetuated by testimonials of successful athletes and coaches, the commercialization of food supplements, and the inadequate distribution of relevant nutritional information.

"Athletes, who select their own diets, often do not get enough to eat nor do they select the proper balance of foods conducive to the demands of their sport. Most coaches seem to base their nutritional recommendations on past experience and seldom consult with physician or nutritionist."

WHAT THE BODY NEEDS

Since the human body is complex, its nutritional needs might be expected to be complex, too. They are, in this sense: Many nutrients are required and no one nutrient is preeminent. All nutrients, in fact, are interrelated and together, jointly constructive.

Moreover, if one should be deficient, supplying it in adequate amount will be helpful, but an excess may be harmful. For example, calcium is a vital nutrient. But increase its intake to abnormally high levels and you may induce deficiency of zinc, another vital nutrient. Similarly, an excess of phosphorus in the diet can limit iron absorption.

In short, an excess of one nutrient may interfere with the activity of one or more other nutrients. Although this should serve as a warning against fads that put emphasis on this or that particular nutrient as if it were something special, unfortunately, as we have seen, too often it does not.

What anyone's body needs—and certainly that is true for the body of the young athlete—is a proper mix of protein, carbohydrate, fat, vitamins, minerals, and water. Proper in proportion—and, no less important, coming from a variety of foods. That variety can help assure that there will be an adequate intake of other vital nutrients—still undiscovered vitamins, minerals, and perhaps other nutrients.

PROTEIN

Let's consider protein first. Although the need for protein is often grossly exaggerated, it is a basic requirement.

Muscles, heart, liver, kidneys, and brain tissue are all mainly made of protein. No body cell can survive without adequate protein supply. The very wall of a cell is protein, and protein makes up 20 percent of the total cell mass.

What is a protein? The characteristic element is nitrogen. And protein also contains carbon, hydrogen, oxygen, and usually sulfur and phosphorus.

Proteins are in fact the most complex of natural compounds. They are always built up of small constituent units called amino acids which contain nitrogen, carbon and other elements.

It's the number and arrangement of the amino acids (often referred to as the building blocks of protein) which determine the nature of any particular kind of protein. Egg white (albumen), for example, consists of 418 amino acids strung together in a particular way to form each albumen molecule.

While proteins are complex, it is not their complexity but rather their amino acid constituents which count in the diet. Digestion quickly breaks down the complex arrangements in food into the amino acid units and the body then builds up from them its own particular types of needed proteins: its enzymes, disease-fighting antibodies, hormones, blood and other cells.

More than twenty different amino acids are found in proteins. Some are produced by the body. But there are eight which the body cannot manufacture—isoleucine, leucine, lysine, methionine, phenylalanine, threonine, tryptophan, and valine—and these are known as essential amino acids that must come from protein foods.

Many foods contain protein. All flesh—from fish, fowl, and mammal—is rich in it. Cow's milk has a high content—with three times as much as human milk. Cheeses often have still more. Cereals contain some—about 5 to 10 percent by weight. Fruits contain a little—about 1 percent by weight. Vegetables, particularly peas and beans, have a greater proportion than fruit.

The protein foods that contain large amounts of the

essential amino acids are known as complete proteins and include those from animal sources, such as meat, eggs, fish and milk. Vegetable proteins are incomplete; they do not contain all essential amino acids. But it is possible to get all amino acids with a mix of vegetables.

How much protein is necessary?

Studies have shown that half a gram of mixed protein for every kilogram (2.2 pounds) of body weight not only should be adequate for normal maintenance in an adult but also should provide a good margin of safety.

For growing children and adolescents, the studies suggest a protein intake of two to three grams per kilogram of body weight.

Even using the three grams per kilogram figure, that would mean that a 100-pound youngster would need no more than about 135 grams, or five ounces a day.

As we noted earlier, perhaps the myth most difficult to dispel in the sports world is that substantial protein supplements are required to meet the demands of heavy exercise.

There is a mistaken belief, subscribed to by many coaches and trainers who pass it on to their athletes, that protein is needed to increase muscle mass.

But many studies have established that muscle mass can be increased only by special exercises and not by consuming a lot of protein, and that exercise does not increase the requirements for protein. Investigators who have evaluated the effects of protein supplements on muscle strength and growth concluded that such supplements did nothing to increase strength or muscle mass.

Does a growing athlete need as much as three grams of protein per kilogram of body weight a day? "These needs," emphasizes Dr. Serfass, "can easily be met without supplements by the natural increase in food intake necessary to meet the athlete's energy demands or by slight modification of the distribution of foodstuffs in the diet. Excess protein intake can deprive the athlete of more efficient fuel and can induce dehydration, loss of appetite, and diarrhea."

Dr. Mayer, too, has pointed out that, contrary to popular opinion, "vigorous sports do not increase the need for protein. One hundred years of experiments and measurements have failed to show any beneficial effect of high-protein diet. Our muscles run on fats and sugars, and physical labor does not make them lose substance. If anything, muscles hang on to their protein a little better if they are exercised. An amount of protein reasonable for a nonathlete is quite adequate for the athlete, too. So the practice of serving enormous slabs of steaks at training tables has no nutritional justification whatsoever. All it does is condition young men to keep on consuming a high-fat diet which will raise their cholesterol when they are no longer very active, to the great peril of their hearts."

Not only do protein requirements not increase with exercise, but protein is never a source of immediate energy—and the body has no way to store extra protein.

When protein is presented to the body, it must be used immediately or it is broken down by the liver and excreted through the kidneys. If you take in more protein than your body can use, in addition to giving short shrift to other important nutrients, you force your liver and kidneys to work harder.

Dr. Cooper makes other significant points:

"In terms of efficiency of utilization of oxygen, it must be noted that one liter of oxygen yields five calories if used to burn carbohydrates, but only four and one-half if used to burn protein or fat. This is a 10 percent difference in the utilization of oxygen and may be an important factor in competitive performance under certain circumstances.

"Another important factor," Dr. Cooper goes on to emphasize, "is the protein of pregame meals. The digestion and metabolism of protein produces a residue of ammonium acid which can be excreted only by the kidneys. Carbon dioxide is the main acid produced in the metabolism of carbohydrate and fat and can be blown off via the lungs and excreted by the skin. During strenuous exercise effective kidney function ceases because blood is shunted around the kidneys (to the muscles), thus preventing the excretion of acid by this route."

What happens then as the ammonium acid remaining after the body's handling of protein can't be eliminated?

"Increased acid in the muscles," says Dr. Cooper, "causes fatigue, cramps, and inability to function at peak efficiency, so it is easy to see why the athlete who eats a large steak, eggs, or other protein foods before a contest will have greater fatigue and acidosis than one who eats food consisting largely of carbohydrates."

CARBOHYDRATES

Carbohydrates have long been the major sources of calories for people throughout the world. For many, 60 to 75 percent of total food calories are in this form, although in the United States we get less than half from carbohydrates.

For athletes, or anyone else engaged in vigorous activity, carbohydrates are the primary sources of energy, the most efficient fuel for energy production at high levels of oxygen consumption.

All carbohydrates are made up of carbon, hydrogen and oxygen. As in water, there are two hydrogen atoms for each atom of oxygen, and carbohydrates are so-called because in effect they are hydrated (watered) carbons.

Carbohydrates include all sugars and starches.

There are many sugars, including the sweetest, fructose, in honey, ripe fruits, and many vegetables; lactose, a sugar in milk; maltose, a sugar from malt or digested starch; and sucrose, the table sugar from sugarcane and beets and maple trees and sorghum.

Starches, which are made up of complex rather than simple sugars, are not sweet. Starches are found in tubers such as potatoes; in seeds such as peas, beans, peanuts, and almonds; and in roots such as carrots and beets. But our biggest sources are cereal grains—wheat, rye, rice, barley, corn, millet, oats.

Starches cannot be absorbed as such from the gut and so enzymes there convert them to glucose, or blood sugar. The energy from carbohydrates is quickly available and quickly used. Usually, within a dozen hours or so, the last of the carbohydrates in the last meal is burned up.

The starchy foods we eat provide more than calories alone. Potatoes, for example, contain significant amounts of vitamin C and the B vitamin, nicotinic acid, and whole-grain cereals contain many vitamins as well as protein.

When carbohydrates are eaten, a relatively small amount of the glucose absorbed from them is converted to glycogen, a form of carbohydrates which can be stored as back-up in muscles and liver.

Glucose is essential—constantly needed to supply not only the muscles, but other organs as well—especially the brain. Without adequate glucose to nourish the brain, the quick reflexes needed for athletic performance are impaired. An inadequate supply for the brain and nervous system also leads to feelings of weakness, dizziness, nausea, and hunger.

Carbohydrate storage in the body is small. There is usually only enough glucose in the bloodstream and glycogen in the tissues to meet energy needs for about half a day of even sedentary activity. That's apparent to anyone who has missed breakfast and lunch and felt unable to concentrate and lethargic in the afternoon.

An adequate intake of carbohydrates is important in all sports and especially in those calling for efforts of long duration. A critical factor in performance is the amount of oxygen reaching muscle tissue to help produce energy. As already noted, the oxygen goes further—we get about 10 percent more calories of energy per oxygen unit—when we burn carbohydrates than when we burn protein or fat.

Commonly, Olympic athletes are fed a high carbohydrate diet in the days before an event such as a marathon or the thirty-kilometer ski race. The success of Korean marathon runners who train on rice has been attributed to their high carbohydrate intake.

FATS

Fats serve several functions in the body.

They are essential in every body cell, required for many cell operating mechanisms. The fat content of cells accounts for about one percent of total body weight, and fats largely remain in the cells, not consumed even during starvation.

Fat consumption for energy occurs, using fats stored as reserve, mostly in layers under the skin. Such fat layers serve another purpose, insulating the body against cold.

Fats provide an efficient way to store energy. An ounce, pound, or any other weight of stored or depot fat will yield about two and one-quarter times as much energy as an equivalent weight of protein or carbohydrate.

When fats are mustered from depots for use, they are converted to carbohydrates.

A little less than half the fat calories in the American diet come from obvious, visible sources, such as butter and margarine (80 percent fat), oils and shortenings (100 percent fat), and bacon (50 percent fat).

The larger portion comes from so-called invisible sources, including nuts (as much as 50 percent fat), doughnuts (50 percent), whole milk cheeses and fat cuts of meat (30 percent and more), frankfurters and luncheon meats (as much as 30 percent, and cakes, pies and ice cream (as much as 13 percent). Even lean pork contains about as much fat as cakes, pies and ice cream. In lean lamb and most fish, the fat content is 8 percent or less; in milk and shellfish, 2 to 4 percent; in fruits, vegetables, and most bread, less than 1 percent.

Nobody knows what may be precisely the ideal amount of fat in the diet.

Without a certain amount—perhaps as much as 15 percent—there may be difficulties in absorbing the fat-soluble vitamins A, D, E and K.

On the other hand, with too much fat, to the exclusion of carbohydrates, a condition known as ketosis can develop. Lacking adequate carbohydrates to burn, the body has to burn or oxidize fats. Large quantities of fats must be handled, beyond the ability of body cells to oxidize them fully. As a result of the incomplete oxidation, substances called ketones are formed and accumulate in blood and tissues. Whereupon, the kidneys try to get rid of them but, in so doing, excrete important minerals as well, including large quantities of sodium. As a result, the alkaline part of the body's buffer system is depleted and the balance is upset in favor of acidosis. If this is uncorrected, it may produce disorientation, coma, even death.

The healthiest diets, based on animal studies, provide between 20 and 40 percent fat. In the U.S. and other Western countries, the overall diet has for some decades hovered around 40 percent. Some authorities believe this is too much, considering the possible role of fats, particularly certain types, in provoking heart disease.

Fatty acids and the fats they form can be classified as saturated or unsaturated. All the common saturated fatty acids are liquid at room temperature. Through a process in which hydrogen is added, they can be made saturated and converted into solid fats. Margarine is one example of the hydrogenation of unsaturated fatty acids into a solid material.

Research suggests that unsaturated fats (also called polyunsaturated) may be less likely than saturated to be used in injurious ways by the body. The theory is that blood concentration of cholesterol is increased by saturated fats, which are found mainly in animal fats, such as in meat, butter and eggs. On the other hand, unsaturated fats, found in large amounts in vegetable oils such as corn and safflower oil, may help reduce the amount of cholesterol in the blood. Cholesterol is believed by some investigators to be a major factor in the artery disease leading to heart attack.

VITAMINS

It has been said that American athletes have the most expensive urine in the world, because of the vast amounts of supplementary vitamins they consume. Because most vitamins are soluble in water and are not stored by the body, any in excess of what the body actually needs are excreted rapidly in the urine.

Vitamins aren't really nutrients in themselves; they only act *on* nutrients. As part of enzyme systems, they help to regulate the rate at which chemical reactions go on in the body. Only very small amounts are needed.

Virtually all foods contain vitamins. And even a diet providing no more than 1,500, or even 1,200, calories, provided it is balanced and varied, offers all the vitamins even the most vigorous athlete requires.

Yet athletes often gobble vitamin supplements which are worthless to them. You can spend a small fortune on such supplements—a fortune which would be better spent for good equipment and perhaps lessons in a sport.

At various times, there have been claims that large intakes of B vitamins, particularly B_1 and B_{12}, can retard fatigue in prolonged exercise. But scientific experiments in which athletes were sometimes given the vitamins and sometimes given, instead, dummy look-alike pills, failed to support the claims. Nor has any proof ever been demonstrated for claims that large intakes of vitamin C, or massive amounts of A and E have any value.

MINERALS

Minerals play many important roles in the body. They are required for contraction of muscles, control of the heartbeat, and conduction of nerve impulses. And they are provided in adequate amounts by any well-balanced and varied diet.

Occurring in soil, minerals are picked up by plants, from which they are absorbed by animals, and humans get minerals from both plants and animals.

Sodium, potassium and iron are the minerals most often affected by heavy exercise or poor diet.

Sodium, which is a constituent of salt, is lost through

sweat at a rate of about 1.5 grams for every two pints of water lost. But this can be made up for by more liberal salting of food. Many scientists now believe that salt tablets are not needed until water loss has reached six pints.

Potassium needs can be met in most cases by including potassium-rich foods, such as oranges and bananas, in the diet.

Iron is a relatively common deficiency in girls and women who menstruate heavily. Adolescent girls are more likely to be iron-deficient than boys because, although their iron needs for growth are comparable, they often do not eat as much.

Yet if attention is paid to including good iron sources in the diet, deficiency can be avoided.

Meats are good sources. Most provide two to three milligrams of iron per three-ounce serving. Liver is an especially good source: beef liver has five milligrams of iron in a two-ounce serving; calf liver is half again as rich in iron as beef liver, and pork liver has twice the iron of calf liver. Liverwurst, made from liver, is a good source, and so is chicken liver. An egg contains one milligram of iron. Oysters, sardines, and shrimp provide two and one-half to five milligrams per three-ounce serving. Most green vegetables provide one to four milligrams per cup, and other good sources include dry beans, nuts, prunes, dates, and raisins, each containing about five milligrams of iron per cup.

WATER

Most people don't think of water as a nutrient yet it is the most basic of nutrients and must be regularly available.

Water is a main component of cells, urine, sweat, and blood. If it is lacking in adequate amounts, much goes wrong in the body. Cells become dehydrated and are unable to carry out their normal chemical reactions, use energy efficiently, or build tissue.

Without adequate water, urine output is diminished and

that means a buildup of toxic materials in the blood. The volume of blood also decreases, impairing the transport of oxygen and nutrients throughout the body, leading to weakness and fatigue. Without adequate water, sweating is impaired and body heat regulation can be seriously affected.

Years ago, it used to be fairly common practice for coaches to ban water during practice sessions and athletic contests. There was a grossly mistaken belief that drinking water during exercise could produce cramps and "water logging." Some coaches also had the notion that water deprivation could toughen up an athlete.

Fortunately, most coaches now know better, or they should. Water deprivation is clearly hazardous to both health and performance.

Even someone who does not exercise needs at least six glasses of fluid a day, and with exercise the need is increased.

Loss of water through sweating is obvious. But other losses occur—through the skin without apparent sweating, and also through breathing.

Any young athlete should drink at least a glass of fluid at each meal and whenever thirsty. But it's important to realize that thirst alone cannot be depended on to signal water need. After a period of exercise and fluid loss, thirst may not call for complete replacement of body water.

The rule for any young athlete should be: Don't wait for thirst before you drink.

SOUND DIET

During World War II, the U. S. Department of Agriculture set about developing a simple, sound diet plan and, with later improvements, it is now recognized to be simple and sound, indeed. Flexible and well-suited to foods available to Americans, it meets all nutritional needs.

The basis for it is that the body requires many kinds of nutrients, and it doesn't matter whether this or that vitamin, protein, or other nutrient comes from this or that food. The body doesn't care. No matter what the food, it will break it down before it can utilize its content of nutrients.

All that does matter is that every day, through proper choice of foods, the body gets those that will give it all the nutrients it requires.

The Department of Agriculture plan—called the Four Food Group Plan—does that.

These are the four food groups:

Group 1: Milk and other dairy products. Included here are cottage cheese, yogurt, cheeses, and ice cream, all contributing calcium, vitamins B_2 and B_{12} and vitamin A, many minerals (but not iron), and protein. Low fat milk can be substituted for whole milk.

Group 2: Meat and high protein foods. This group includes meat, fish, poultry, eggs, and even such vegetable items as dried beans, peas and nuts. All contain large amounts of protein. Fish and poultry have less fat than most meats. Eggs contain virtually all vitamins and minerals but large amounts of cholesterol. Liver is rich in iron and vitamin A but also cholesterol.

Because of the saturated fat content of meat and eggs and the concern that such fat may contribute to heart disease, it is prudent to limit red meat consumption and eggs to four servings or less of each per week, with most protein coming from chicken, fish, legumes and nuts.

Legumes—which include navy, kidney and lima beans, stringbeans, soy beans, lentils, black-eyed peas, peas and peanuts—are a commonly overlooked good source of protein.

Group 3: Vegetables and fruits. Green, yellow, and leafy vegetables are excellent sources of minerals and A, B and E vitamins, and include spinach, kale, Swiss chard, watercress, collard, mustard and turnip (the greens), and carrots, pumpkin, squash of various types and yams (the yellows). Citrus fruits, tomatoes, raw cabbage and salad greens contribute vitamin C. Lettuce, cabbage and salad greens provide somewhat less of vitamin C than do tomatoes, oranges, grapefruit, tangerines, and other citrus fruits. Potatoes and other vegetables and fruits—including broccoli, Brussels sprouts, green peppers, cauliflower, berries, cherries, melons and peaches—contribute vitamin C, minerals, some protein, and energy.

Group 4: Cereals and grains. Bread, cereals and pasta provide proteins, iron, and B vitamins as well as carbohydrates. They help fill energy requirements. Enriched flour and cornmeal offer vitamins B_1 and B_2, niacin and iron. And wholegrain flour, bread and brown rice contain the B vitamins, minerals, and desirable dietary fiber.

Any young athlete who consumes four daily servings of groups three and four and two daily servings of the other groups will be getting a well-balanced diet providing essential carbohydrates, fats, proteins, vitamins and minerals. If the choices from each group are varied from one day to the next, all the better.

If more food is needed—that is, more calories—extra helpings can be used.

HOW MUCH FOOD IS NEEDED?

An average American may consume as much as 3,000 calories a day. Athletes, of course, need more food than people who do not exercise.

One study of the Australian Olympic team found that most consumed in the range of 3,000 to 4,000 calories a day; a lesser number had intakes of 4,000 to 5,000; and about 6 percent consumed more than 6,000.

Some professional athletes in training camp have been known to eat as many as 10,000 calories a day and still lose weight.

The total amount of energy (calories) required depends on several factors: body size, age, type of activity engaged in, and the length of time each spent in that activity.

For example, volleyball takes about three and one-half calories a minute and swimming the crawl about fourteen calories a minute. Tennis can consume seven to ten calories a minute; squash, ten to twelve; skiing, fifteen; running at ten miles an hour, eighteen to twenty. The heavier the athlete, the more calories consumed in any given activity.

Says Dr. Jean Mayer: "In practice, we have found that the athletes who require the greatest calorie intake day in and day out are those training for long-distance running events. Even slightly built boys training for events such as the 5,000 or 10,000 meters, or the marathon, require 6,000 calories. By contrast, much beefier football players during the football season rarely need more than 4,500 calories."

HOW MANY MEALS A DAY?

Many studies have established that the body uses calories more efficiently and performance is better if at least three meals a day are eaten.

Too many Americans, young and old, athletic and non-athletic, have a habit of just gulping coffee for breakfast, a sandwich for lunch, and then consuming a heavy evening meal.

Says Dr. Cooper, at whose school there is a mandatory rule that no varsity athlete can omit breakfast: "I feel certain that academic failures and poor athletic performance may occur in students who regularly skip breakfast, eat a hamburger at noon, and then eat whatever is left over in the evening. A day in and day out diet of this type is deficient in what is needed for the growing teen-ager and is no small problem today in the general school population as well as in athletes."

And Dr. Cooper goes on to note: "Some experiments have suggested that five smaller meals spaced throughout the day were even more efficient than our standard three meals a day. The increase in performance was small and not as marked as the difference between three and two meals per day. If an athlete eats three meals a day containing adequate amounts of protein, fat and carbohydrate, he should do well and except for the precontest meal his diet does not need any modification."

THE PREGAME MEAL

Competition should always be entered on an empty stomach. That's because when digestion is going on the heart must pump large amounts of blood to the gastrointestinal tract but, when more blood is needed by the muscles during exercise, the amount going to the stomach is significantly decreased and cramps may develop.

If a preevent meal is eaten no later than three hours before an event, there is time for more complete digestion of the food and yet not so much time as to cause feelings of hunger.

The preevent meal should be easily digestible in order to avoid problems of competing on a full stomach. Various studies have shown that in keyed-up athletes, normal digestive processes are slowed and a heavy pregame meal may never get out of the stomach until well after the event.

Fats should be avoided in the pregame meal because they tend to slow stomach emptying. Because carbohydrates are the best source of immediate energy, the meal should be high in such high carbohydrate foods as bread, spaghetti, macaroni, potatoes, porridge, fruit, and fruit juices.

Many professional teams use carbohydrate pregame meals. One major football team, for example, uses toast, pancakes, salad and fruit juice.

The meal should be low in sugar. Sugar is absorbed very quickly—and very quickly gets into the bloodstream in the form of glucose. The body immediately responds with an outpouring of insulin to clear the excess glucose out of the blood and the result can be rebound hypoglycemia, or low blood sugar, impairing energy and performance. A teaspoon or so of sugar—sugar or honey, maple syrup, or molasses, for example—usually causes no problems. But anything more may have effects even in addition to hypoglycemia, drawing water into the intestinal tract and causing cramps.

Rather than sugar, fruits can be used. Although fruits contain a sugar (fructose), that kind of sugar must go to the liver to be converted to glucose and gets into the bloodstream more slowly.

The pregame meal should be low in protein. Since protein cannot provide immediate energy, it is not needed. Moreover, the products remaining after protein is digested can only be eliminated through the kidneys and so increase urination.

It's now generally recognized that to compensate for the fluid losses during the event, the preevent meal should include at least three glasses of liquid.

Recommends Dr. Cooper: "Extra salt intake is advisable when sweating is profuse and bouillon cubes provide a good source. If salt tablets are used, they should be taken with the pregame meal and not just before the game since salt can irritate the stomach and may cause vomiting."

WHERE THE "MAGIC" IS

There is no "nutritional magic wand." Many people would like to believe there is—and perhaps none more so than young athletes and many of their coaches. Certainly, it is easy enough for salesmen for "remarkable" products—"energizers," "body builders," and "fatigue fighters" to make beguiling claims.

They don't hold up when subjected to scientific inquiry. What does hold up is very simply stated.

Dr. Jean Mayer has done it well: "There is no magic

involved in athletic nutrition: the good diet and abundant fluid which the nonathlete needs are also what the athlete needs—only more."

And Dr. Gabe Mirkin has also stated it well: "The same rules for eating apply universally to those who exercise and those who don't. The only difference is that people who are physically active require more calories and more fluids."

CHAPTER 9

MAKING WEIGHT FOR SPORTS

He is sixteen, a high school junior, with an ambition to make the wrestling team. At the start of the school year, he is among the candidates called together. With the others, he goes through skin-fat fold measurements, estimate of fatness, and a determination of desirable competing weight.

He weighs 154 pounds. The estimate is that about 15 percent of that is fat—about average for American boys from middle-income families.

The decision is that he could be more fit and compete best with only 5 percent of body weight in fat. He is advised to reduce his weight by 10 percent, to about 139 pounds.

Because of the conditioning program he will follow, he will increase his muscle mass; and that increase, along with his normal growth, will produce an increase of a bit more than two pounds in lean body weight.

So the suggestion is that he aim to compete in the 145-pound weight class.

And with two months to go before the first December

weigh-in, there is enough time to reach competing weight by losing fat at a rate of about two pounds a week.

For a young athlete, that loss rate often is practical, achievable with a modest decrease in food intake and an increase in energy expenditure through the conditioning program.

What exactly will he have to do? How should he eat? What else should he do?

It's very much worth looking into what sports medicine physicians recommend when a young athlete needs to reduce weight—or when it's necessary to gain weight. Too often, in both situations, youngsters—and older athletes as well—resort to practices which can be harmful.

HARMFUL WEIGHT-LOSS PRACTICES

They use rubber or plastic suits during exercise. They spend long hours in the sauna. Some induce vomiting. Not infrequently, diuretic drugs and cathartics are taken.

All of these measures result in weight reduction all right, but only a very temporary loss of pounds and at high cost. All involve dehydration.

Sweating at an increased rate thanks to rubber or plastic suits or sauna sessions causes loss of body fluids. So do cathartics. And diuretics, of course, are drugs designed for specific medical use in ridding the body of excess fluids in people with health problems which cause the excess fluid accumulation.

But these are not measures for any healthy person, let alone a young person who wants to participate in vigorous sports.

Altering body fluids, for one thing, achieves nothing positive because the body in a healthy person closely regulates fluid balance and when the individual drinks water or anything else, the body will tend to sop it up eagerly and weight is regained.

Altering body fluids does nothing to change body fat content. And it is body fat weight which should be lost.

But, aside from being foolish, dehydration is potentially dangerous.

Dehydration causes important changes to occur in the body. There is a decrease in blood volume, heart output, blood flow through the kidneys. Muscle strength diminishes. Other body functions may be impaired.

The dehydrated athlete is more prone to heat stroke or heat exhaustion. He or she may suffer, too, from fever, nausea, and weakness, and most likely will not perform at maximum capability.

Most of the time, the physical damage is not permanent and body strength is restored with rehydration and the regaining of the pounds.

But sometimes there are more serious, even life-threatening hazards.

Recently, in the *Journal of the American Medical Association*, Dr. Philip H. Croyle of St. Joseph Hospital, Denver, and colleagues reported on a sixteen-year-old high school wrestler who suffered a massive blood clot in a lung as a result of excessive, rapid weight loss.

The youngster, who weighed 109 pounds, underwent rapid dehydration twice in one week, losing a total of thirteen pounds, or 12 percent of his body weight.

That brought on a condition in which a minor bruise suffered during the wrestling bout triggered a sizable blood clot. The clot blocked a lung.

Bypass chest surgery saved his life. He recovered and was well later, eighteen months later. To make matters even worse, he was defeated in his match by an opponent he had handily beaten before. In weakened condition, his strength and skill were drastically reduced.

SOUND PRINCIPLES

There are about 3,500 calories stored in each pound of body fat. If fat weight is to be lost, it's necessary to spend 3,500 calories in excess of what is taken in.

Actually, 3,500 calories may be about the total daily

average energy expenditure of an active, high school athlete. If such a person ate nothing at all and maintained his normal activities, he would lose a pound. But he wouldn't remain a healthy young man, let alone a vigorous athlete, very long if he tried that.

Nor would he if he resorted to any of the multitudinous fad diets which, foolishly, his elders often use with unending frustration.

Dieting has been called the number one pastime in the United States. At any one time, some 20 million adults are on some reducing diet or other.

"Magic" reducing regimens are not only numerous; they are almost unbelievably bizarre, self-defeating, and health-impairing.

There are magic duo diets: lamb chops and grapefruit; or eggs and spinach; or bananas and skim milk—and nothing else. Other crash diet notions include grapefruit and coffee and nothing else for days on end; or celery and virtually nothing else; or cottage cheese and little more.

There are high-protein diets which, with intake limited to steak, eggs, and other high-protein foods, are supposed to reduce. But any single-category diet can be dangerous because it omits other necessary food groups and their nutrients.

There is an "eat-fat" diet which is supposed, somehow, to put the fats eaten to work melting away the fat deposits in the body. There is a low-carbohydrate diet, which restricts intake of carbohydrates while allowing eating just about anything else. But restricting carbohydrates severely may upset both digestion and body fluid balance and the usually much higher fat intake that goes along with such a diet may have harmful effects on the arteries.

Even for a nonathletic adult, such diets, when not outrightly dangerous, are self-defeating. They appear to be successful briefly but the loss is usually the result of fluid, not body fat, and the fluids are quickly replaced with no change in the body fat situation.

If anything, such gimmicky regimens may be even

worse for the young athlete who, because of his sports activities and his still-growing body, needs sound nutrition at all times, including the times when he may need to lose weight.

It bears emphasis that nearly fifty nutrients—including all of the amino acid constituents of proteins, carbohydrates, vitamins and minerals—are essential for health.

Ample dietary protein is certainly essential at all times, and never more so than during childhood and adolescence when protein, which largely makes up muscles, heart, liver and other organs, is needed for development and growth. Even after growth is over, body tissues which are continually being worn out must be replaced, and for this, protein is required.

Similarly, calcium and phosphorus, which go into bone, are essential for bone maintenance and can be especially critical in youth when bones are still growing.

At all times, carbohydrates are needed for quick energy, and some fats for energy reserve and to help absorption of some vitamins. Of course, vitamins are required.

All of which spells a balanced diet which, as we noted in an earlier chapter, requires selection of foods each day from the four basic food groups: milk and milk products; cereals and breads; fruits and vegetables; and meat and protein-rich foods.

LOSING THE WEIGHT PROPERLY

How then can a young athlete go about achieving a sound and healthy weight loss?

According to experts, as we've noted, a rate of weight reduction of about two pounds a week can be compatible with a good diet and good conditioning. Under special circumstances, the rate might even be somewhat higher.

Usually, what is desirable is to have the calorie intake fall about 1,000 below calorie expenditure. That means a 7,000 calorie deficit a week, or two pounds of loss.

And the calorie deficit should not depend entirely on

reduced food intake. Calorie intake can be reduced by 500 to 750 a day but it should never be cut to a level of less than 2,000. Anything less, as Dr. Nathan J. Smith of the University of Washington School of Medicine Division of Sports Medicine has advised in a report in the *Journal of the American Medical Association*, can lead to increasing use of body muscle mass as an energy source. Anything less, he emphasizes, will not be adequate to support a training program, school work, and a healthy active life-style.

In his report, Dr. Smith recommends that the dietary intake include twelve servings of the four food groups—and, as an example, proposes a menu such as this:

	CALORIES
Breakfast or night snack	
Fruit (2 servings)	100
Bread group (2 servings)	250
Lunch	
Sandwich or cheeseburger	400
French fries (20 pieces)	230
Milk (1 carton)	170
Dinner	
Meat (6 ounces)	450
Potato (1 med. size)	80
Vegetable (1 serving)	40
Roll and Butter	125
Milk (1 8-oz. carton)	170
Total	2,015

A young athlete usually can keep to a diet containing about 2,000 calories by eating moderate servings of three family, dormitory, or training-table meals and by avoiding second servings, desserts, and between-meal snacks.

Avoidance of snacks can be especially important because snack foods are usually high in calories. Some typical examples:

Foods	Amount	Calories
Chocolate bar	1 small bar	155
Chocolate creams	1 average size	50
Cookies	1 medium size	75
Doughnut	1 plain	135
Popcorn	1 cup popped	55
Potato chips	8–10	100
Peanuts or		
pistachio nuts	1	5
Peanut butter	1 tbsp.	100
Olives	1	10
Ice cream	½ cup	200
Chocolate nut sundae		270
Ice cream soda		255
Chocolate malted milk	1 glass	450

Beyond the relatively modest decrease in food intake, an increase in activity is essential. What's needed is an hour or more of a suitable conditioning activity which can involve an expenditure of 250 to 750 calories and will maintain muscle competence and contribute to conditioning for competition.

Exercise is important both for its effect in increasing the caloric deficit and because it helps to make certain that weight is lost in the form of fat rather than lean muscle tissue.

Some suitable form of exercise activity usually can be found. It might, for example, be an hour of bike riding a day—perhaps a half-hour ride to school and another half-hour ride back. Over a period of a week, that extra energy expenditure could mean a pound of weight loss.

SOLVING THE WEIGH-IN PROBLEM

Some young athletes have the problem of being over weight limit at the time of weigh-in—during the wrestling season, for example.

The problem usually can be minimized or even eliminated by avoiding the water retention that can be induced by salty foods. Avoidance of such foods while still maintaining a good water intake, and temporary avoidance as well of high-residue foods, can, at once, avoid the weight problem while contributing to fitness for competition.

For seventy-two hours before competition or weigh-in for weight control sports such as wrestling, Dr. Smith advises generous water intake—no less than eight full glasses each twenty-four hours—coupled with limiting the intake of the following foods:

Anchovies, herring, sardines
Bacon and bacon fat
Bologna
Bouillon cubes
Bread and rolls having a salt topping
Canned soups
Catsup
Celery or onion salt
Cheese, all kinds
Chili sauce
Chipped and corned beef
Crackers
Dry cereals
Frankfurters, ham, koshered meat, luncheon meat, salt pork
Garlic salt
Heavily salted foods
Horseradish
Instant cocoa mixes
Meat tenderizer
Olives
Peanut butter
Potato chips, corn chips, other salted snacks, pretzels
Prepared mustard
Relish, pickles

Salt and monosodium glutamate
Salted cottage cheese
Salted nuts and popcorn
Salty and smoked fish and meats
Sauerkraut
Sausage
Soy and Worcestershire sauces

The list, as you see, is extensive. But so is the salt problem. The American diet is full of salt. Not only do we add it at the table—some of us reaching for the salt shaker even before tasting what's in front of us—but it is present naturally in many foods.

It is present in fresh vegetables such as artichokes, beets and beet greens, carrots, kale, dandelion and mustard greens, spinach and Swiss chard.

It is present in milk, eggs, cheeses and meats.

Canned vegetables are rich in it.

It is in baking powder and soda, in the flavor intensifier monosodium glutamate, and in the preservative sodium benzoate. It is added to many prepackaged prepared foods.

Although the human body needs only one gram or less of salt intake daily, we commonly take in as much as fifteen grams a day. There is evidence that excessive salt intake not only leads to water retention but also may be a significant factor in the development of high blood pressure.

In addition to limiting salt intake, limiting the intake of foods of high residue for three days prior to competition is desirable, says Dr. Smith.

Among high residue foods are raw fruits and vegetables; salads; dried fruits such as raisins and apricots; nuts; whole-grain cereal products including whole-grain breads, granola and bran; berry and fruit pies; desserts with raisins and other dried fruits.

But, he cautions, these are good foods. They contribute essential nutrients to a normal diet. *And their use should be limited only during the particular period of preparation for top performance.* The residue of these foods adds what he calls "nonfunctional" weight and may sometimes produce an undesirable feeling of heavy fullness during competition when a "light" feeling in the abdomen is preferable.

GAINING WEIGHT

Young athletes who want to gain weight to improve their performance need to understand how properly to go about it and to avoid potentially serious pitfalls.

To begin with, is the weight gain really needed? Some experts question whether it usually is. The best, most efficient athletes, they point out, are lean.

True, in some competitive situations, smallness may be a disadvantage. But the smallness may be normal for the young person's present level of maturity.

In pointed advice to coaches, Ronald Byrd of the University of Alabama writes: "Retarded growth may occur from malnutrition, but usually maturation and normal growth take care of what is probably only a temporary inconvenience rather than a serious problem. Don't automatically recommend an increase in food intake; there is seldom a good reason for simply padding the body with fatty tissue. First, look at the parents for genetic influence. Are they also small or lean? If not, find out if there is a possibility of poor dietary habits."

It's advice youngsters and parents could well heed.

If there is real reason for a youngster to gain weight, it should still be noted that probably in no other nutritional aspect of sports is there as much abuse as in weight gain.

No small part of the abuse relates to the use of drugs— anabolic steroids. We shall have more to say about these compounds in the next chapter, but a word about them here.

Anabolic steroids are synthetic, or man-made, chemicals designed to have some of the effects of male hormones. The latter have two major actions: (1) they foster the development of male secondary sexual characteristics;

and (2) they help in the development of muscle mass. The anabolic steroids have been developed to have maximum effect on muscle and minimum effect on sexual character-istics.

But are they effective? And what of their dangers?

Their effectiveness is very much in question. There have been studies which indicate lack of any real evidence that they make any contribution to increasing muscle mass or strength that is not attributable to conditioning and in-creased food intake.

As for dangers: in adolescents and preadolescents, they can lead to permanent stunting of growth by affecting the growth centers of bones. In older athletes, they can cause testicular wasting and disturbed sperm formation. In girls and women, they may produce masculinization. There are additional potential side effects: possible poisonous ef-fects on the liver, and development or worsening of acne.

Another potential for harm lies in the use of undesirable diets to gain weight—diets high in saturated fats and cho-lesterol. Such diets may contribute to development of high blood fat levels and heart and blood vessel disease. That potential may be somewhat greater if there is a family history of early heart and blood vessel disease.

Any young athlete who wants to gain weight has to realize that his or her aim should be to increase lean body mass—that is, muscle—not just body fat. For that, there needs to be an increase in calorie intake plus muscle work. Without the latter, there can be no increase in muscle mass and the increased calorie intake will lead to more body fat.

Generally, the addition of 750 to 1,000 calories a day to the usual diet will provide the energy requirements both for gaining a pound or somewhat more per week and for the increased physical activity going into muscle training.

The muscle training program should be designed by the team coach or trainer, taking into account the young athlete's age and condition.

The diet, experts urge, should be recommended by a

physician and, moreover, the athlete should be checked regularly by the physician.

What the American Heart Association calls a "prudent" diet and recommends for American adults is also one, experts say, which is desirable for the young athlete. It contains less than 35 percent calories as fat, and that fat is low in animal fats and cholesterol. Any physician can obtain educational materials, including sample menus, for such a diet from the American Heart Association.

The young athlete should be seen at least briefly at regular intervals by the physician. At those visits, dietary records should be reviewed—and estimates should be made of the level of body fatness through skin-fat fold measurements to detect any increases. If there is an increase in fatness, then caloric intake must be reduced or muscle work increased, or both.

CHAPTER 10

DRUGS AS ATHLETIC AIDS: FACT OR FICTION?

Some years ago, the trainer for one of the major league baseball teams developed a remarkable drug program. He fed any player who wanted them—and almost every player did—any one or all of three differently colored pills.

One was a red "shut-out" pill; the second, a potent green "hitting" pill; and the third, a yellow "RBI" (runs batted in) pill. The results were beautiful.

The pills worked so effectively that the team won the pennant that year. Moreover, in each of the next two years, with the pills in constant use, the flag was won again.

What was in the pills? Nothing but inert ingredients. Placebos. But they worked because the players thought they were potent stuff. That was the beautiful part: they worked without causing any harm.

But many real drugs have been used in considerable quantities in professional and amateur sports—and many are still in use. Some, if they do no particular good, may do no particular harm. But others, concerned medical authorities report, do no good and may do much harm.

THE SIZE OF THE PROBLEM

Nobody knows the full extent of drug use and abuse in sports.

Recently, the *New York Times* carried a special report on "Mounting Drug Use Afflicts World Sports," in which it noted, on the basis of interviews with members of the sports medicine task force of the U. S. Olympic Committee for the 1980 games, that "the use of stimulants and steroids in international sport has reached 'epidemic' dimensions."

According to one task force member, Dr. Daniel Hanley, "The problem is worse than it's ever been."

Agreeing, Dr. Tony Daly, another task force member, remarked that "Athletes are trapped. Based on peer pressure and folklore, they feel that in order to improve they have to experiment."

A number of recent events illustrate the problem:

• In a European meet, five track and field athletes were disqualified after tests showed they were using anabolic steroid drugs. Among the disqualified: Nadechda Tkacenko of the Soviet Union who was ordered to return her gold medal in the women's pentathlon and Yevgeny Mironov, a teammate, who lost a silver medal in the men's shot put.

• At a world aquatic championship meet in West Berlin, the bronze medalist, Viktor Kuznetsov, for the 100-meter backstroke was disqualified after tests showing he had been using steroids.

• Almost at the same time, Ilone Slupianek, a women's shot-putter from East Germany, and Marku Tuokko, a men's discus thrower from Finland, lost gold medals in the European Cup and were suspended, along with three other athletes, for eighteen months because of steroid violations.

To many leading sports medicine authorities, it appears that a chemical technology race is under way, with trainers, coaches, and athletes continuously experimenting with drugs.

AT YOUNGER AGES

Has the use of drugs percolated down to younger age groups?

Half a dozen years ago, the American Academy of Pediatrics felt it necessary to issue an official statement on "Drugs and Sports."

"Young people today," the Academy noted, "grow up with the notion that there is a drug to hasten recovery from practically every illness and that a healthy person can be even better off if he has something special in his diet or his manner of living.

"The result of these beliefs is a host of misconceptions about ways by which a healthy individual can be improved by a miracle drug, a special diet, a vitamin, a hormone, particular exercises, or some other procedure.

"There is no scientific basis for any such practices, although they are usually not actually hazardous. However, a number of drugs, including those allegedly capable of increasing performance, may indeed be harmful."

The Academy added that in their eagerness to excel, some athletes and their coaches are using varied "ergo-genic" aids, including nutritional, physical and drug agents.

As for the nutritional or dietary aids, they could be dealt with in a few words, cutting right through the nonsense: "There is no evidence to support claims that any special food, vitamin or other nutritional supplements can improve athletic ability of an individual already receiving an adequate diet."

Similarly, no scientific evidence supports the use of such physical ergogenic aids as breathing oxygen, mas-sage, ultraviolet light, or mechanical devices of various kinds.

Oxygen, the Academy emphasized, cannot be stored

in body tissues and its inhalation before exercise has no effect on performance. Massage, ultraviolet light, vibrating machines, ultrasound and other mechanical devices have never been shown to have beneficial effects on performance.

As for the use of drugs as an aid in improving performance, that cannot be condoned. "No drug," the Academy statement pointed out, "can safely make the athlete better than he normally would be. The facts and dangers regarding the use of anabolic steroids, stimulants and sedatives should be made available to athletes, coaches, parents of young athletes, and physicians. All of them should know that the misguided use of ergogenic aids to improve athletic performance is contrary to good medical care, harmful to physical and mental health, and counter to ethical and sportsmanlike participation in athletics."

THE ANABOLIC STEROIDS

One group of drugs causing great concern are the anabolic steroids. These, as we noted in the preceding chapter, are derivatives of the male sex hormones, the androgens.

When androgens first became available for use, there was some interest among scientists in determining whether they could help maintain or restore strength in aging men with presumably low androgen concentrations. During World War II, they were given to victims of starvation to help restore a positive nitrogen balance.

Anabolic steroid derivatives were developed as less masculinizing substitutes for androgens and were first used by weight lifters on the mistaken assumption that they would somehow increase the formation of muscle tissue from protein in those with positive nitrogen balance and access to plenty of protein.

Actually, anabolic steroids are produced in small amounts by the body. And, as drugs, the compounds were originally prescribed for people who because of serious health problems—severe burns, cancer, malnutrition—could not produce adequate amounts of their own.

But in healthy people who do produce their own, most physicians feel that their administration has no positive value. Yet many young athletes convince themselves that somehow the drugs enhance their performance.

It has to be remembered that the mere taking of anything, no matter what, provided there is belief in its value, will provide a psychological boost. But if any increase in performance does accompany use of anabolic steroids, it is undoubtedly intensive training and dedication which are the most important factors.

More than a dozen years ago, three investigators carried out a careful scientific study with groups of young men, athletes and nonathletes. The study found essentially no difference in effect between anabolic steroids and placebos (look-alike but inert preparations) in both groups. But exercise consistently produced improvement in performance. The conclusion of the study was that it is good training, not anabolic steroids, that brings about better performance.

Still, the drugs are being used by football players, weight lifters and others. East German women gymnasts allegedly use them to delay adulthood.

According to the American Academy of Pediatrics, research has not shown any increases in strength, motor performance, body measurements, or working capacity after use of androstenolone—a popular anabolic agent—by young men.

Moreover, says the Academy, "athletes who claim gain in weight and increased athletic performance appear to have taken self-administered doses of steroids far beyond the therapeutically recommended amount of these drugs; the results are questionable at any age and highly undesirable in adolescence."

In youths who have not achieved their full growth, the

steroids can stop the process of bone growth and there may be precocious sexual development. In girls, there is the possibility of masculinization.

In 1976, the American College of Sports Medicine, after analyzing claims made for and against anabolic steroids, reported that there is no conclusive scientific evidence that even very large doses aid performance. It noted that prolonged use of the drugs has caused liver disorders in some people, some reversible after cessation of drug usage, others not.

Still another report in the *Journal of the American Medical Association* noted studies which showed no improvement in either physical fitness or athletic performance. It also pointed out that some cases of enlargement of the prostate gland in young men using steroids in large doses or for long periods and, occasionally, loss or diminution of libido have been reported.

Still other reports indicate that the drugs can have other effects: bleeding from the intestinal tract, increased risk of future heart attack, development or intensification of acne, abnormal hair growth on face, legs and abdomen in girls, hoarse and raspy voice, headache, lethargy, increased blood pressure, and abnormal rise in blood sugar.

AMPHETAMINES

These drugs have been the most commonly employed stimulants. Their users claim that they provide a sense of heightened alertness and relieve fatigue and lassitude. But do they improve performance?

In a study by Dr. P. V. Karpovich of Springfield College, fifty-four young athletes were asked to perform five strenuous physical activities. Some received amphetamines while others were given placebo. There was no essential difference in the overall performance between the two groups.

The drugs have powerful effects on the central nervous

system. They stimulate the breathing center, elevate blood pressure. More work can be accomplished, but complex tasks are not improved. Physical performance is improved if the athlete is fatigued. The drugs produce prolonged alertness, a feeling of well-being, and decreased awareness of fatigue; but an individual's judgment and his own estimate of his performance are impaired.

The U. S. Army has a training film showing a recruit completing an obstacle course in five minutes—then, after taking amphetamine, requiring nine minutes to complete the same course. But now, after staggering across the finish line, the recruit boasted: "I must have broken the course record."

How dangerous are the drugs?

One hazard is their masking of the signs of fatigue and exhaustion, removing the normal body restraints intended to prevent hazardous overexertion; and there is risk that heart, blood vessels, and musculoskeletal systems may be overextended, leading to irreversible damage to tissues.

Because the drugs decrease sensitivity to pain, they may lead to injuries—muscle pulls, cramps, and strains. And many heatstroke deaths have been attributed to amphetamine use.

In large doses, the drugs can cause abnormal heart rhythms, which sometimes can be fatal. Users may suffer from headaches and stomach upsets. Mood changes occur. Users often become aggressive and hostile. Central nervous system effects include wakefulness and loss of ability to concentrate.

The drugs are habit-forming. When their use is stopped, people have difficulty working and relating to other people, and there is a psychological need to keep using the compounds. But the more they are used, the less effective they become, and so there is a tendency to take more of the drugs all the time.

Actually, amphetamines got an undeserved reputation for at least some efficacy for athletes because of a study some years ago which went wrong and suggested, mistakenly, that the drugs did at least slightly improve the performance of runners, weight lifters, discus throwers and swimmers.

After the study was duly reported, other investigators looked into it carefully and found the fault. In the study, there had been some reliance on athletes making their own measurements of results, with some of the runners, for example, timing themselves.

Since amphetamines make users feel they are performing better than they actually are, the slight improvement reported in the study could be attributed to the athlete's own impressions.

Indeed, the original investigators did acknowledge later—in a second study concerned with the psychological effects of amphetamines—that athletes taking the drug felt they ran and threw faster than what the stopwatch and tape measure actually showed.

Since then, numerous other studies have failed to show any improvement in athletic performance from amphetamines.

But many young athletes, always looking for some panacea, have kept using them.

BLOOD DOPING

Still other "aids" are in use, or misuse.

Blood transfusion—sometimes called blood doping—is one of the latest fads in performance-boosting. In this procedure, the athlete has from 450 to 1,200 milliliters—approximately half a quart to a little more than a quart—of blood removed about three weeks before an important event. The blood plasma is returned immediately and the red cells separated out from the plasma are stored until one or two days before the event. Meanwhile the athlete's body replenishes the supply of red cells. Then, before the event, the stored cells are injected.

The theory is that with the now-extra red cells the oxygen-carrying capacity of the blood is increased and that should mean improved performance and increased endurance. But, as some authorities point out, a large number of the blood cells will have died during the storage period and so the transfusion effect, if there is any, must be largely psychological.

It's important to note that blood doping is not without hazard. In fact, it carries the risks that go with all blood transfusions—of infection, mismatching, and serum hepatitis.

SEDATIVES, TRANQUILIZERS, AND PAINKILLERS

Sedatives and tranquilizers are frequently employed to ease tension and anxiety in athletes. Most commonly, barbiturates are used, but tranquilizers also are often taken.

Considering the problem, the American Academy of Pediatrics warns that "while occasional use of a short-acting sedative to obtain restful sleep the night before a performance may be justifiable, the frequent use of 'downers' in preparation for participation in sports is hazardous because of detrimental effects on performance and the possibility of psychological dependence."

Pain-killing agents such as the local anesthetics Xylocaine and procaine have come to be known as the "lubricants" of football. Their use is not restricted to that game.

The chief hazard associated with them is that they may mask pain and permit an athlete to put more stress on injured limbs when they should be healing.

Recently, a Washington, D. C. football player, Mike Thomas, made the news when he was asked to take an injection of one of the agents in order to continue playing with a fractured ankle. When he refused, he was berated in newspaper columns by his colleagues and employers.

There is also considerable use in pro sports—and perhaps in amateur—of butazolidin or "bute." The drug is forbidden for use in racehorses in some states but it is the number one drug, in terms of amounts used, in the National Football League, for example.

Bute is used as an anti-inflammatory agent to reduce pain and swelling in joints and ligaments. It should be noted that racing commissions forbid it because its effects are not even entirely predictable; horses with sore knees may run better on it but their knees sometimes give way unexpectedly.

According to Dr. Edward Percy, a member of the American College of Sports Medicine, bute is used as commonly as aspirin among football players not so much because it is needed but because it is available. Its chronic use can cause stomach problems, ulcers, nervous disorders, hepatitis, kidney disease, serious anemia and, according to some reports, leukemia.

Cortisone is another anti-inflammatory agent often used in football and basketball. Like bute, it can cause stomach disorders and it may also increase susceptibility to infection and cause osteoporosis, or thinning and fragility of bones. Some studies also indicate that it may retard the healing process in ligament injuries.

Perhaps as good a summation as any on the use of drugs by athletes was given at a recent special symposium on sports medicine held in Canada.

"As with any individual," observed Dr. E. C. Percy of Montreal, "the athlete strives to win in his or her chosen field, but in their particularly intense desire to achieve victory, athletes tend to be superstitious, gullible, impressionable, and hypochondriacal. They are apt to try almost anything to improve their performance, be it dietary, physical, psychologic or pharmacologic."

But, as Dr. Percy emphasized, "Improved athletic performance from the taking of drugs is fiction, not fact. Performance can only be improved by determined effort, proper conditioning, and dedicated training."

CHAPTER 11

THE EMERGENCE OF SPORTS MEDICINE

Throughout this book, we have referred to sports medicine and sports medicine physicians.

Sports medicine is certainly not entirely new. In a limited sense, it can be looked upon as virtually as old as sport itself. For when the first sportsmen injured themselves they required some form of medical care.

Later, the care and preparation of athletes for competition attracted some attention as it became apparent that good preparation and training produced better results in sports.

Early Greek physicians became interested, both in the good health to be derived from athletic activity and in the rational preparation of Greek sportsmen. One Greek physician, Iccus, even developed a dietary system.

Among the Romans, sport became less of an activity of the well-to-do, as it had been for the Greeks, and developed as an activity for the amusement of the masses, becoming lethal as the gladiatorial system was developed.

The Dark Ages followed. It was not until the Renaissance and the redevelopment of Western civilization that the concept of a relationship between health and physical activity had a resurgence. In a famous poem, John Dryden, the English poet, wrote:

"Better to seek in fields for health unbought
Than fee for the doctor for a nauseous draught."

Yet, according to some medical historians, it was not really until after the Second World War that sport came into its own as a universal human activity.

In developing countries, sport offered opportunities for individuals to achieve status within their nations, and it offered individual countries the opportunity to achieve some status among other nations.

In many countries, especially in Eastern Europe, sport took on an idealistic aspect and even became something of an instrument of national policy.

Levels of performance were pushed higher and higher. And to help achieve and maintain those levels, biological sciences were applied.

Writing not long ago in an American Medical Association publication, *The Medical Aspects of Sports*, Dr. J. G. P. Williams of England, Secretary-General of the Federation Internationale de Medicine Sportive, observed:

"The preparation of the top-class international athlete is now approaching the level of intensity and involvement previously seen only under restricted circumstances in the preparation of such individuals as astronauts.

"Nowadays, thousands of young men and women throughout the world are submitting themselves to programs of sports preparation of an intensive nature with resultant problems."

And sports medicine has been developing around the world because of those problems.

In East Germany, sports medicine has for some time been a recognized medical specialty with a well-defined training program requiring physicians to go through three years of postgraduate study before qualification.

More recently, the United Kingdom became the first of the Western European countries to establish a formal qualification in sports medicine through its inclusion as a special subject in the Diploma of Medical Rehabilitation.

In the United States, a number of organizations have sprung up and the American College of Sports Medicine is the group presently recognized as the national association.

Sports medicine has been termed a science that attempts to explain how the body works during physical activity. It deals with many aspects and effects of exercise— biochemical, physical, psychological. It is concerned as well with training methods, nutrition, and the prevention, as well as more effective treatment, of injuries.

It is not limited to physicians but is also practiced to some extent by nurses, physical therapists, trainers, coaches, physical educators, nutritionists, chemists, and podiatrists.

SOVIET SPORTS MEDICINE

In the Soviet Union, there are now more than 350 regional medical offices for athletes as well as several thousand special departments at polyclinics in cities and rural hospitals.

Not long ago, in *World Health*, a publication of the World Health Organization, Dr. Vyacheslav Nikolayev, himself a sports physician in the Soviet Union, expounded on the virtues of Soviet sports medicine.

Among other things, he told of a trip all the way to Murmansk, within the Arctic Circle, and being present in the regional medical office for athletes there during a discussion between the chief physician and the trainer of the local athletic team.

"The coach," wrote Nikolayev, "complained that the results returned by his pupil, star athlete Alexei Baskakov, were getting progressively worse. He asked for an explanation.

"The athlete was duly given a thorough medical examination, using the most up-to-date equipment. The results showed that he had a low oxygen consumption; he had little capacity for work and his weight was on the increase. His body reacted by slowing down his speed in running heats. The physician offered an appropriate set of recommendations."

Nikolayev doesn't tell what those recommendations were but he does go on to assert: "This was a typical example of the close contact that is maintained between coach, doctor and athlete throughout Soviet sport. Without this relationship, it is broadly speaking impossible to aim for record-breaking results without risking dangers to health because of the strains imposed.

"The work loads," Nikolayev pointed out, "have to match each individual's physical capacity, and that in turn can only be determined by doctors with access to the very latest in investigative equipment. Soviet physicians who work at the sports clinics are often referred to as 'trainers in white,' and they are frequently credited, quite justifiably, as 'co-authors' of new track records."

Nikolayev went on to say that "Nobody in the Soviet Union may take part in a sports contest without getting the go-ahead from the doctors. Leading athletes undergo a full medical check every year, carried out as a rule at the local sports clinic. It is considered perfectly normal for a physician to specialize in sports medicine in this way, since the prime goal of the Soviet physical education system is to boost the health of millions of individuals. As for track records—they are just one of the incidental by-products."

U. S. SPORTS MEDICINE

Here in the United States, sports medicine has had its most obvious and dramatic growth in the care and treatment of professional athletes, the million-dollar sports stars.

It probably is not entirely fair to say, as a recent series of articles in The New York Times suggested, that "In the

United States, the practice of sports medicine is devoted largely to the care and treatment of some 3,000 highly skilled professional athletes who make football, baseball, basketball, and hockey a paying proposition. The major concern—and perhaps the best definition—of sports medicine is finding ways to get these athletes back into action as quickly as possible after injury."

Certainly, many sports medicine specialists are very much engaged in that business. But there are other aspects to American sports medicine.

We might as well take a look here, briefly, at what sports medicine has, in fact, been able to do for the injured pros.

There is, for example, the case of Eric Soderholm, Chicago White Sox third basemen, who won the American League's comeback-player of the year award in 1977. Soderholm made his comeback after an Atlanta sports medicine physician operated on his knee and developed a rehabilitative exercise program for him. During his comeback season, Soderholm achieved a .280 batting average, hit twenty-five home runs, and batted in sixty-seven runs.

It was the same physician specialist who designed a series of exercises to help Dick Butkus, Chicago Bear linesman, to play on a knee that had suffered degenerative arthritis damage from repeated past injuries.

In 1973, thanks to a sports medicine physician, Charlie Waters of the Dallas Cowboys played a football season with a fourteen-inch rod in his arm to hold together a bone he had broken in a game months before.

In 1974, Tommy John of the Los Angeles Dodgers had a tendon transplant in his pitching arm. That year, too, Denis Potvin of the Islanders had a lightweight cast inserted in his skate boot to allow him to play about thirty games with a broken bone.

As Dr. Joseph S. Torg, director of the University of Pennsylvania Center for Sports Medicine, puts it: "If you have a million-dollar ballplayer sitting on the bench with a splinter in his butt, it may not be a medical crisis but it is an economic one."

Today, almost every professional team employs at least one staff physician—usually an orthopedist with a bent for sports medicine—and has consulting physicians as well, on retainer. The New York Rangers have a staff of four specialists.

Says one sports medicine physician, Dr. James Garrick, medical adviser to the National Football League's Joint Safety Committee: "To have an orthopedist, an internist, two trainers and two assistant trainers for the forty members of a professional football team is very luxurious. The same number of people would take care of 500 college athletes and 5,000 high school athletes. I'm not saying professional athletes get better care, just more of it."

Another prominent sports medicine physician observes: "Twenty years ago players played and played until they couldn't play any more. Then somebody else came and took their place and you never heard of them again. Now they are treated like kings."

Actually, to no small extent, the highly publicized care, especially the surgery, given to professional athletes, is simply the use of standard orthopedic medical principles for special problems of athletes.

Dr. John L. Marshall, who is director of sports medicine services at the Hospital for Special Surgery in New York City and also physician for the Giants, has said: "Orthopedists laugh at all the attention we get for doing bread-and-butter operations. All we've done in sports medicine is popularize preexisting techniques."

But this, he adds, "is a great public service. Now people know to come in and ask for Larry Czonka's operation."

REHABILITATIVE CONTRIBUTIONS

Sports medicine has undoubtedly made significant contributions in the area of rehabilitation. Physicians specializing in sports medicine tend to be less conservative than others who advise patients to rest after injuries or surgery, because that has been considered the safest thing to do.

Specialists in sports medicine have learned to urge their patients to start rehabilitation very quickly, exercising even while in casts. This often is of great benefit, and some of these principles are being more widely adopted by other physicians thanks to their successful use in sports medicine.

The specialists have also pioneered or furthered the use of many rehabilitation devices. Among them: fiberglass and plastic casts; small, two-and-one-half-ounce transcutaneous nerve stimulator packs which can be taped to the body to emit tiny electrical charges to relieve pain; and ultrasound equipment to increase blood supply to an injured area.

The effort to speed recovery from injury in the case of pro players has led to advances in surgical and rehabilitative techniques; but it has also led to controversial practices, such as use of injectable anesthetics to let players perform while injured.

PERFORMANCE ANALYSIS

Sports medicine has other potential, including the capacity to help improve performance through scientific analysis.

In 1976, the U. S. Olympic Committee, deciding to make as much use as possible of that capacity, set up experiments in biomechanics and exercise physiology at its national training center in Squaw Valley, California.

Out of those experiments have come a number of significant developments.

One finding, for example, showed that American kayakers, although bigger and stronger than their European rivals, continually finished behind them. The reason had been unknown. But after thorough analysis it was discovered that Americans were driving their paddles into the water too hard in the beginning; the emphasis should come in the last half of the stroke.

Another finding was that top U. S. volleyball players,

although excellent jumpers, have been weak in their upper arms and chest, and the deficiency—a correctable one—has hindered their effectiveness as spikers and setters.

Still another finding was that American women runners tend not to utilize potential strength in their arms to maximum efficiency. This, too, could be corrected.

A few years ago, at the request of the U. S. Ski Association, the University of Colorado established a sports medicine team, consisting of a physician, two exercise physiologists (one of them a certified athletic trainer), a psychologist, and a kinesthiologist (a specialist in the study of the movement of body parts).

One function of that team is to establish and emphasize methods to minimize ski injuries and improve treatment for any injuries sustained. Another is to analyze the many components—developmental, kinesiological, physiological, and psychological—that contribute to performance in Nordic and Alpine events. Through film evaluation and computation, muscle function and biochemical principles necessary to each event have been analyzed. Physiological and psychological test data on more than 200 ski racers have been compiled and are now available to identify factors related to success in ski racing.

A third effort is to measure the physical and behavioral factors important in ski racers of all levels and age groups. Physical tests given include tests for muscular strength and power, aerobic capacity, body composition, and various motor abilities. A battery of psychological tests is used to draw up a psychophysical profile for each competitor. The idea is to educate both athlete and coach about what influences performance and allow each competitor to gain the most from his or her individual capabilities. From the test results, the team has been able to recommend changes or additions to the training program of many of the skiers with resulting improvement in performance.

The University of Colorado team also functions as an educational resource group. It disseminates its findings through publications and travels to various areas of the country for a series of clinics attended by coaches.

THE WIDENING APPLICATION
OF SPORTS MEDICINE

The potential of sports medicine is vast. Its research findings can help young amateur athletes as well as the pros. Those findings—in regard to good nutrition and suitable conditioning activities, for example—have been noted throughout this book. Undoubtedly, there will be many more valuable findings coming as sports medicine research intensifies.

It is intensifying and producing valuable information for treatment and rehabilitation as well, as we have noted.

Many medical schools have been setting up sports medicine departments and centers.

A survey in 1978 disclosed eighty-five sports medicine centers in the U. S.—up from just one in 1955. Of the eighty-five, most were established since 1970.

A very good indication of the help in store for young athletes is the experience of North Carolina. Through the Sports Medicine Division of its Department of Public Instruction, the state has been developing a medical delivery system within local communities to help in the prevention, treatment, and rehabilitation of sports-related injuries, aiming to reduce injuries among public school students participating in sports.

The Division succeeded in enlisting the help of many physicians. It did so through the State Medical Society which contacted local medical societies and requested them to appoint physicians to be responsible for coordinating sports medicine within each local community.

That coordination involves arranging with school officials for the administration of medical examinations for all students participating in interscholastic athletic programs and for the assignment of game and/or team physicians for all home football games.

Television-assisted courses of instruction have been set up for prospective public school teacher/trainers and include anatomy, identification of more common injuries, and general treatment and rehabilitation procedures. The instructors are physicians actively involved in sports medicine throughout the state, most of them from the faculties of the state's three medical schools, at the University of North Carolina, Duke, and Bowman Gray.

There has been dissemination of information about modern techniques of athletic training through a variety of media. Newspapers across the state have received periodic releases identifying actions to be taken to prevent injuries. TV stations have provided time for announcements.

Within a few years of its start, the North Carolina program led to the development of a basic corps of over 120 teacher-athletic trainers serving local high schools, with each local community providing supplementary funds as salaries for them.

CHAPTER 12

COMMON QUESTIONS AND ANSWERS

What effect does athletic activity have on a child's final height and weight?

This is an area which needs more study.

According to animal studies, while a certain minimum level of exercise is required for growth and development, an excessive level may retard growth. Theoretically, then, there may be some ideal level of training between extremes that could provide for optimal development.

Thus far, available evidence in humans indicates that exercise has little effect on final height and weight. But it appears likely that children who exercise will, as adults, have lower percent body fat.

Some investigators report that an active, vigorous childhood leads to a stronger, more supple, and sturdier physique than a sedentary childhood.

One study did find that boys and girls aged eight through eighteen engaged in a year-round swimming program had larger physical dimensions and lung capacities than did others. But it is possible that another factor was involved: that the youngsters may have entered into the program because, to begin with, they were better endowed.

Is there any real basis for the idea that girl athletes may become masculinized?

Apparently not. No evidence indicates that they do.

For example, when investigators at Bowling Green State University compared 275 nonathletic women college students with 328 others who participated in various sports (many of them in the 1972 Women's Intercollegiate Championships or the 1972 Olympic gymnastics tryouts) they found the athletic women only slightly larger—5'6" in height and weighing 129 pounds on average—than the nonathletic women, who averaged 5'5" tall and 126 pounds.

In her book, *Women: Psychology's Puzzle*, Dr. Joanna Bunker Rohrbaugh of the Harvard Medical School noted that there is no truth either in the so-called "muscle myth."

"For when women engage in organized swimming, or even in weight-lifting programs," she points out, "the major changes in body composition, involve decreases in subcutaneous (under-the-skin) fat. Exercise physiologists also point out that athletic competition does not cause excessive muscle development. No matter how often a woman lifts weights, she won't look like a scaled-down Arnold Schwartzenegger."

Is it advisable for a youngster to take part in sports when sick?

No.

The body may well need all its energies to combat illness and shake it off more rapidly and completely.

During illness, it is better to rest than train.

And when activity is resumed, it is usually advisable to start at a lower level and work up to the level attained before illness.

Some experts believe that in case of an illness with

fever, such as flu, it's advisable not to exercise until at least several days after all symptoms are gone.

What's overtraining? How can it be recognized? How can it be avoided?

Many youthful athletes, and even older ones, take their training a bit too far, pushing themselves too hard.

They get into a state of staleness akin to a state of physical and psychological exhaustion.

Unfortunately, too many young athletes, when overtrained, worriedly try to push themselves even harder. Not only are they likely to prolong the period of staleness; they also increase the likelihood of injury.

With overtraining, there may come warning indications such as feelings of fatigue and sluggishness, loss of appetite, nervousness, irritability, muscle soreness, sleeping difficulty, and elevation of pulse.

Once staleness develops, no treatment is likely to help very much other than rest for several days or even sometimes longer.

Often, taking the pulse while still in bed on awakening in the morning can help pick up an indication of approaching staleness so it can be headed off.

If the pulse, taken for one minute, is more than seven to ten beats faster than usual, it can be helpful to omit athletic activity that day or at least take it very easy.

A rest in time can do much to head off staleness.

How can common muscle pulls and strains be prevented?

One measure that can go far to prevent most such injuries is stretching.

"Stretch exercises should be a way of life for any athlete," says Dr. Donald L. Cooper, team physician and director of student health services at Oklahoma State University in Stillwater and past chairman of the American

Medical Association Committee on the Medical Aspects of Sports.

"They [stretch exercises] should be done year round, day in and day out, both before and after workouts," Dr. Cooper notes.

And in advice to physicians in an article in the professional journal, *Emergency Medicine*, he goes on to add:

"You must emphasize to all coaches that they should spend at least ten minutes per practice working on flexibility. And remember: you don't want to see the guys bouncing up and down; that's called ballistic stretching and is not very good. What I mean is slow, static stretching where you stretch until you can feel the muscle pull, then back off and hold it for about ten seconds. Then repeat, stretching a little bit further, and hold it again.

"I can't emphasize strongly enough how important static stretching is. When a muscle has good longitudinal flexibility it's much less likely to be injured."

What are shin splints and what can be done about them?

"Shin splints" refer to pain in front of the lower leg resulting from muscle injury.

They are common in runners, especially when the running is done on hard surfaces, and/or when there is inadequate training and too much is done too soon.

Other possible causes include anatomic abnormalities of the foot, or other foot and leg problems which may require the use of special foot supports, and imbalances in the strength or flexibility of muscles of the lower leg.

Treatment for shin splints may include resting the injured leg and ice massage of the painful area.

Also helpful as a means of treatment and prevention: strengthening the shin muscles by running upstairs, and stretching the calf muscles. The stretching can be done with wall push-ups in which, facing a wall and standing about four feet away, with palms on the wall and back straight, elbows are bent so the upper body approaches the wall. With heels kept on the ground, this will stretch the calves. The position should be held for a count of ten, after which elbows are straightened. Several repetitions are needed.

When shin splints fail to respond within two or three weeks, medical help should be sought since another problem, such as a stress fracture, may be involved. After about two weeks, such a fracture will usually be visible on X rays though not before. Stress fractures take longer to heal than shin splints but treatment may be similar to that for shin splints.

What's athlete's heart?

It's an enlarged heart, but not at all the same kind of condition that occurs in some forms of heart disease.

Vigorous physical activity may enlarge the heart gradually, and the increase in size is beneficial.

With such enlargement, the result of training, the heart becomes stronger. Its pumping activity becomes more efficient and it is capable of pumping more blood with each beat than an untrained heart. That assures a good supply of oxygen and nutrients to body tissues.

It also means that even at rest the heart need pump less often—in effect, giving it increased rest between beats.

Why do weakness, nausea and light-headed feelings sometimes appear after vigorous exercise?

Such symptons and others, such as throbbing head and blurred vision, are sometimes referred to as "athletic sickness."

They result from a temporary hypoglycemia, or low blood sugar, which may develop when sugar in the blood is used up at such a rapid rate during heavy exercise that the liver doesn't keep pace in replenishing the blood sugar supply.

The symptoms usually disappear after a brief rest.

Is it wise to try to direct a child to lifetime sports rather than those most popular among kids?

If a youngster wants to play and has a talent for such sports as football, baseball and basketball, fine.

Even in that case, it could be wise to try to interest him in other activities as well.

There is no question that football, baseball and basketball are extremely popular with kids. These are the glamor games, and professional sports help to make them so. But these are not games that many adults play.

Upon growing up, a youngster who has focused entirely on one or another of them usually finds himself a spectator rather than active participant. This does nothing for his or her health and physical fitness.

On the other hand, any youngster who in youth has had a chance to sample other sports—either instead of or as well as the glamor three—can keep playing one or more of them all through life.

Among such potentially good-for-a-lifetime sports are badminton, tennis, handball, jogging, cross-country skiing, biking, swimming, and even soccer and volleyball.

Is "getting the wind knocked out" a serious matter?

Not usually.

The phenomenon is common in sports as the result of collisions with other players or objects and produces a feeling of great difficulty in breathing.

What's involved is a blow to a network of nerves, called the solar plexus, in the center of the abdomen. As a result, the diaphragm, which is involved in breathing, temporarily does not function normally.

The plexus usually recovers quickly and normal breathing returns in a few minutes. Often discomfort is relieved and the return of normal breathing may be hastened by taking short breaths and short exhalations.

In the rare situation where spontaneous recovery does not occur, mouth-to-mouth resuscitation may be needed.

Is it ever advisable to use a rubberized warm-up suit?

Despite a popular notion, use of a rubberized warm-up suit while exercising will not get rid of pounds permanently and may be harmful.

During vigorous activity, the body produces a lot of heat which should be transferred to the environment, primarily by evaporation of perspiration, in order to keep body temperature within a tolerable range.

Rubberized clothing can increase sweating and some weight loss does occur, but it is only temporary, since the loss is due to dehydration and the weight is regained as soon as the fluid level in the body returns to normal.

Rubberized clothing can be hazardous because it leads to overheating, causing a large amount of blood to be diverted to the skin for cooling. This, along with the excessive fluid loss through sweating, reduces blood plasma volume and puts a great strain on the heart and blood vessel system.

Is complete rest essential after an injury?

Immediately after an injury, rest and immobilization often are necessary. A minor injury can turn into a major one when aggravated.

As long as the injury hurts at rest, continued rest is needed.

Often, when the injured area no longer hurts at rest, it can be exercised, starting very slowly, keeping movements minimal, stopping immediately if pain reappears.

If minimal exercise is possible without discomfort, the exercise can be gradually increased.

It's wisest to make rehabilitation of an injured part a slow, gradual matter and not to jump back into full activity prematurely.

During the rest and rehabilitation process, it is often possible to maintain fitness by engaging in activities that do not involve the injured area. With an aching shoulder, for example, it is still often possible to jog. Rowing is possible if a leg hurts. Other injuries may not be aggravated by swimming.

Isn't there any danger in drinking water or other fluids during competition?

No.

On the contrary, under some circumstances, it could be dangerous not to.

Fluid during vigorous activity is often necessary; it does not cause cramps.

During vigorous activity, especially in hot weather, the body loses huge amounts of fluid through sweating and exhalation of vapor.

On hot days, an athlete playing baseball, basketball, soccer, tennis, football, or other sports can lose four, five or even more pounds of fluid.

Drinking too much water or other fluid at any one time may distend the stomach and cause discomfort.

But drinking a cup or two before an event and every fifteen to twenty minutes during the event will be beneficial without causing any discomfort.

And it can be important, especially on a hot day and during very vigorous activity, to do the drinking without waiting for thirst to signal you to drink. Thirst can lag behind until considerable fluid has been lost.

Is it OK to drink iced water?

A common belief that it's unhealthy to drink iced or very cold water when overheated from exertion is not valid, according to two sports-oriented American Medical Association consultants.

At Alvarado Medical Center, San Diego, Dr. John L. Boyer took body temperatures of subjects after strenuous physical activity and then again immediately after they drank refrigerated drinking fountain water in the gymnasium and found no significant temperature change due to the cold water.

Says Dr. Allan J. Ryan of the University of Wisconsin: "I am aware of no evidence that drinking ice water is harmful to athletes in the course of their participation in sports."

One common misconception appears to be that icy cold drinks can cause stomach cramps. This is not borne out at all by the experience, for example, of many professional teams which customarily now drink ice drinks during competition.

Are liniments of any value?

Liniments—liquid preparations to be rubbed on the skin—can be useful for many common muscle aches and pains that stem from exercise, according to Dr. Ernest W. Johnson of Ohio State University College of Medicine.

Usually, they contain methyl salicylate as a principal ingredient, along with oil of wintergreen or camphor.

Rubbed on over an aching muscle, they help to bring more blood to the area, producing warmth and helping to reduce discomfort.

They also have some tendency to increase muscle work capacity.

But an important caution should be observed: During or immediately after liniment is applied, heat should *not* be applied or a skin burn may result.

If a young athlete experiences a heat stroke episode, should he be excluded from any sport in which there is a risk of exposure to excessive heat?

Not necessarily.

A youngster who suffers from heat stroke and makes a complete recovery does not harbor any long-term effects, according to a report in the *Journal of the American Medical Association*.

Such a youngster apparently loses a large amount of fluids when exposed to high heat and humidity while exercising vigorously.

That need not mean recurrence is likely as long as large amounts of water are taken before and during play.

Is there ever any justification for injection of a local anesthetic such as procaine (Novocain) so a player can stay in a game?

In a forthright answer, one expert, Dr. T. B. Quigley of Boston, saw no place whatever for using procaine to abolish pain so a player can keep playing.

"Whatever the injury may be, it is almost certain to be made worse," wrote Dr. Quigley in the *Journal of the American Medical Association*.

"Pain," he added, "is nature's way of imposing rest, and rest is essential for the normal healing of injury. No one has yet discovered how to make a wound heal faster than nature intends, but there are many ways to delay the process and the injection of procaine is one of them."

As Dr. Quigley also noted, the practice has been condemned by every organization and group interested in athletic injuries, including the American Medical Association Committee on the Medical Aspects of Sports.

In soccer, can repeated contact between head and ball cause brain changes similar to those in punch-drunk prizefighters?

In answer to that question, Dr. Otto C. Kestler of New York, an American Medical Association consultant, has noted that in his thirty years' experience, he has never encountered anything to indicate changes in soccer players similar to the brain changes in prizefighters.

For one thing, a soccer ball is somewhat elastic and softer than a prizefighter's gloved hand and not capable of producing the brain structure changes sometimes seen in the case of fighters.

In soccer, too, the head is used only occasionally and even children playing soccer gradually train themselves and develop skill and resistance in such use of the head.

"Plays involving the head are used in passing the ball, in scoring, and in intercepting shots," notes Dr. Kestler. "All

this is done with active positive motions which are antici-
pated by the players. A misjudged force of impact or an
accidental blow on the head of a player or even a spectator
can cause a transient moderate cerebral concussion which
is usually shortly resolved. It should be pointed out, moreover, that using the head in soccer particularly in nonprofes-
sional and school children's games can be reduced to a
minimum."

**Old records are constantly being broken in many
sports? What accounts for that? Will it go on for long?**
Records are, indeed, being broken, in virtually every sport.

When, for example, Johnny Weissmuller achieved a
100-yard free-style swimming record of fifty-two seconds,
it seemed remarkable. Today, hundreds of swimmers beat
that time.

The sub-four-minute mile achieved by Roger Bannister
in 1954—the time was 3:59.6—today would not win many
important mile races.

In many sports, new records are set every year and
in some cases almost every week.

There are many reasons to account for the remarkable
improvements.

For one thing, more people are participating. Once
largely limited to the relatively few, usually the wealthy,
sports now are for the masses—and not just in the U. S.
and other Western countries but around the world.

Improved diets also help to improve size and strength.
Undoubtedly, too, better sanitation and medical advances
contribute.

There have been and continue to be many improvements in equipment—among them, for example, livelier
baseballs and bats, livelier golf balls, improved football kicking shoes, starting blocks in track and better track surfaces,
the fiberglass pole, and certainly not least of all, motion
picture films which allow analysis of form, movement, timing,
coordination, and errors.

Training techniques, too, are no longer based on old tradition but rather on research and are much improved and undoubtedly will continue to improve.

There is no indication at this point that record breaking, as the result of all these factors, will not continue to go on for some time yet at a fast pace although eventually the pace may slow and while new records will be established, they may be less startling.

How does one find a doctor knowledgeable about sports and sports-related problems?

Many physicians of course are concerned with varied injuries. They are trained to provide relief from pain whenever possible.

But athletic injuries can be different from other injuries. They can be sudden and accidental. Often they result from overuse.

And usually a young athlete wants something more than just pain relief. He or she is concerned, too, about performance.

So, ideally, the physician tending to the health and any injuries of a young athlete should understand exercise. Often such a physician is one who is athletic himself or herself.

If you're in need of such a physician, you may get good recommendations from other young athletes or parents.

Failing that, you may want to choose the team physician of a local school or college.

You may also get recommendations from the nearest medical school or the local county medical society.

PART II

SPECIAL NOTES ABOUT INDIVIDUAL SPORTS

BADMINTON

If some of its enthusiasts are right, badminton may be the fastest of all court games.

Developed centuries ago in India where it was known as "Poona," badminton was introduced into England by English army officers who had served in India and was really launched there at an 1873 party at "Badminton," the Duke of Beaufort's country place in Gloucestershire.

The game soon spread to the United States, Canada and elsewhere. And although first played by men, it soon became popular with women as well.

By 1878 the first organized badminton club was established in the U. S. in New York City.

Played vigorously, badminton is a high-energy activity which demands—and can contribute to—heart and lung fitness, leg muscle endurance, some degree of arm and abdominal strength, and back flexibility.

A vigorous game calls for fast and furious volleying of the bird or shuttlecock, with the players in almost continuous motion as they bat the bird over the net.

Because the shuttlecock is given to eccentric flights and sudden, often unexpected descents, there are demands for speed and dexterity and, some hold, for even more endurance than is required for tennis.

Like many other sports, badminton can give rise to injuries such as sprains and strains.

Yet, with proper training and good conditioning, it is a relatively safe game and one with lifetime value, playable at any age by anyone who maintains good physical condition.

The badminton singles court is seventeen by forty-four feet—twenty by forty-four for doubles. The net which bisects the court is five feet high at the top.

The shuttlecock, which weighs only seventy-three to eighty-five grains, has fourteen to sixteen feathers, each two and one-half inches long.

The racket is lighter and slightly larger than the racket used in squash.

The game can be played both indoors and outdoors.

BASEBALL

Baseball is often referred to as the "national pastime", and it's the rare child who hasn't played it at some point.

According to popular tradition, the game was invented in 1839 by Abner Doubleday at Cooperstown, N. Y., now the site of the Hall of Fame and the National Museum of Baseball.

But research indicates that a game called "Base Ball" was played before 1839 in this country and in England.

The game of course has evolved over the years. The first curve ball is believed to have been thrown in 1867. Two years later, the first all-professional team, the Cincinnati Red

Stockings, played sixty-four games without a loss. The ball now considered standard was adopted in 1872; the first catcher's mask was worn in 1875; the first chest protector in 1885; the three-strike rule was adopted in 1887 and the four-ball pass to first base came two years later.

Although baseball has gotten something of a bad reputation at the grade and junior high school levels because of "Little League Elbow," elbow injury is hardly inevitable. A help has been restriction by official Little League baseball on the amount of pitching a youngster can do. Still needed: ways to discourage prolonged practice sessions and awareness by coach, parent and child of possible harmful effects from excessive throwing.

Preseason conditioning is important.

One sports medicine authority who is also physician to a major league club recommends that young players and would-be players do some light weight lifting and also wind sprints (running full out for ten or fifteen yards), stopping, repeating, doing half a dozen such sprints daily to help strengthen arm, leg and trunk muscles. Side-stepping exercises, and backward and forward running can help coordination.

Most injuries in baseball are caused by the ball which is both hard and propelled at high speed. Even twelve-year-old Little League pitchers have been known to throw baseballs as fast as seventy miles an hour—and the speed of a batted ball is faster.

A study by the Consumer Product Safety Commission indicates that an estimated 900,000 injuries occur to the 46 million people, young and old, who play baseball and softball each year, with as many as 7,200 injuries a day during May and June. The injury incidence estimated by the CPSC study—1.96 percent—is the same as found in a Little League study of 5 million players aged eight to fifteen.

Of the 900,000 CPSC estimated injuries, 243,000 are to the head; 234,000 to fingers, hands and wrists; 72,000 to the trunk; 275,000 to legs, ankles and feet. Little League actual injuries in 5 million players: to the head, 38 percent; upper extremities, 39 percent; trunk, 4 percent; lower extremities, 19 percent.

The Little League study also shows the proportion of injuries according to position played: pitcher, 5 percent; catcher, 16 percent; first baseman, 5 percent; second baseman, 6 percent; third baseman, 5 percent; shortstop, 5 percent; outfielders, 14 percent; runner, 17 percent; batter, 22 percent; on-deck, 7 percent; miscellaneous, 3 percent.

Still, a "hazard index"—drawn from CPSC figures— puts baseball and softball in fifth position, preceded by bicycles, stairs, lawnmowers, and football in that order.

The breakdown of the types of injuries found in the Little League 5-million player study: Bruises, 40 percent; fractures, 19 percent; sprains, 18 percent; cuts, 10 percent; dental, 5 percent; abrasions (scrapes), 3 percent; concussions, 2 percent; miscellaneous, 3 percent.

And the mechanisms of injury as found in the Little League study: Pitched ball, 22 percent; batted ball, 19 percent; catching, 14 percent; thrown ball, 10 percent; sliding, 10 percent; collisions, 10 percent; hit by bat, 4 percent; falling, 4 percent; running, 2 percent; throwing, 2 percent; miscellaneous, 3 percent.

The mechanism breakdown from the CPSC study: Of the 900,000 estimated injuries, 374,000 are from being hit by the ball; collisions account for 99,000; being hit by a bat, 81,000; catching batted balls, 68,000; catching thrown balls, 56,000; catching spikes, 45,000; running bases, 45,000; sliding, 36,000; coming down hard on foot, 36,000; being spiked, 18,000; hard tags and miscellaneous, 10,000.

Can baseball injuries be reduced?

They can be, significantly, according to Dr. Creighton J. Hale, president of Little League Baseball, Williamsport, Pa., writing in *The Physician and Sportsmedicine*—by a number of measures:

• Eliminating steel spikes in favor of soccer-type cleats;

● Eliminating sliding—or using the breakaway base, a conventional base which, instead of being strapped to steel stakes in the ground, is Velcro-attached to the base plate and can dislodge when struck with enough force;

● Eliminating the on-deck circle and keeping players in dugouts until their turn at bat, and screening the dugouts (or where dugouts are not available, seating players behind a protective screen) to help prevent injuries from a foul or overthrown ball or a bat that slips from a batter's hands;

● Using face protectors (a recently developed polycarbonate face mask which attaches to a batter's helmet protects the face without interfering with vision);

● Prohibiting any intentional contact between base runner and infielder making a play at a base;

● Motivating players to use proper equipment.

BASKETBALL

The game is said to be the only one devised in the U.S. with no roots in the sports of other nations. It was conceived in 1891 by Dr. James Naismith, an instructor at the International YMCA Training School in Springfield, Mass., now Springfield College. The game started with two peach baskets fastened to a gymnasium balcony.

Basketball is a fast sport, good for conditioning. One problem with it is that too often a player's size is a significant factor.

As in most sports that involve running for sustained periods, lower extremity injuries are most common, particularly ankle injuries, with sprains and strains predominating.

Girls are participating increasingly in basketball. And in 1978, Drs. Alfred Moretz, III and William A. Grana of the University of Oklahoma reported a study of injuries for both boys and girls engaging in a basketball program at a large Oklahoma City high school.

The study covered two seasons (1975–76 and 1976–77) and focussed on fifty-one boys and sixty girls with a mean age of sixteen.

There were forty-three injuries in thirty-two girls, eleven of the injuries being classed as major (persisting for seven days or more). There were eight injuries, four of them major, in seven boys.

Ankle injuries were most common, accounting for thirteen of the total forty-three injuries in girls, three of the eight in boys. In addition, the boys experienced three arm, one knee, and one foot injuries while the girls had four arm, two back, four face cuts, two hip, six thigh, five knee, four leg and three foot injuries.

Sprains accounted for half of the boys' injuries and for nineteen of the forty-three in girls. There were no strains in boys, eleven in girls. Fractures and dislocations were limited to one in boys, three in girls.

Injuries occured more commonly in practice—thirty-nine for the girls and six for the boys—than in games. And most occurred during the first half of the season.

All told, the girls had a higher injury rate—0.72 injuries per player to 0.16 injuries per player for boys. But a greater proportion of their injuries were minor. And the girls especially tended to be injured early in the season.

Drs. Moretz and Grana have some recommendations. Writing in *The Physician and Sportsmedicine*, they say:

"Our findings suggest that the girls were in poorer condition at the onset of the season, so they were injured frequently until they were conditioned and more experienced.

"Therefore, a major step in prevention would be to begin a preseason four- to six-week conditioning program designed for the girls and specifically aimed at preventing these early-season problems. With the conditioning program, the number of injuries might be reduced, bringing the girls' statistics in line with the boys'."

BICYCLING

Cycling is an excellent conditioning activity and an increasingly popular one.

A 1978 nationwide survey of Americans over seventeen years of age indicated that 19,500,000 cycled regularly, ranking cycling fourth—behind only walking, swimming and bowling—in total numbers participating on a regular basis.

And when medical experts, at the request of the President's Council on Physical Fitness and Sports, were asked to assess the contributions of various activities to physical well-being, they rated cycling as second only to jogging.

In recent years, more bikes have been sold than passenger cars.

Injuries are all too common among bicyclists, now running at the rate of about a million a year, about 460,000 of them serious enough to require hospital emergency room treatment.

Yet studies indicate that the vast majority of accidents are preventable, with most due to the cyclist's carelessness—failure to choose a suitable bike and keep it in good working condition, to observe sensible riding precautions, and obey traffic laws.

A California study found that in 70 percent of bicycle-car accidents, the cyclist had disregarded traffic laws.

About half of serious accidents involved youngsters aged five to fourteen. In nine out of ten, the accident was the child's fault, with the most common circumstance being the youngster emerging precipitously from an alley, driveway, or parking lot, and ignoring stop or yield signs.

One common error in cycling is riding on the wrong side of the road. This is actually illegal in most states, and less safe than riding with traffic. If there should be a collision between bicycle and car, the force of impact will be less if the bicycle is traveling in the same direction as the car. Considering that a good young athlete can easily be traveling 20 to 25 mph on a level stretch with a modern bike, this is important.

Among major accident patterns associated with bicycles are: loss of control because of riding too large a bike, difficulty in braking, stunting, and striking a rut, bump or obstacle; mechanical and structural problems such as brake failure; wheel wobbling; gear-shifting difficulty; chain slippage, pedals falling off, and spoke breakage; entanglement of feet, hands or clothing in the bicycle; foot slippage from the pedal.

From the U. S. Consumer Product Safety Commission and other expert sources come the following tips on selecting, using and maintaining a bicycle:

Selecting the bicycle

● If you're buying a bicycle for a child, buy one that fits—not one he will "grow into" but one that is suitable for him or her today. Feet should reach the ground while seated on the seat.

● Ask for reflectors that will make the bike visible at night from front, back and sides.

● Tape retro-reflective trim to the fenders, handlebars, chainguards, and wheel sidewalls to make it recognizable in the dark as a bike.

● Attach headlight and taillight.

● Check hand and foot brakes for fast, easy stops without instability or jamming.

● Avoid slippery plastic pedals; look, instead, for rubber-treaded pedals, or metal pedals with serrated rattrap edges or with firmly attached toeclips.

● Don't buy a bicycle with sharp points and edges, especially along fenders, or with protruding bolts that could scrape or tear clothing.

● Don't buy a bike with gear controls (or other protruding attachments) mounted on the top tube of a man's bike.

Using the bicycle
Teach the child to:

● Observe all traffic laws and signals, just as cars must do.

● Not ride double or try stunts.

● Ride near the curb in the same direction as traffic.

● Find alternative routes rather than ride through busy intersections and heavy or high-speed traffic.

● Walk—not ride—the bike across busy intersections and left turn corners.

● Avoid riding in wet weather when handbrakes may require a long distance to stop.

● Avoid loose clothing or long coats that can catch in pedals or wheels; leg clips or bands keep pants legs from tangling in the chain.

● Apply retro-reflective trim to clothing for increased visibility in the dark or wear reflective vests and jackets.

● Avoid crossing raised sewer grates.

● Ride with both hands on the handlebars. If books or other items must be carried, equip the bike with basket or pannier bag or both.

Maintaining the bicycle

● Regular maintenance is essential for safe riding. At least twice a year there should be a thorough maintenance check of tires, gears, spokes, steering, brakes, chain (which should be lightly oiled), pedals, reflectors, and handlebar and seat tightness. Parents should inspect the bikes of young children. An experienced repairman should do complicated work if that is necessary.

● Cover sharp points and edges with heavy, waterproof tape.

● Replace any protruding bolts with shorter bolts, or add crowned nuts or other protective devices to prevent catching on bolts.

● Align or "true" wobbly wheels for better control. Adjust spokes if necessary.

● Tighten and/or adjust any loose parts.

● Inflate tires to recommended pressure—and replace worn tires.

● Lightly oil and clean all moving parts, taking care to keep oil off rubber.

● Keep the bike indoors when not in use to avoid rust and weakening of metal parts from moisture.

BOXING

Although boxing has many things to recommend it, many physicians as well as parents find it difficult if not impossible to approve of a youngster's participation.

It is a fact that not only the actual boxing but the rope skipping, road work and other exercises that go with the sport all are excellent conditioning activities.

It is also a fact, of course, that boxing teaches self-defense, which may have value.

Yet many, perhaps even most, physicians would agree with the feeling of one sports medicine authority that "it is difficult for a physician to approve of the sport because its ultimate goal is a knockout—or, in essence, the infliction of brain damage."

If a youngster must participate, headgear should be worn.

If you can find a good instructor for the child, by all means do so.

While learning the science of boxing, the boy should be conditioning himself. Running and brisk walking, if possible over hilly ground, can help to develop leg muscles and stamina.

Rope skipping is good for footwork as well as stamina.

Working at a heavy dummy bag can help develop punching power.

A punching bag—at shoulder level or a little higher—can provide practice for hitting a moving target and strengthening arm and shoulder muscles. The youngster should wear light gloves or old gloves with fingers cut out and should dance around and hit the bag hard.

Because a boy's hands are not very strong, learning how to punch correctly from the beginning is important. Hands should be held open—and the fist should be closed only in landing a punch. Constant clenching of the fist puts a strain on forearm muscles. The thumb, of course, should never be used in hitting. In landing a straight punch, the palm of the hand should be turned inward and downward so the blow is landed with the top of the knuckles.

Many experts urge avoidance of use of heavy weights, dumbbells, medicine balls. Speed, agility and suppleness—not tight bunchy muscles—are what count most.

FOOTBALL

Football, of course, is the number one autumn sport. It's the glamor game, played each Saturday by hundreds of college and thousands of high school teams, attracting huge crowds, accounting for most sports scholarships, and providing high salaries at the professional level.

Almost every Saturday afternoon from late September to early December, hundreds of thousands of eight- to fourteen-year-old youngsters play Little League football. There is even a Midget program for five- and six-year-olds.

Since football is a collision sport, injuries are expected. The U. S. Consumer Product Safety Commission estimates that each year over 230,000 people receive hospital emergency room treatment for injuries associated with football.

The National Football League has reported a 90 percent injury rate per year, meaning that 90 percent of players in the League every year have some kind of significant injury.

Deaths from organized football have declined in recent years. A study published in 1979 by the National Football Head and Neck Injury Registry at the Sports Medicine Center of the University of Pennsylvania in Philadelphia shows that in a five-year period, 1959 to 1963, during which 820,000 youths played football each year, there were 86 deaths as a direct result of football. During the five-year period of 1971 to 1975, with 1,275,000 players in the games each year, 77 deaths occurred.

Despite the contact nature of tackle football, the catastrophic injury as well as fatality rates have remained low, and there are relatively few serious injuries in relation to the total number of players involved during a given season. So reports Dr. Joseph S. Torg of the Registry and the University of Pennsylvania.

Of great value has been the evolution of protective coverings for the head. As recently as 1905, the only protection was a full head of hair. Present-day helmet-facemask systems provide excellent protection to the head and face. In the past deaths have been primarily from head injuries and the helmet-facemask systems have reduced the risk of death considerably.

On the other hand, even as deaths and many types of catastrophic injuries have declined, there has been an increase in broken necks resulting in complete paralysis. By effectively protecting the head, the protective helmet-facemask system has allowed it to be used as a battering ram in tackling and blocking, thus causing more broken necks.

From 1971 to 1979, the Registry has documented 1,129 serious injuries, mostly among high school and college players. Of these, 550 were broken necks, of which 176 resulted in permanent paralysis from the neck down.

The reason for the paralyzing injuries, as Dr. Torg reports, is that, given the excellent helmet-facemask protection for head and face, "coaches have developed playing techniques that use the head and helmet as a battering ram in blocking, tackling and butting. Such techniques fail to account for the potential danger of injury to the cervical (neck) spine when the head is the primary point of contact in a high-impact situation."

Fortunately, some progress is being made in combatting the problem. In 1976, the National Federation of State High School Associations implemented a rule change to prohibit butt blocking and face tackling, and the American Football Coaches Association Ethics Committee went on record opposing this type of blocking and tackling.

Checking on catastrophic head and neck injuries, Drs. Frederick O. Mueller and Carl S. Blyth of the University of North Carolina found that the fatality rate, which reached a peak of 3.4 per 100,000 players in 1968, was down to .55 per 100,000 in 1978.

In 1978, there were forty-two catastrophic head and neck injuries, according to the Mueller-Blyth study. Twenty-nine involved neck fractures, twelve subdural hematomas, and one a brain stem injury. These injuries led to permanent paralysis in sixteen players, death in fifteen, recovery in eleven.

Of the forty-two catastrophic injuries, six occurred in youngsters aged ten to fifteen. The greatest number by far, twenty-eight, occurred in players aged sixteen to eighteen. The concentration of the injuries in the sixteen to eighteen age group may be due to lack of neck muscle strength, improper playing fundamentals, or both.

Most (thirty-six) of the catastrophic injuries occurred in games; only six occurred in practice. Tackling apparently is the most dangerous activity in football; twenty-six of the forty-two players injured were making a tackle, and five were being tackled.

What of injuries to younger football players? Little League and Midget programs are usually well-organized, requiring the youngsters to wear helmets, face masks, mouthpieces, plastic soccer-type cleats, and hip, kidney, shoulder, tailbone, knee and thigh pads.

There is evidence that preadolescents in organized contact sports such as football have less risk of injury than high school athletes.

But the injury rate may be higher in youth leagues than commonly believed, according to a study by Barry M. Silverstein, head athletic trainer at the University of Tampa, Florida. For two years, he followed the three games played each Saturday by a youth league organization.

Silverstein found that the average injury rate was 15 percent for all participants on the three teams.

The peewee group—eight to eleven-year olds up to 90 pounds—had a 10 percent injury rate in 1977 and 14.4 percent in 1978.

The junior varsity group—twelve- and thirteen-year-olds up to 110 pounds—had an injury rate of 28.3 percent in 1977 (attributed to having only twelve players on the squad most of the season) and 13 percent in 1978.

The varsity group—players fourteen years old up to 130 pounds—had a 20.6 percent injury rate in 1977 (attributed to small numbers on the squad), and 11 percent in 1978.

Most injuries were not serious. Bruises and sprains accounted for upwards of two-thirds. There were seven head injuries in 1977. They included one bruise, two mild concussions, and four moderate concussions, only one (a mild concussion) occuring in the peewee group; one (bruise) in the junior varsity, and five (one mild and four moderate concussions) in varsity players. In 1978, there were also seven head injuries, all concussions. The peewee group had one mild concussion; the junior varsity, two mild; and the varsity, two mild and two moderate concussions.

Silverstein's study shows that helmet spearing continues despite prohibitions. Approximately 30 percent of all injuries in 1978 were caused by spearing incidents producing bruises or other injuries.

The study also revealed: at no game was a physician present. At only three of the six game sites were emergency phones available. For most teams, pregame and posthalftime warm-up and flexibility programs were poor.

Should youth league football be condemned because injuries are endemic to such a contact sport? No, says Silverstein.

"Rather," he writes in *The Physician and Sportsmedicine*, "attention should be focused on the discrepancy between the reported rates of injuries in little league football and the data presented (in the study).

"We should consider how preadolescents are being treated at games across the country. Perhaps youth leagues should be required to provide emergency medical services during games, and pay or emergency phones should be required at all game sites. Physicians, certified athletic trainers, paramedics, or emergency medical technicians should be required at games." ·

Adds Silverstein: "Responsible officials and parents committed to the health and safety of their young weekend sportsmen should consider these points. Their responsibility does not end with athletic insurance—it also demands care, concern, and action for children playing adult games."

GOLF

A golf course has been defined as an "outdoor insane asylum peopled with madmen suffering from the delusion that they will finally master the game."

Nonetheless, as its devotees are quick to inform you, golf is a fascinating and challenging, even if an often frustrating, game. It is as much a game of mental relaxation as of physical workout.

Chasing a little white ball around for several hours can lead to complete absorption. It requires much standing and walking, interspersed with moments of intense concentration and the exertion of taking a swing at the ball.

It provides a good walk and fresh air but relatively little conditioning and tends to be a relatively expensive game.

More and more youngsters are taking up golf. In fact, its skills may best be learned early.

Young people seem to have an advantage over adults. As some experts put it, because the average boy or girl may not have the strength to swing a club hard, he or she is likely to let the club head drop of its own weight and volition, and in the process, may not develop the bad free swinging habits of older people.

GYMNASTICS

Gymnastics—a wide range of exercises including tumbling, vaulting, climbing and balancing—has been a booming sport in recent years, especially since the 1972 Summer Olympics in Munich when a diminutive Russian girl, Olga Korbut, made a remarkable impression on millions for her flying, hurtling and dancing in gymnastic events.

Because of a high injury rate, gymnastics has engendered a considerable amount of controversy and, among parents, concern over whether the benefits outweigh the risk.

The sport has its assets. It helps keep joints loose. According to some sports medicine physicians, gymnasts as a whole have healthier bodies than other athletes when they're older.

In studies by the Institute of Sports Medicine at Lenox Hill Hospital, New York City, with male high school athletes, gymnasts were by far the most flexible. In tests of lower body flexibility, the gymnasts topped other athletes with a score of 93 percent, with football players second at 57 percent.

Unlike some other sports which may overdevelop some one part of the body, gymnastics does not. Both gross and fine muscle development occurs as a gymnast practices to achieve the strength, flexibility and timing required for good performance.

On the other hand, compared with other noncontact sports, gymnastics has a relatively high incidence of injuries. However, they tend to be less serious than those incurred in other sports.

On the Consumer Product Safety Commission's hazard list, accidents on gymnastic equipment rank 69 out of a total of 369 product-accident categories. Strains and sprains account for 34 percent of the gymnastics-related injuries; lacerations, 19 percent; fractures, 18 percent.

The trampoline has occasioned most concern. A relatively new American addition to the sport, bouncing on a trampoline is fun and good exercise and allows for exciting stunts.

But each year, according to the Consumer Product Safety Commission, more than 19,000 persons are treated in hospital emergency rooms for injuries associated with trampolines.

A recent national survey of sports injuries in high schools and college showed that from 1973 through 1975, spinal cord injuries with permanent paralysis resulted more often from trampolines than from any other gymnastic activity.

The survey, covering sports programs at 15,356 high schools, 683 junior colleges, and 1,125 four-year colleges, found that of eighty-six permanent spinal cord injuries reported, most (forty-six) occurred in football. Next came gymnastics (twenty-two) and trampolines were, next to football, the most frequent cause of permanent paralysis.

Some states—among them, Colorado and Illinois—have barred trampolines from high schools.

Yet the trampoline has its defenders, some of whom believe that most of the trouble lies with the somersault (as a cause of paralysis), improper teaching, and youngsters' fooling around.

In 1979, the Committee on Medical Aspects of Sports of the Medical Society of the State of New York issued a statement of policy about the trampoline:

"There is considerable adverse publicity about all bouncing apparatus. The committee feels that some of these criticisms are unjust and lack foundation...

"The committee feels there is safety in the use of the trampoline under proper supervision. It is urged that every school district be required to adopt the new certification developed by the U. S. Gymnastics Safety Association, and only those teachers be allowed to teach the trampoline who acquire the certification.

"The committee encourages school districts to adopt a program of activities which eliminates the somersault and other dangerous twists from all day-to-day physical education classes.

"The role of the spotter should be eliminated since in most instances the spotter is no better trained than the novice trampolinist. The spotter requirement (to make sure the jumper stays in the middle of the trampoline bed and provide other help) should be fulfilled by having the instructor at or on the trampoline at all times. If the participant is only doing the maneuvers at which he is competent, there is little chance he will fly from the equipment. Dangerous tricks should be completely avoided until a level of competence is reached allowing these, and only under proper supervision."

The Consumer Product Safety Commission has published a number of suggestions to help make use of a trampoline safer, with some important to note if you are buying, or have bought, a trampoline for home use:

EQUIPMENT

The trampoline should be equipped with frame pads of firm, yet flexible, resilient material, wide enough to cover the frame and the outer hooks of all springs. The pads should be securely attached to the frame.

If there is a covering over the springs between the frame pad and jumping bed, it should be of a color which contrasts with that of the bed.

The trampoline should be set up on a level surface and only in a well-lighted area. If it is to be used outdoors at night, there should be outdoor lighting adequate to light up evenly the entire trampoline.

Safe jumping requires a minimum ceiling height of twenty-four feet measured from floor to ceiling. Gymnasiums with high ceilings can accomodate indoor jumping; *most homes cannot.*

Inspect a new trampoline carefully before using it and check the condition of all parts every time it is used.

Look especially for any of the following which could be hazardous:

- Punctures or holes worn in the bed.

- Deterioration in the stitching of the bed.

- Sagging bed.

- Ruptured springs.

- Missing or insecurely attached frame pads.

- Bent or broken frame.

- Sharp protrusions on frame or suspension system.

Use

No tricks or stunts should be attempted before you can perform basic bounces, drops and body positions.

Control your bounce by flexing knees slightly when you

contact the trampoline bed. Bend them more to stop bouncing.

Safe use of a trampoline absolutely requires appropriate supervision—more supervision for less skilled users and for the more difficult jumps being attempted.

Spotters are essential (note above the more recent suggestion of the New York State Medical Society committee for spotter replacement by a well-trained instructor) for all novice or beginning jumpers and for advanced jumpers developing new skills. Spotters stand on the ground around the trampoline frame and watch the person jumping. There should be at least four spotters (one on each side of the trampoline). Spotters should be instructed how they can be most useful in preventing injuries. Their task involves the following:

• Making sure the jumper stays in the middle of the trampoline bed. They tell the jumper to move back to the middle if he or she begins to 'travel' or move to the outer parts of the bed.

• Telling the jumper to "break bounce" or bend the knees and drop immediately to the bed if the jumper looks as though he or she has lost control or is off balance.

• Gently pushing the jumper back to the center of the bed if he or she comes too close to the springs.

Spotters should never stand or sit on the trampoline frame.

Keep bounces low until you can control your bouncing and consistently land in the center of the trampoline.

If you feel nervous about jumping or executing a stunt, don't do it. Being tense makes it more difficult to control bounce and maintain balance.

Consider a trick thoroughly before trying it. Changing your mind in midair is dangerous.

Only one person at a time should be on a trampoline.

A "spotting" or "twisting" belt can greatly increase safety when attempting new tricks. More often found in a gym than at home, this device is worn by the jumper and is attached by a series of ropes to an overhead pole or rig and is used to control the jumper's movements. The ropes are controlled by spotters who should be expert in their use, able to stop you in the middle of a trick if you lose control and lower you gently to the trampoline bed. The belt doesn't guarantee that no injury will occur, but does make the activity safer than without a belt.

Keep jumping periods short, especially when you are a beginner, and don't jump when tired.

Wear socks, pants and shirt while jumping, to avoid mat burns.

Climb, don't jump, off the trampoline.

When supervised use of the trampoline is over, secure the trampoline to prevent unauthorized and unsupervised use.

In general, injuries from gymnastic activities are being reduced to some extent by the redesigning of equipment with safety in mind. For example, until a few years ago, tumbling tricks set to music ("free exercise") were done on hard floors with a few movable mats spread about. Now tumblers can use forty-by-forty-foot mats that grip the floor during activity, with less risk of ankle sprains.

About the safety of gymnastics, it may be worth noting the comment of one orthopedic specialist, team physician for professional basketball, soccer and lacrosse teams and for a college football team and a competitive gymnastic squad: "Supervision is the key and with a good program and well-trained personnel you rarely see serious injuries. Here you have a sport that builds muscles and body control, that doesn't penalize the little guy and builds confidence. When parents ask my advice about sports I always tell them 'No' to football, but gymnastics—I'd never discourage that."

HANDBALL

This is an excellent conditioning game, always popular with kids, increasingly so with adults who use it to keep in trim.

It's a vigorous activity that exercises heart and lungs,

and many muscles. Players have been known to lose several pounds in a strenuous match.

It's inexpensive. Not only are courts found in YMCAs, athletic clubs and school gymnasiums, but, because all that is needed is a ball and a wall, kids often play against a building, marking off a court with chalk on a sidewalk. And many youngsters play against themselves matching one hand against the other.

The game was originated by the Irish back in the tenth century, and some credit it with being the parent of tennis. Its early name—in Ireland and England—was "Fives" (for the five fingers in the hand).

Handball has long been popular in English schools, especially at Eton.

It was a Tipperary player, one Meham Biggs, who is credited with bringing new excitement to the game about a century ago when he astounded opponents by his ability to make the ball spin, curve and do tricks on the rebound. The competition soon imitated his skills.

Two kinds of handball are played: four-wall, the original Irish game; and one-wall, which originated in Brooklyn, New York, about 1913.

One-wall is considered to be the faster game, with more speed and stamina required to cover the court. Four-wall is regarded as more scientific.

Because ankles can be easily sprained in handball, good shoes, preferably high ones, firmly laced for ankle support, are important. Also, heavy white woolen socks to absorb perspiration. And soft leather gloves to protect the hands (most have drawstrings to keep them tight around the wrists.)

The official ball of black rubber, inflated, is $1\frac{7}{8}''$ in diameter, weighs 2.3 ounces, and should rebound forty-two to forty-eight inches when dropped from a height of seventy inches at sixty-eight degrees temperature.

The standard one-wall court is thirty-four by twenty feet, with a sixteen-foot-high wall. Sidelines extend three feet past the backline. A "short" line is drawn across the court sixteen feet back from the wall. And nine feet back of this line, on each side of the court, a small line extending inward four inches from the sideline designates the serving area.

ICE HOCKEY

This has been called the fastest game on earth. As played by professionals, it has also been called the roughest.

Nobody knows the actual number of young persons playing hockey. As of 1976, 216,000 youths from the age of seven up to college age were registered with the Amateur Hockey Association of the United States. The actual number is undoubtedly far higher, and there are, in addition, college and pro hockey teams and many amateur leagues.

Like any other body-contact sport, hockey produces its share of bruises, fractures, and joint injuries.

In addition, there are injuries peculiar to hockey—including head and face lacerations, punched out teeth, and eye injuries. Almost all of these are preventable.

Because hockey-connected facial injuries had become a significant health problem, special studies have been made of them.

One study covered 299 members of the Lake Region Hockey Association (LRHA) of St. Paul, ranging in age from seven to seventeen; 200 varsity players in the St. Paul High School System (SPHS) ranging in age from ten to nineteen; 180 in the Western Collegiate Hockey Association (WCHA) ranging in age from seventeen to twenty-six; and 174 players in the National Hockey League (NHL) aged eighteen to forty-one.

Facial injuries were more frequent among older players, with the rate rising from 7 percent in the youngest players to 54 percent to 66 percent of players in the LRHA and SPHS groups, and to 95 percent of nongoalie players in the WCHA and 93 percent of nongoalies in the NHL.

The three main types of injuries were facial fractures, facial lacerations, and loss of teeth.

Facial fractures, mainly of the nose, in the youngest

(LRHA) group became more frequent in the next oldest (SPHS) group and included some jawbone and cheekbone fractures in the nongoalie players. The college level WCHA group had six times more fractures than the SPHS group; six of ten nongoalie WCHA players had had a facial fracture, most commonly of the nose, and one-third of the goalies had had a broken nose or jaw. NHL players had twice the fracture rate of the WCHA group, with one facial fracture per man, most nasal, followed in frequency by cheek and jawbone fractures.

Facial lacerations—of the cheek, chin or forehead—were sustained by about 40 percent of nongoalie players in the youngest (LRHA) group. This happened to goalies only occasionally in both this and the SPHS group. Among the SPHS players, the laceration rate was one per player among nongoalies—mostly to forehead and chin—by the time they had played five or six seasons. In the WCHA, the nongoalie laceration rate was almost five per man. Even the college goalies averaged more than two each. In the NHL, the goalies' laceration rate was seven per player and that of other players almost fifteen. One player had more than 600 stitches in his head.

Loss of teeth did not occur frequently in the LRHA group, for whom dental guards are mandatory. In the SPHS, although dental guards are required, more than one of ten nongoalie players had lost a tooth, mainly after seven or eight seasons of play; goalies had lost no teeth. In the college group, six of ten nongoalie players had lost teeth as compared to three of ten goalies. And in the NHL, the rate of tooth loss was two per man for both nongoalies and goalies.

"In spite of the aggressive nature of hockey, most injuries are accidental," reported the physicians who carried out the study, Drs. Eugene and Michael Rontal of the University of Michigan and Drs. Ken Wilson and Barclay Cram of the University of Minnesota.

The physicians pointed to certain practices with the

stick—spearing, high sticking, slashing, hooking, boarding, and butting—as being particularly offensive. They also noted that fighting, skate injuries, and collisions with goal posts and boards resulted in some injuries.

Prevention? "The game can be made safe without emasculating it," the investigating physicians reported.

One vital preventive measure: mandatory facial protection, including a full face mask, padded chin strap, and dental guard. Good masks are available: One problem, especially for high school, is the cost of new equipment.

A second important preventive measure: modification of some of the equipment. This includes padding the butt end of the stick, cushioning of sharp edges along the boards; use of a tall, flat protective surface about the entire rink rather than wire mesh to prevent lacerations during collisions with the barrier.

And third: Rules already on the books should be firmly enforced. For example, the stick should be kept on the ice; it wasn't intended to be a weapon. Severe penalties should be enforced for players who high-stick, slash or spear.

Eye injuries have been of concern, too. U. S. Consumer Product Safety Commission data and some Canadian studies have indicated that up to 10 percent of hockey injuries involve the eye.

And it has been estimated that damage to 3,600 eyes could be prevented in the U. S. in a single year by requiring masks and imposing stronger penalties for fighting on the ice and also for raising a hockey stick above the level of another player's waist.

ICE SKATING

This can be an enjoyable sport for people of all ages. Some children are introduced to it shortly after they learn to walk. Many people in their seventies and eighties continue to enjoy it.

It can be excellent exercise if strenuous enough, increasing heart and lung fitness and working out many major muscle groups of the body.

Although some people—both youngsters and adults—believe they cannot skate because of weak ankles, experts say that ankles so weak as to make skating difficult or impossible are rare. More often, the problem lies with skates that don't fit properly. Skates should be fitted, and there should be no assumption that their size should be the same as shoe size. Particular attention should be paid to heel fit.

Speed skating is an excellent conditioner. But places where it can be done, good surfaces free of cracks in the ice that may catch skates and cause injuries, are not easy to find.

Figure skating is no less beneficial and more available. It is also one of the most exacting of sports.

Many hours must be spent on the ice, perfecting basic stroke, stopping motion, backward motion, turns, jumps, and spins.

But figure skating is fun as well as good exercise—and although the competitive years usually range between the teens and early twenties, the sport can be enjoyed by people of all ages.

Interestingly, Sonja Henie, the Norwegian girl who did much to popularize figure skating, took up the sport when she was seven and proved to be so clumsy at it then that her older brother urged her parents to take the skates away or she might break her neck. But in 1924, at the age of ten, she won her first title, the Norwegian figure skating championship, and thereafter went on to win the European title eight times, the Olympic championship three times, and the world title ten times.

One of the great American male skaters, Richard T. Button, won the U. S. championship in 1946 at the age of sixteen, the youngest ever to hold the title. He subsequently won five straight world championships, seven consecutive U.S. titles and two Olympics. In 1949, while a Harvard student, Button possessed five major titles—Olympic, world,

North American, European, and U. S.—an unprecedented feat.

Like any other physical activity, skating can produce injuries. Most are relatively minor—bruises and scrapes from falls on the ice. Occasionally, fractures occur. And sprains and strains of knee and ankle may result from jump turns.

Suggestions from the U. S. Consumer Product Safety Commission to minimize the likelihood of serious accidents:

● Learn to perform basic skating maneuvers well before attempting more complicated moves.

● On outdoor ice rinks and ponds, look out for patches of grass and rocks in addition to ruts and thin ice.

● Try to break any fall with your hands and avoid landing on the flat of the back or the head.

● Keep equipment in good repair. Don't skate on blades that need repair.

ROLLER SKATING

Always a popular children's activity, roller skating today is enjoying a boom as an adult sport as well.

One reason for the boom: the increasing adult interest in physical fitness. Another: the new skating wheels made of polyurethane instead of steel, or fiber-hard plastic combinations, which provide a smoother, quieter ride, added maneuverability, and even an illusion of floating through space.

Roller skating gets high marks as an exercise. Provided it lasts at least thirty minutes, it contributes to heart and lung endurance and also improves leg muscle endurance. Arms and upper body get involved. The demands of balancing while rolling also lead to improved agility and posture.

When the President's Council on Physical Fitness and Sports asked seven medical experts to rate exercises according to overall contribution to physical well-being, skating ranked third, just behind jogging and bicycling.

There are more than 3,000 roller-skating rinks across the country and the number has been growing steadily. And street skating is popular, especially among the young, with one favorite—roller hockey—often played with considerable skill.

Competitive roller skating is now included in the Pan American Games and there is an effort to make it part of the Olympics.

As a competitive sport, roller skating includes speed or racing, hockey, and artistic. The latter includes figure, freestyle, pair skating, fours, dance and novelty events.

Amateur meets on local, state, regional, and national levels are sanctioned and supervised by two organizations—the U. S. Amateur Roller Skating Association and the Roller Skating Rink Operators Association.

Competitive skaters usually start serious practice in the early fall, but the season for most major competition is the spring.

A recent Gallup poll found that roller skating is the fifth most popular participation sport among teen-agers—right behind basketball, baseball and softball, swimming, and bowling. According to another survey, 28 million Americans skated in rinks last year.

Injuries? The Consumer Product Safety Commission estimates that approximately 128,000 persons require hospital emergency room treatment each year for injuries suffered while skating. Roller skating accounts for the majority of injuries—an estimated 93,000—and ice skating, 34,395.

Injuries include broken fingers, wrists, arms, ankles, legs and collarbones, banged-up faces, and cut-up arms and legs. Actually, serious injuries are less likely among young children who are closer to the ground and have more break-resistant bones than adults, but children are not by any means immune.

From medical experts come a number of suggestions to help minimize the likelihood of injuries:

● Use knee and elbow pads to protect against bad scrapes.

● Skating in shorts and a T-shirt is asking for trouble; wear long pants and long-sleeved shirts.

● Practice stopping and falling in a safe area. When falling on skates, try to bend elbows to cushion the blow to arm bones. Rolling with a fall may be better than sliding on a hard surface. And if you feel a fall is coming, aim if possible for grass or another soft place to land in.

The Consumer Product Safety Commission has additional suggestions:

● Avoid skating too close to others who can stop abruptly in front of you or skate across your path.

● Look where you're going. Environmental hazards such as cracked or uneven cement sidewalks, streets, rocks, tree branches, or other debris can cause tripping.

● Buy skates that fit well. For children, choose shoe skates that fit their present foot size, not a pair they can grow into.

● Carefully run a hand over metal parts to check for any sharp edges and points that can cut in case of a fall.

● Keep skates in good repair, parts tightened, broken straps of strap-on skates replaced immediately.

RUNNING

Considering the relative simplicity and inexpensiveness of running and the fitness values to be obtained, it is not surprising that millions of people are "on the run." Among them now are many youngsters.

Running, which can be a lifetime activity, rates very high for building stamina and muscular strength and endurance, along with cardiovascular fitness.

It's possible to run virtually any time and anywhere. If possible, it's best to run on soft dirt or smooth grass rather than on a hard surface.

The one essential is good, well-fitted running shoes that support the arches and ease foot and leg stress—shoes with pliable tops, firm soles, padded insole, hard rubber outsole. Clothes need only be fairly loose, suitable to the weather. A sweatsuit can be used, with layers added in cold weather.

Correct posture is important. The body should be upright, not leaning forward. A forward lean tends to shorten the stride and waste energy. Arms should be held slightly away from the body—with elbows bent and forearms parallel to the ground, and the arms should be allowed to swing freely.

A major mistake is to land on the toes in running. The effort should be to land on the heel and rock forward onto the ball of the foot to propel the next step. Landing on the toes increases the risk of foot and leg injuries and tends to be more tiring.

A beginner does well to work into running gradually. Overenthusiasm can lead to injury and discouragement.

A starter program suggested by some experts calls for beginning with ten minutes a day of moderately-paced walking, then gradually increasing the pace. The next phase calls for continuing the ten-minute workouts, but now interspersing some jogging with the walking and gradually moving on until the jogging occupies the whole ten minutes.

In the next phase, workout time is extended to twenty minutes, starting with a mix of walking and jogging and working up to the point where the jogging can be done comfortably for the full twenty minutes.

Thereafter, the jogging pace can be increased to the point of running as endurance improves and ligaments and tendons are strengthened so there is less proneness to injury.

There are, of course, other advocated regimens—but

all have in common a relatively slow start and gradual progression.

Injuries can occur in running. A muscle, tendon or bone
may be affected—most commonly in the low back, leg, knee,
ankle or foot.

Such injuries are much less likely with good shoes and
running on grass or dirt, and also if training has been gradual.

Periods of warming-up and cooling-down are important
and can help avoid injuries. Stretching exercises are very
valuable. They help when done on getting up in the morning
and again before running, relaxing muscles so they become
less susceptible to injury. Starting a run slowly and gradually
increasing the pace helps to get muscles ready for all-out
endeavor with less likelihood of injury.

It's helpful, if not essential, for a neophyte runner to
have a companion for the running.

And, especially in the early phases of a running program, having half a dozen different running routes rather
than just one can help maintain interest.

SKATEBOARDING

Skateboarding has become an increasingly popular sport
and, until recently, has brought alarming increases in injuries.

Between 1973 and 1977, there was a thirty-fold increase in the number of injuries sustained.

According to a study by the Consumer Product Safety
Commission, 140,000 skateboard-related injuries were
treated in hospital emergency rooms in 1977. In 1978, however, the injuries dropped 38 percent to an estimated 87,-
000.

The decrease may be due to increased use of skateboard parks and the preventive actions of various skateboard safety groups. The parks often require users to wear
protective gear such as helmets, knee pads and elbow pads,

and require other precautions such as equipment checks before use. Many feature safety patrols trained in first aid.

Still, 87,000 injuries represent a considerable toll.

Most skateboard injuries occur in the ten to fourteen age group. One third of the injuries are fractures involving the forearm and lower leg. Another third are bruises and scrapes. The rest are sprains and miscellaneous problems, including head injuries, concussions and skull fractures, and abdominal injuries.

In a four-year period ending in 1979, at least twenty-five deaths occurred, usually following a head injury or collision with a motor vehicle. Protective equipment was usually not worn by the victim at the time of the injury.

In a skateboard policy statement in 1979, the American Academy of Pediatrics called for education of parents and children as essential. Skateboards are not toys and skateboarding requires complex skills.

The Academy urged that training programs by competent instructors be encouraged; that special training should include the proper methods of falling; that youngsters should perform stunts only within their achieved level of skill, and in areas set aside for that purpose. It underscored the need for skateboarding to be done under supervision. Urged the Academy:

● Make sure your youngster's skateboard is the right size for him, made of sturdy materials, and bought from a knowledgeable dealer.

● Encourage use of protective equipment which should include helmet, gloves, elbow and knee pads, and sturdy shoes. Long-sleeved shirts and long-legged pants can provide added protection.

● Make certain that all equipment is kept in good working condition.

● Ideally, skateboarding should be done in a skateboard park. Short of that, try to see that it is done on a clean surface, free of holes, rocks and sand, and in an area not used by motor vehicles, never on public streets or sidewalks, and never on wet surfaces or without proper lighting at night.

The U. S. Consumer Product Safety Commission has these additional suggestions:

• Padded jackets and shorts are being made, as well as padding for hips, knees and elbows. Wrist braces and special skateboarding gloves also can help absorb the impact of a fall. With protective equipment, it is important to look for comfort, design and function; the equipment should not interfere with the skater's movement, vision or hearing. The protective equipment currently on the market is not subject to Federal performance standards and, therefore, careful selection is necessary. In a helmet, for example, look for proper fit and a chin strap; notice whether the helmet blocks the rider's vision and hearing. Padding should also fit comfortably. If it is too tight, it could restrict circulation and reduce ability to move freely; if too loose, it could slip off or slide out of position.

• Learning how to fall in case of an accident may help reduce the risk of serious injury. If losing balance, the rider should crouch down on the skateboard so he will not have to fall so far. In a fall, even though it may be difficult to relax the body, he or she should try to and also should try to roll rather than absorb the force with the arms.

SKIING

An exciting sport which is becoming increasingly popular, skiing is also a challenging and vigorous one.

As a means of promoting fitness, skiing—either downhill or cross-country—ranks high. Experts of the President's Council on Physical Fitness and Sports put downhill skiing in third place after handball/squash and jogging, and cross-country in fifth place after ice or roller skating.

Both types of skiing are excellent for developing stamina, muscular endurance, muscular strength, flexibility, and balance.

There have been some estimates that skiing dates back thousands of years. One pair of skis exhibited in the Djugarden Museum in Stockholm, Sweden, may be at least 5,000 years old.

The first ski club in the U. S. was formed by Scandinavians at Berlin, New Hampshire, in 1872, and others developed thereafter. However, the sports growth in this country began to accelerate after the 1932 Winter Olympics at Lake Placid in New York which introduced many thousands to the spectacle of skiing and sent many home to take up the sport.

Ski enthusiasts now can be counted in the millions. Older people enjoy it. Most contestants, however, are young.

Ski jumping is the most sensational form of skiing; downhill, the most dangerous; slalom, the most graceful; cross-country, the most grueling.

In jumping contests, distance is only one factor. Judges award points for three additional reasons: control in flight, landing, and finish; courage; and form.

Downhill racing is against time. In major events, the race covers a course containing steep pitches, artificial ruts and bumps, and other obstacles, calling for the winner to take risks to speed along the straightest line.

Slalom racing, which has become increasingly popular, requires the racer to use great skill in following a winding course marked by flags. The emphasis on skill rather than merely speed, reduces danger.

Cross-country races are usually over natural courses; one-third uphill, one-third downhill, and one-third flat or rolling.

Downhill skiing is best learned at an early age.

Expert instruction, starting with basic fundamentals such as how to stop, execute a turn, and fall properly, is of great importance. While a youngster may learn on his own, it will at best take longer, and bad habits may be learned along the way.

The risks in downhill skiing are well known. It's estimated that during any season, more than 200,000 skiers will take tumbles serious enough to cause a fracture, sprain, or cut. This means an injury rate of approximately one per 1,000 skiing hours.

But the risk of injury can be greatly reduced by good equipment and by good physical conditioning before taking to the hills.

As one physician and veteran member of the National Ski Patrol puts it: "Many a broken bone can be avoided by an athlete with the strength and stamina to pull out of predicaments a skier is bound to get into."

Good conditioning can mean greater enjoyment and can help reduce the larger number of injuries which occur late in the day when skiers become tired.

Among preski exercises recommended by some experts:

● Leg lifts and sit-ups to condition the abdomen against hillside bumps.

● Walking upstairs and down—preferably backward—to tone up the Achilles tendon.

● Toe stands, easily done while watching TV or while on the phone, and half knee bends to help guard against knee and ankle injury.

Other experts emphasize that skiers need strong thigh and calf muscles since it becomes difficult, when these muscles tire, to control the skis. For conditioning, they suggest other endurance-stamina exercises as well:

● Rapidly repeated jumps on both feet with knees bent.

● Running in place.

● Squat position with one leg extended and then the other leg in quick succession.

● Jumping rope.

● Running laps and sprinting.

Proper clothing can be important. Absorbent clothing (such as jeans) should be avoided because the danger of frost bite increases when clothing becomes saturated with melted snow. Fabric gloves, too, should not be used since they wear out quickly when a rope tow is employed, increasing the likelihood of rope burns. And, warns one physician, exposed long hair is a danger. Thousands of skiers each season lose some of that hair when it becomes caught in tow mechanisms.

Cross-country skiing is booming—and with good reason.

With adequate snow, it's possible to go cross-country skiing (also known as touring) in a park, on a deserted country lane, even on a golf course when permitted.

Fifteen years ago, only a few thousand Americans had taken up cross-country; by 1978, the number had reached over 2 million and is still climbing fast.

Costs are much lower, only about half as much for cross-country equipment and clothing as for downhill. A youngster's outfit may run about $125. And the cost of travel to a ski area is saved.

The physical exercise in cross-country is excellent. The sport provides a full-body workout.

The basic cross-country movements are relatively simple. On level terrain, a knee-flexed, easy glide—a kind of Groucho Marx motion—is used and is usually easily learned in a couple of hours. More practice is needed for uneven terrain and turns, and good balance and deft use of the ski poles are needed for uphill and downhill moves.

"You can use a herringbone step to go up, or sidestep if the hill is steep enough," advises one expert. "And you come down in a slight crouch for greater stability. Where downhill skiers go forty, fifty, sixty miles an hour, in cross-country, twenty is about tops. You can 'bail out' or fall purposely, to avoid a hazard, and not get hurt."

No special clothing is required. Clothes should simply be layered so they can be taken off and tied around the waist or slipped into a pack when the exertion warms you considerably, then donned again as you cool with rest.

Although cross-country skiing is considered by many to be a perfectly safe sport, it isn't, of course. There can be accidental injuries, notably when going down icy slopes. But it is, relatively speaking, quite a safe sport.

SOCCER

Around the world, this is the most beloved and highly attended game. It is played in more than 140 nations and in most countries, especially those of Europe and South America, it is the predominating sport.

Only in the United States is it commonly called soccer. Elsewhere, it's known as football, or futbol, or *il calcio*.

It has become the fastest-growing sport in the U. S. in recent years.

In 1979, there were 477 colleges playing soccer as members of the National Collegiate Athletic Association. Youth and high school programs have been mushrooming. California, for example, with one of the largest youth programs, has more than 200,000 youngsters participating.

It's an excellent game in many respects. The sustained pace builds endurance and vigor, helps to condition the whole body. It's a good team sport and, by run of the ball, each player can momentarily become leader of the team. It requires a minimum of equipment and expense.

In soccer, size is neither an advantage nor disadvantage. And, because kicking a ball around is almost as natural as playing catch, children can learn the skills readily.

For six to seventeen-year-olds, soccer has been described in one medical study as one of the two best fitness "buys," (the other being swimming) with both having low injury rates and not favoring one sex, or any particular body type, or age over another.

In Norway, soccer has long been the most widely played sport, and a medical study in Norway of soccer injuries in adolescents indicates that the game is relatively safe, with a low injury rate, and with those injuries mostly minor. The study, by Dr. Svein Nilsson of the Beitostolen Health Sports Center in Sandvika, Norway, found that of all injuries, 39 percent were merely blisters and skin abrasions; 36 percent were only bruises; only 20 percent were sprains and strains; with fractures accounting for the smallest percentage.

An American study which examined rates of orthopedic injuries (fractures and dislocations) for various sports found that the injury risk in football is twice as high as in basketball and gymnastics, which are next highest on the list, and the risk in soccer is only one-third that of basketball and gymnastics.

SOFTBALL

When it originated just before the turn of the century, softball was known variously as mush-ball, kitten-ball, and indoor baseball. It acquired its present name in 1926.

In the 1930s, softball flourished as the "depression sport" as unemployed people with no money for high-priced entertainment took up softball as participants and spectators.

It's played by people of all ages and almost from its beginning, female participants have been identified with softball.

One of the outstanding women players, pitcher Bertha Ragan, hurled the Orange (Calif.) Lionettes to a two-one victory in twenty innings over the Fresno Rockets, achieving twenty-two strikeouts in the process. She is credited with pitching more than 100 no-hit, no-run games and scoring 233 shutouts and 4,630 strikeouts.

Softball was mainly a fast-pitch game until the 1960s when slow-pitch became increasingly popular.

Softball may be simpler and easier for many to play than baseball because the smaller field reduces strenuous running; pitching is underhand; and the larger, softer ball may be handled without mitts or gloves.

The official ball weights 6¾ ounces and is 11⅞″ to 12⅛″ in circumference. The pitching throw is forty-six feet and the baselines are sixty feet long.

As a means of promoting fitness, experts of the President's Council on Physical Fitness and Sports ranked softball thirteenth in a list of fourteen, ahead of bowling, but behind golf, walking and many other activities such as tennis, basketball, bicycling, swimming, skating, skiing and handball/squash.

There can be injuries, of course. A study by the Consumer Product Safety Commission, which didn't differentiate between baseball and softball, produced an estimate of 900,000 injuries occurring to the 46 million people, young and old, who play baseball and softball each year.

Among suggestions from experts for reducing risk of injury: boy and girl players should warm up before playing, use a glove, learn to grip the bat tightly so it will not slip from the hands and hurt somebody, and catchers should always wear masks.

Other information which may apply to softball can be found in the earlier entry in this section on baseball.

SQUASH

In recent years, squash has become increasingly popular in the U. S. and elsewhere.

In the U. S., by 1977, the number of players had reached more than 400,000, up from about 130,000 fifteen years before, with half the growth taking place in the most recent years. In England and Australia, squash has become more popular than tennis, and a count in 1977 showed an astounding 800 squash courts in Mexico City.

The game is relatively simple to learn. Two players stand at the same end of a relatively small, white, rectangular court and use a light racquet to bash a hard rubber ball off four walls and the floor. With five playing surfaces, there are long volleys in which both players move all around the court.

It's a fast, demanding sport, capable of providing a complete workout in half an hour or less, excellent for heart and lung endurance.

Eye injuries are of particular concern in squash, but they are preventable.

In squash, a player's eyes are vulnerable to great forces both from the ball and the opponent's racquet.

Conventional eyeglasses, if they are worn, are not sturdy enough to withstand the forces and there have been serious eye injuries among players wearing such glasses. Players are strongly advised by ophthalmologists who have studied the problem to wear industrial plastic safety lenses mounted in a sturdy athletic or industrial frame.

Players who do not wear spectacles or who wear contact lenses should wear an eye protector. Tests have indicated that commercially available eye protectors and industrial plastic lenses mounted in sturdy frames can withstand the impact of a racket blow and there have been reports from players receiving direct blows to eye protectors and safety glasses with no resulting eye injury.

SWIMMING

Swimming has excellent value as a sport for children, including some handicapped children. It's also a good sport for lifetime participation.

In terms of effectiveness in promoting fitness, it has been ranked by experts of the President's Council on Physical Fitness and Sports, ahead of such activities as tennis, basketball and bicycling, with high marks for developing stamina, muscular endurance and strength, and flexibility.

Many physicians consider it to be the best of all sports for asthmatic children. Asthma may sometimes be induced by exercise, but this danger is minimal in swimming. In Australia, which has a program to encourage asthmatic children to get into swimming at early ages, the country's Olympic swimming team at one point recently had asthmatics making up about one-third of the squad.

Swimming is also a sport in which an overweight child is not necessarily penalized and often may compete successfully with his leaner counterparts.

Swimming is also a sport in which progress can be measured by time, and not necessarily by winning over others.

There are, of course, various distances for competitive swimming including 100, 200, 400 and 1500 meters.

Remarkable feats of endurance swimming have been recorded. One of the greatest distance swimmers was Pedro A. Candiotti of Argentina, sometimes called the "shark of Quilla Creek." Although for many years his ambition was to swim 205 miles down the River Platte from Rosario to Buenos Aires, his fifteen attempts were unsuccessful for one reason or another, including his effort in 1943 when, after being in the water for seventy-four and one-half hours, he was forced to quit because of a rising tide. In 1935, however, he made his longest swim, 281 miles in the Parana River in Argentina. It took him eighty-four hours.

Another feat of endurance was that of John V. Sigmund, who in 1940, swam 292 miles nonstop down the Mississippi River from St. Louis in eighty-nine hours and forty-two minutes.

Women swimmers have achieved remarkable feats of

endurance. One Mrs. Myrtle Huddleston of New York, after first continuously swimming in a tank for eighty-six hours and sixteen minutes, went on to break her record in 1931 by swimming continuously for eighty-seven hours, twenty-seven minutes.

Swimming is not a high-injury activity. It gives rise to muscle pulls occasionally and sometimes to mild shoulder and knee injuries. It is possible for these to be avoided by suitable conditioning and proper warm-up and stretching exercises.

In a study at Fort Leavenworth, Kansas, with the children of service people, Dr. Richard B. Chambers ranked swimming and soccer as the two best fitness "buys" for six-to seventeen-year-olds.

Not only did Chambers find that "swimming probably provides the most balanced form of exercise. . . . Endurance as well as power can be developed along with agility and coordination"; he also found that swimming had a zero rate of orthopedic injuries such as fractures and dislocations.

Underwater swimming does have a serious—but needless—risk. Some youngsters—and adults—think that taking rapid deep breaths (hyperventilating) can increase the time they are able to swim underwater. And it may do so. But it also increases the risk of drowning, even for an expert swimmer.

In filling the lungs with oxygen, it's necessary to blow out a lot of carbon dioxide, an excessive amount. And carbon dioxide is essential for stimulating the breathing process. Without it, there is a grave risk of losing consciousness and drowning.

Youngsters who swim underwater should be cautioned—and this goes for adults as well—to take a normal breath, then swim, exhaling slowly. They should also be warned that if they start to feel dizzy or find themselves developing tunnel vision, they must get to the surface immediately.

TENNIS

Once a game for aristocrats, tennis numbered its players in the hundreds a century ago. Today it is played by millions of all ages and social classes.

By 1973, the U. S. Lawn Tennis Association estimated that more than 11 million Americans were playing the game.

Tennis is capable of meeting the needs and desires of just about everyone, with the amount of activity in it variable according to individual needs.

While a high degree of heart and lung endurance is required for a competitive player who may need to condition his or her body with activities such as running or skipping rope to meet the demands of a long and tough match, it's possible for people to play the game throughout life with a minimal degree of endurance.

Tennis is not likely to produce great increases in muscular strength but does increase muscular endurance, particularly of leg muscles and muscles used in serving and stroking.

Although tennis doesn't increase muscular strength to any marked degree, strength can improve tennis play—and some players make use of weight training in their conditioning programs.

Among other exercises often used in conditioning for tennis are chin-ups, shoulder dips on parallel bars, jogging and sprinting, rope skipping, squat thrusts, sidestepping, and squeezing a tennis ball in the racket hand.

With good conditioning, tennis is a safe sport. Tennis elbow, commonly associated with tennis, is an injury that often may be preventable (see TENNIS ELBOW in Part Three.)

TRACK AND FIELD

Except for relay races, track and field is an individual sport.

The sport is divided into two types of events: Track contests, which consist of running and hurdling, are usually held on an oval track, about one-fourth of a mile in length and eighteen to thirty-two feet wide, topped with cinders, with one side of the oval marked for dashes; indoor tracks are shorter, usually requiring eight to eleven laps to the mile and have board, clay, or dirt surfaces.

Field events such as jumping, vaulting, and weight throwing are usually held on the field inside the track.

The shortest races usually are 100, 220 and 440 yards (90, 180 and 400 meters) outdoors, and 50, 60 or 70 yards indoors.

Distance races commonly include the mile and two miles.

In relay races, four participants make up a team. In nonmedley relays, each runner covers the same distance as other runners while in the medley relays, distances vary. Commonly, nonmedley relays are 440 and 880 yards, with each runner covering 110 or 220 yards, and one and two miles, with each runner covering one-quarter or one-half mile. Medley relays usually are one mile (with runners covering, respectively, 440, 220, 220 and 880 yards) or two and one-half miles, with runners covering one-half, three-quarters and one mile respectively.

In hurdling, the runner goes over a series of ten barriers spaced an equal distance apart on the track. In a high hurdle race, the distance is 120 yards with hurdles spaced ten yards apart and three and one-half feet high for college men and adults, three and one-quarter for high school boys and two to two and one-half feet for girls and women. The low hurdle race for college men and adults is 220 yards with hurdles twenty yards apart and two and one-half feet high. In high school events, the distance is 180 yards with eight hurdles spaced twenty yards apart.

The broad jump is usually made after a fast short sprint and takeoff from a wooden slab four feet long and eight inches wide. High jump and pole vault also are made from a running start over a horizontal pole supported on two upright standards, with the pole vaulter using a pole about twelve to sixteen feet long.

The shot put, a metal sphere weighing sixteen pounds (twelve pounds in high school events) is thrown from the center of a seven-foot-diameter circle.

The discus, a wooden disk with metal rim, which is at least eight and five-eighths inches in circumference and weighs at least two kilograms (four pounds, six and four-tenths ounces) is thrown from a circle measuring eight feet two and one-half inches in diameter. In high school competition, a slightly smaller discus is used.

The javelin, a spear-shaped stick at least eight and fifty-three hundredths inches long and weighing at least one and seven hundred sixty-five thousandths pounds, is hurled from behind a starting line.

Cross-country, a special kind of running, is usually over a gently sloping course of grass or dirt roads and paths, containing pebbles and rocks, crossed by ditches or streams, and blocked by gates and fences.

Field events, except for pole-vaulting, are generally fairly safe. So are track activities. But no sport of course is entirely free of some risk or injury. The risk can be reduced considerably by good coaching and conditioning, and proper warm-up.

VOLLEYBALL

According to some estimates, volleyball is a team sport played by more people around the world than any other game except soccer and football.

Adaptable to both sexes and all ages, the game requires a minimum of equipment. A net or rope, a ball and a relatively smooth surface are all that are needed.

Among its other distinctions, volleyball has been said

to be the only truly amateur sport remaining in the world today.

The game has relatively simple rules. It can be played in the back yard, at picnics, and as a recreation sport—with even the most unskilled joining in. It has always been one of the favorites on military bases, even at the front lines in wartime. In World War II in the Pacific, often volleyball nets were strung up on the beaches soon after beachheads were established.

The game became part of the Olympic program in 1964.

As played today by skilled players, the game takes as much speed, stamina, conditioning and training as many other sports.

Played at highest levels, the game has great value for fitness. Muscle strength is needed in legs, back, shoulders and arms. A volleyball hit by a strong spiker has been known to travel faster than the fastest baseball pitch.

Muscle endurance is needed because of the jumping required. A player may have to jump with hands above the eight-foot net hundreds of times during a game.

Great speed and flexibility are needed for defensive play. Wrist and finger flexibility is essential for making the pass and for pass and set up, great body control, involving foot, ankle, knee, spine and pelvic areas, is needed.

According to some top coaches, it may take as long as six years for a player to develop to the point of being able to compete well in national competition.

A regulation team consists of six players—left, center, and right forwards; and left, center, and right backs.

An official court for both indoor and outdoor play is sixty by thirty feet. The net is three feet wide, thirty-two feet long. It's stretched so the top at the center is eight feet from the ground and the bottom five feet. In women's games, the top height is seven and one-half feet. The ball is twenty-six to twenty-seven inches in circumference, weighs nine to ten ounces, and is inflated to seven or eight pounds pressure.

WRESTLING

This is one of the most universal of sports, and an ancient one. Throughout history, every nation has had its wrestlers. The sport has always been popular because it needs no complex paraphernalia and it can build muscles and health.

Professional wrestling, which once had great appeal, has deteriorated to the point today where it is often considered no more than a farcical exhibition.

Amateur wrestling, however, has maintained its status and is popular in high schools, colleges, and sports clubs.

Although sometimes considered to be a rough sport, wrestling is not dangerous for a youngster who is well coached and in good condition. Conditioning for wrestling, starting shortly after start of school in the fall, may include easy jogging on the road and wrestling on odd days, with careful, repeated practice of basic takedowns, escapes, falls, and other maneuvers.

Strains are fairly common injuries. Knee injuries occur occasionally.

It's important that headgear be worn to protect the ears. Injuries may otherwise be caused by head scissors and headlocks and cauliflower ears may develop.

A problem in wrestling may be "making" weight—that is, losing enough weight to make a classification.

Efforts to lose a lot of weight quickly through excessive sweating and extreme reduction of food and liquid intake not only may harm the body, but are likely to badly weaken the wrestler for his event.

According to some sports medicine experts, it is generally unsafe and possibly dangerous for any youngster to try to lose more than 10 percent of body weight to qualify for a weight classification.

PART III

COMMON
ATHLETIC
INJURIES
AND THEIR CARE

WHEN TO SEE A PHYSICIAN

It would be difficult if not possible to engage in any sport or other physical activity without risking an occasional injury.

More often than not, the injuries are minor and may yield to relatively simple measures, without need for a physician.

But some injuries require medical care. If untreated or improperly treated, they may cause serious problems, interfere with, or even prevent, further sport activity.

When should medical help be sought?

Certainly, you should seek it for any injury you are worried or have any kind of doubts about concerning its nature, or how it should be treated.

A cardinal rule is to trust your intuition; to be safe, rather than sorry.

It is a fact that diagnosis of the exact nature of an injury is sometimes difficult. It can be difficult even for a physician without resorting to X-ray studies or other special diagnostic tools. In such circumstances, you certainly cannot be expected to put your finger on the real trouble.

It is wise to seek help for any of the following:

● Any injury to a joint or its ligaments.

● Any severely painful injury of any kind.

● Any bone or joint pain, even if moderate, that continues beyond a week or so.

● Any injury that fails to heal within two or three weeks.

● Any infection as indicated by pus, fever, redness, or swollen lymph nodes.

IMPORTANT BACKGROUND INFORMATION ON BODY TISSUES

Bones. Bone ranks among the body's hardest structures. It is strong, light, capable of withstanding loads as much as ten times or even more than it is normally called upon to carry.

Bone is composed of two kinds of tissues. One, an outer dense, ivory-like layer, is known as compact bone. The other, the inner layer, is known as cancellous bone and is a spongy, honeycomb-like substance. The honeycomb structure provides strength. Cancellous bone contains the red marrow, the pulpy substance where red and white blood cells are produced.

Much of the main surface of bone, except for the areas forming joints, is covered by the periosteum, a tough fibrous membrane which carries blood vessels and nerves.

Joints. Generally, joints have four components. First, there are the adjacent bone ends which are covered by gristlelike cartilage to help prevent damage from jarring movements. Second, attached to and linking the bone ends together is a capsule of fibrous material. Third, reinforcing the capsule at some points are ligaments—tough, very strong, thick bands of fibers designed to help prevent excessive movement but flexible enough not to interfere with normal activity of the joint. Fourth, lining the joint capsule and covering parts of bone within the capsule is the synovial membrane. The membrane produces a whitish synovial fluid which serves as a lubricant.

Some joints have an articular disc, composed of fibrous tissue which has some cartilage cells, lying between bone ends. The disc helps to diffuse the synovial fluid during movement and also aids in assuring proper contact between moving surfaces at any position of the joint. The knee has two such discs, called the semilunar cartilages or menisci.

Muscles. More than half the body consists of muscles, more than 600, which make possible everything from sucking air into the lungs and pushing food through the digestive tract to supporting the spine and carrying out all movement.

The skeletal muscles are attached to bones. Each muscle consists of many bundles of striped fibers which can shorten and lengthen. The bundles are parallel. Each is enclosed in supporting connective tissue. Such tissue also binds the separate bundles together and forms a loose sheath around the entire muscle, carrying blood vessels and nerves.

Muscle contraction is brought about by a complex system. From the motor area in the brain, impulses go out to stations in the spinal cord. From the cord, other nerve fibers transmit the impulses to the muscle, with each nerve fiber branching in order to supply the many muscle fibers.

Although only about the size of a hair, each muscle fiber is capable of supporting 1,000 times its weight. All told, there are six trillion fibers.

Muscle tissue is formed before birth and a baby's supply of muscle fibers is his or her supply for life.

The fibers grow as the child grows and strength develops as the fibers do their job of contracting. But the number of fibers per person remains constant. The fibers in the arms of a prizefighter or weight lifter number the same as those in the arms of a little girl, though much stronger and thicker through use.

Tendons.   These are tough cords or bands of strong white fibrous tissue that connect the ends of muscles to bones. When a muscle contracts, it pulls on a tendon, which moves the bone. Tendons are so tough that they are seldom torn, often remaining intact when an injury is severe enough to tear a muscle or break a bone. One of the most prominent tendons is the Achilles tendon, which can be felt at the back of the ankle, just above the heel.

Fascia.   Muscles are covered by a strong inelastic membrane known as the deep fascia. The fascia's job is to provide firm pressure so that when a muscle contracts it does not bulge outward so much as to lose much of its force.

Above the deep fascia, there is another protective membrane, the superficial fascia. It's made up of loosely meshed connective tissue containing fat cells. The superficial fascia blends with the skin and facilitates skin movement. It has another purpose as well, helping to retain body warmth through its fat cells which are poor heat conductors.

Skin.   Actually, the largest organ of the body, the skin performs many vital functions. It acts as a barrier against disease organisms, helps shield delicate tissues underneath from injury, acts as an insulator, helps eliminate waste in the form of perspiration. It also helps produce the body's supply of vitamin D, and the sense receptors it contains enable the body to feel pain, cold, heat, touch, and pressure.

It consists of two main parts—an outer layer, the epidermis, and an inner layer, the dermis, or true skin.

The epidermis has several layers of cells which are constantly being shed, worn away by friction, and replaced by new cells from bottom layers of the epidermis. As long as the horny outer layers are intact, microorganisms cannot enter.

The dermis, which is the thicker part of the skin, is made up of connective tissue containing blood vessels and nerves. It also has sweat glands that collect fluid containing water, salt and waste products from the blood and transport it away in canals ending in pores on the skin surface where it is deposited as sweat. There are also sebaceous glands in the skin which secrete oil that keeps the skin surface lubricated.

Nerves.   Found in all body tissues, nerves are white, cord-like structures made up of many fibers bound together in bundles by connective tissue and covered by connective tissue sheaths.

The motor nerves carry information from the brain and spinal cord to the muscles, stimulating them to contract. Sensory nerves carry information from the outside world—sensations of heat, cold, pain, etc.—to the brain and cord. Still others, mixed nerves, are composed of both motor and sensory fibers, and carry messages in both directions at once.

Blood.   Blood consists of a fluid, plasma, and blood cells. The plasma is 90 percent water, the remainder being made up of various proteins and salts.

Blood is the chief means of transport in the body. It carries oxygen from lungs to body tissues and waste carbon dioxide from tissues to lungs; foods from the digestive tract to the tissues and waste products to the kidneys. It also distributes hormones from the glands and helps in regulating body temperature by carrying excess heat from the interior to the surface layers of the skin where it can be dissipated to the air.

The red cells in blood contain hemoglobin, a red iron pigment, which provides the characteristic color and is also responsible for attaching to and carrying oxygen and carbon dioxide.

The white cells, or leukocytes, larger than the red and fewer in number, help in combatting infection and injury. When tissue is damaged, they engulf and remove damaged cells to facilitate repair.

There are also platelets in blood—oval discs that play a role in clotting blood to stop hemorrhage when a blood vessel is damaged.

Blood vessels.   There are four main types of blood vessels: arteries, arterioles, capillaries, and veins.

Arteries, which transport blood from the heart to tissues, range in size up to a little more than an inch in diameter. They are found all over the body, dividing and subdividing to supply all areas.

The smallest arteries divide into arterioles, very much smaller vessels. In turn, the arterioles divide into networks of miscroscopic vessels called capillaries where oxygen and carbon dioxide are exchanged with tissues. A capillary is so small that red blood cells must pass through in single file.

Veins return blood to the heart. They are larger than arteries and there are more of them. Many have valves which allow blood to flow through in the right direction and close behind to prevent backflow.

Blood varies in color from a bright red in the arteries to a duller red in the veins.

Lymph and lymphatics.   As blood flows through the capillaries, allowing oxygen and nutrients to move through the thin capillary walls to the tissues and waste products from the tissues to seep into the capillaries, some plasma seeps outward to facilitate the exchange.

The plasma fluid, along with waste products not removed through the capillaries, drains away from the tissues through a system of vessels called the lymphatics. The fluid is called lymph and it is carried by the lymphatic vessels to the blood.

At some points in the lymphatic vessels, small bodies called lymph glands act as filters to prevent any microorganisms which may have entered the lymph stream from getting into the bloodstream.

When there is an infection, lymph vessels and glands draining the infected area become tender and swollen as they filter the infecting microorganisms.

TYPES OF INJURIES AND BODY RESPONSES

Sports injuries can be considered to occur in two main categories: the trivial, such as muscle and tendon strains which involve no real tissue damage; and more serious, such as muscle tears and ligament sprains, which do damage tissue.

Trivial injury reactions. The main symptoms usually are mild local inflammation and pain and stiffness. Many such trivial injuries result simply from overuse of a part, and they heal with rest. Some may need bandaging or strapping.

More serious injury reactions. When some part is crushed by a blow or torn, small blood vessels in the area break and blood oozes into the tissue. There is often some diffusion of the blood so that bruising may appear at some distance from the injured area.

Soon, blood clots form to seal the damaged vessels and bridge torn tissue fibers. Connective tissue cells, known as fibroblasts, then grow in to repair the damage. And the fluid part of the blood from the broken vessels is drained away by the lymphatics and eventually gets back into the general blood circulation.

Even as this is going on, undamaged capillaries near the injured area dilate to hold more blood than usual. Their walls also become more porous. As a result, a substantial amount of both plasma and white blood cells moves into the tissues and makes up what is known as an inflammatory exudate which helps to stimulate the growth of fibroblast repair cells. The white cells in the exudate carry out another important job: they engulf and remove destroyed tissue cells and the clotted blood.

Local heat, redness, swelling, and pain mark all of these activities. The heat and redness come from the extra blood in the capillaries in the injured area; the swelling is due to both the dilation of the capillaries and the fluid accumulation in the tissues; and the pain stems from pressure on nerves or, in some cases, injury to them.

Adhesions and thickenings may occur if the amount of blood and exudate escaping into the tissues is not controlled. With excessive amounts, the tissues, in effect, become water-logged and some fibers may stick together, thickening and forming adhesions. The thickenings and adhesions may interfere with movement and lead to pain.

All these reactions can occur when joints or tendons are injured and there is damage to the synovial membranes. The remaining undamaged membrane cells then produce more than usual amounts of fluid, leading to swelling of joints and tendons.

DETERMINING
WHAT HAS BEEN INJURED

Except in such obvious situations as when the skin has been injured, this is not always easy.

But there are some general guidelines that can be helpful.

You can suspect the possibility of a joint, ligament or cartilage injury if it hurts to touch or move an injured area such as ankle, knee, hip, wrist, elbow or shoulder.

If a muscle mass under the skin is painful when touched or moved, the injury is likely to be to a muscle.

Similarly, if pain occurs on touching or moving a tendon, the fiber extending from a muscle, the probability is a tendon injury.

Bone breaks are among the most painful of injuries, and the pain will be severe when a broken bone is moved or touched.

THE 1, 2, 3, 4, OF
TREATING ATHLETIC INJURIES

There are four simple, but important steps to follow in the case of all athletic injuries, whether they are muscle pulls, strains, joint injuries or broken bones.

All can be used immediately, even if a physician will be needed.

1. Rest the injured area. Stop using it immediately. Continued activity risks making the problem worse.

2. Apply cold. Cold has several values (see below) but a particularly important one is that it causes any injured blood vessels in the area to become constricted so there is less bleeding. The less blood in a wound, the less time it takes for healing.

3. Compress the injured area to minimize swelling which, if uncontrolled, can extend the time needed for healing. A good procedure is to apply ice, then wrap an elastic bandage snugly over the ice—not so tightly as to cause pain, numbness, or cramping, which may indicate you're shutting off the blood supply.

Some sports medicine authorities recommend leaving ice pack and bandage on for half an hour and, after about a fifteen-minute interval, rewrapping and repeating the whole procedure for about three hours. If the area is still swelling or pain is increasing, get a physician.

4. Elevate. By raising an injured part to above the level of the heart, you help get excess fluid draining away from the area.

IMPORTANT FACTS
ABOUT HEAT AND COLD
AND WHEN TO USE THEM

Heat and cold are valuable remedies, but confusion about them is widespread and commonly one is used when the other should be.

Cold first. Applied as soon as possible after many kinds of injuries, cold has several valuable effects.

It helps to relieve pain through its action on the nerve endings in the skin. Cold also helps to restrict the swelling accompanying local inflammation by constricting the dilated capillaries and reducing effusion of fluid into the tissues.

And cold also helps to relax muscles and reduce the spasms, or involuntary muscle contractions, that often accompany injury.

Depending upon where the site of injury is, cold may be applied by immersion in a pail or bowl of cold water, perhaps with some ice cubes added, or by use of wet towels, cold packs, or pieces of crushed ice placed in a pillow case.

Heat. Heat should NOT be used immediately after an injury. It causes capillaries to dilate and if used too soon may aggravate inflammation and encourage bleeding from torn blood vessels.

When used at the right time—no sooner than twelve to twenty-four hours and, according to some authorities, no sooner even than forty-eight to seventy-two hours, after the injury—heat can help relieve pain and muscle spasm and may also help in the repair process by increasing blood flow to the injured area.

Heat can be applied by immersion and by hot compresses. An electric heating pad produces dry heat which often is not as effective for pain relief as moist heat.

ABRASIONS (SCRAPES)

An abrasion is the rubbing or scraping off of an outer layer of skin. There may be oozing of blood. Sometimes, nerve endings may be exposed enough to cause pain.

The first thing to do is to remove any splinters or other foreign material that may be imbedded in the skin. Tweezers may be useful. Make certain they are clean; a five-minute dip in alcohol is a good safeguard.

Then wash the area with soap and water. Although hydrogen peroxide can be used, it offers no particular advantage over a good soap-and-water cleansing.

If the scrape is large in size or if blood continues to ooze, you can cover with a sterile dressing—applied so it does not adhere to the wound. Otherwise, a dressing is usually not needed.

Chances are that the abrasion will scab over and heal well, but keep an eye out for possible infection. Among the indications of infection are marked swelling or redness, fever, pus. If infection does develop, let a physician treat it without delay.

See a physician, too, if you can't remove an imbedded object.

Is a tetanus shot needed? Usually not for a mild scrape but it may be if the abrasion is extensive or if any material had lodged under the skin.

ATHLETE'S FOOT

This is a common problem for athletes and for many others as well. There is now important new information about the nature of the condition and its more effective treatment.

Athlete's foot starts out as a fungus infection which can be picked up in a locker room, public shower, or swimming pool walkway. It usually develops between the toes and the early manifestations are scaling and itching.

Treated without delay, the infection usually can be overcome by a nonprescription antifungal remedy obtainable at any drugstore (one such is Tolnaftate). Clearance may require a week or two. Of major help in treatment is good foot care, which includes gentle removal of scales, bathing followed by thorough drying, and the wearing of cotton or wool socks (which are absorbent) rather than those made of synthetic materials.

If not cured early, athlete's foot can change its nature. Bacteria intervene and even drive the fungi out. When that happens, athlete's foot becomes wet, malodorous, and painful. At that point, antifungal agents do no good. You will probably need a physician's prescription for a suitable drying lotion, and an oral antibiotic.

Both types of athlete's foot—fungal and bacterial—are encouraged when the feet are wet from exercise, hot weather, and perspiration.

For prevention, the feet should be dried thoroughly after showering and socks should be changed after any athletic activity.

BLACK EYE

This is a frequent injury in boxing. It also occurs quite often in racquetball and squash, or any game played in an enclosed area where it is easy to get hit in the eye during the heat of the game.

A black eye involves the bruising of tissues around the eye and the breaking of blood vessels and bleeding under the skin which causes the discoloration.

Immediate application of cold compresses can help slow the bleeding, minimizing both discoloration and swelling. Later, warm wet compresses may help absorption of the blood.

Usually, a black eye is a trivial injury. But it's wise to check for any vision disturbance such as blurring or increased sensitivity to light, any changes in the appearance of the eye, or any indication that the pupil is not the same size in the injured eye as in the other. Any of these findings may indicate more serious injury and the need to see a physician, preferably an ophthalmologist, or eye specialist, immediately.

BLEEDING

Prompt control of severe bleeding can be lifesaving. It is almost always possible.

Although bleeding is often classified as arterial, venous or capillary, the classification isn't necessarily valuable since there may be bleeding from all three types of vessels when a wound is large.

In bleeding from capillaries, the tiniest blood vessels, blood oozes. Blood from a vein is dark red and flows steadily while arterial blood is bright red in color and spurts from a wound.

In an emergency, what counts is the amount of bleeding and how it can be controlled rather than the source.

There are three major methods of control: direct pressure, elevation, and pressure at pressure points. Only when all else fails should a tourniquet be used.

Direct pressure: This, the simplest and preferred method, works for minor bleeding and very often for severe.

You place a dressing over the wound and press directly on the bleeding site with the palm of the hand. Ideally, use a sterile dressing; if one is not available, apply the cleanest available cloth or, if necessary, just the bare hand.

It takes three to ten minutes for blood to clot. Apply pressure at least that long.

If a dressing is used and it becomes blood-soaked, do not remove (that would disturb clotting); add another dressing over the first and apply firmer hand pressure.

Elevation.   If there is a severely bleeding wound of the head or an arm or leg, it helps to elevate the area as well as apply direct pressure. With the elevation, gravity reduces blood flow to the wound site.

Pressure points.   When control can't be achieved with direct pressure and elevation, pressure can be applied to the artery supplying the wound site.

While there are many pressure point sites where you can apply your fingers to help control bleeding, the two most important and effective are the brachial artery in the upper arm and femoral artery in the groin.

The brachial artery pressure point is midway between elbow and armpit on the inner arm between the large muscles. With thumb on the outside of the arm, and fingers of the same hand on the inside of the arm, apply pressure by moving the flattened fingers toward the thumb.

The femoral artery pressure point is on the upper leg, on the inner thigh just below the middle of the crease of the groin. Press there with the heel of the hand while keeping the arm straight.

When using pressure points, apply pressure only long enough to control bleeding.

Tourniquet. This should be used ONLY as a lifesaving measure, to control bleeding after all other means have failed.

A tourniquet cuts off all normal circulation beyond the site where it is applied and tissue damage from the lack of blood and oxygen may result in need for amputation.

For a tourniquet, you can use folded triangular bandages, clothing or other material—folded about two inches wide and long enough to go around the limb twice or more.

Place the tourniquet slightly above the wound, fold around the limb twice, tie a simple knot.

Place a strong stick or similar object about 6 inches long over the knot and tie it in place with a square knot.

Twist the wood several times to produce enough pressure to stop the bleeding and secure the wood in place with the free ends of the tourniquet or another bandage.

Don't loosen the tourniquet unless told to do so by a physician.

Never cover the tourniquet with clothing, bandages, or hide it in any way. And attach a piece of paper to the patient's clothing or extremity indicating the tourniquet's location and the time it was applied.

Get medical help immediately.

Because SHOCK can follow loss of large amounts of blood, treatment for it may be needed. See SHOCK.

BLISTERS

Blisters of the hands and feet tend to be particularly common at the start of a playing season.

For treatment, gently clean the blister itself and the area around it with soap and water.

Then, using a needle sterilized over a flame, prick one side of the blister. Place a piece of sterile gauze over the blister and apply gentle pressure to squeeze out the fluid.

Follow with a sterile gauze pad and adhesive.

When a blister has already broken, wash the area and apply the sterile gauze pad and adhesive.

BRUISES (CONTUSIONS)

Often the result of either a kick, contact with another player, or a fall on a hard surface, a bruise usually involves no break in the skin. But because of damage to small blood vessels, bleeding occurs under the skin and leads to the typical black-and-blue mark.

Sometimes, there may also be stiffening of the injured area because of pain and muscle spasm.

Applying cold packs or ice in a towel helps reduce the swelling and pain and hastens healing. With healing, as the blood is gradually reabsorbed, skin color gradually changes from blue to green to yellow to normal over a period of two or three weeks.

If pain persists for more than twenty-four hours, hot applications—hot water bottle, heating pad, or towel soaked in warm water—can help.

In the case of a very severe bruise immediately over a bone, there is a chance that there may be a bone fracture and an X ray may be required.

BURSITIS (See also TENNIS ELBOW)

A bursa is a small fluid-containing sac around a joint that helps make joint motion smooth.

Bursitis is inflammation of a bursa.

Although a bursa anywhere in the body may be affected, the most frequently involved is the subdeltoid bursa in the shoulder which may be injured because of improper use of the shoulder joint or because of a direct blow on the shoulder in body contact sports.

With injury, the bursa becomes distended with synovial fluid and there is great pain with any effort to move the shoulder.

The bursitis often will clear in a few days if the shoulder is immediately put at complete rest, with arm and forearm supported in a sling.

Cold compresses or ice packs applied the first day help to minimize swelling. Later, moist warm heat may be helpful.

Once acute pain on movement is gone, the shoulder can be exercised gently.

If pain is very severe from the beginning or fails to moderate in a few days, a physician often can speed relief by prescribing an oral anti-inflammatory agent such as phenylbutazone. In some cases, under local anesthesia, he may use a needle to withdraw some of the fluid from the inflamed sac and instill an anti-inflammatory cortisonelike drug. The injection treatment sometimes can provide almost immediate pain relief.

CHEST INJURY

The ribs and their muscles are often bruised in sports. Sometimes, the ribs may be fractured.

And even though there is no rib fracture, the ribs in young people tend to be quite flexible and, after a severe blow to the chest, the chest may be compressed enough, because of the rib flexibility, to break blood vessels or even possibly to injure lungs or heart.

If there is any suspicion of a possible fracture, or if there is breathing difficulty, persistent chest pain, or marked restlessness after a heavy blow to the chest, a physician should be seen immediately.

CONTUSIONS (See BRUISES)

CUTS (LACERATIONS)

Most often, cuts are minor, affecting only the skin and superficial tissues.

In such cases, they can be washed with soap and water and sterile tape strips can be applied so that the edges of the cut are brought and held together.

For a minor cut, a physician will not usually be needed unless, after twenty-four hours or so, pus, redness, swelling, or fever indicate infection, which then will need medical treatment.

Medical treatment also should be obtained if there is vigorous bleeding suggesting major blood vessel damage, or if numbness, tingling, and weakness occur, suggesting possible nerve damage.

If a cut is deep or extensive, stitching by a physician may be required.

DISLOCATION

In a dislocation, a bone end is displaced from its normal position in a joint, and there may be some injury to surrounding ligaments.

Dislocation may follow a fall, a blow against a joint, a sudden twisting, or even a sudden muscle contraction. The most common sites are fingers, thumb, elbow, and shoulder.

With a dislocation, there may be an obvious deformity, along with swelling, tenderness to the touch, and pain on motion.

Let a physician put the bone end back where it belongs. Unless done properly, there may be repeated dislocations.

Until medical help is available, handle a dislocation much as you would a fracture (see FRACTURES). Apply cold compresses to minimize swelling and inflammation, and splints to hold the joint steady in the dislocated position so there will be no potentially damaging movement.

FRACTURES

A fracture, or break in a bone, may or may not be obvious.

Sometimes, the bone is felt, or heard, to snap, and there may be a grating sensation as the broken ends rub against each other. Sometimes, there is an obvious deformity.

Other possible indications of a fracture include swelling, discoloration, and pain and tenderness to the touch. But, in many cases, there can be no certainty whether the problem is really a fracture or a sprain (see SPRAIN).

If you're in the slightest doubt, act as if the trouble is a fracture.

No one except a physician should try to set a fracture.

Until medical help is available, the aim should be to prevent further injury by keeping broken bone ends and nearby joints from moving.

Apply cold, preferably an ice bag, to the painful fracture area to help reduce swelling and inflammation.

If a broken bone protrudes through the skin and there is bleeding, apply a sterile compress—or, for lack of that, a clean hankerchief or cloth—over the bleeding site and press to stop the blood flow. Cover the area with a sterile bandage or clean towel or sheet.

Don't try to clean the wound or straighten the broken arm or leg.

If the victim must be moved in order to get medical attention, use a splint—a straight stick, board, rolled-up newspaper or magazine—to prevent movement of the broken bone.

Make certain the splint is long enough to go beyond joints above and below the break.

Pad the splint, if possible, with any soft objects available, and tie it in place with a belt, necktie, or bandage—snugly but not so tightly as to cut off circulation.

Properly attended to by a physician, even the most severe fracture is likely to heal, although the healing may take a month or more.

HEAD INJURIES

Any head injury deserves careful attention. Even if it seems trivial, it should not be passed over lightly.

Of course, it may be minor.

In a minor injury, there may be quick development of a bump and perhaps brief stunning without loss of consciousness.

You can apply ice to minimize swelling.

If there is a bleeding scalp wound, raising the head and shoulders will help to control the bleeding. Apply a sterile dressing and, when bleeding stops, bandage the dressing to hold it securely in place.

Even if the injury seems minor, it is safest to restrict activity for twenty-four hours. Keep alert, too, for any late-developing signs that may indicate that the injury is more severe than it appeared to be at the beginning. These include increasing lethargy and excessive sleepiness; any difference in the size of the pupils of the eyes; severe and repeated vomiting; irregular, slow and deep breathing; arm or leg muscle weakness; blurring of vision or double vision; persistent or severe headache; drooping eye or mouth.

If any such manifestations appear—even several days after the injury—get immediate medical help.

If you have even the slightest doubt that the injury is minor, medical help should be sought without delay.

Get immediate help if any fluid drains from the nose or ear (a possible indication of skull fracture) or in case of unconsciousness. Until help is available, keep the victim lying down, as quiet as possible.

In case of unconsciousness or any difficulty in breathing, turn the head gently to the side so any blood or other material can drain from the corner of the mouth.

HEAT CRAMPS

Heat cramps are very painful muscle cramps that begin suddenly and most often occur in the muscles that bend the arms and legs, sometimes in the abdominal muscles.

They develop because of profuse sweating and failure to replace the loss of salt that accompanies the sweating during vigorous activity in hot weather.

Often the patient will lie down with legs drawn up, crying out from the severe pain. The skin may be wet and pale.

Although an attack of heat cramps, if untreated, may last for hours, it is not considered dangerous.

Massaging the cramped muscles gently may help relieve the cramps. If not, try pressing firmly.

Also, give the victim salt water immediately—about half a glass containing half a teaspoonful of salt—and every fifteen minutes for an hour or until the cramps are relieved.

HEAT EXHAUSTION

Also known as heat collapse and heat prostration, this condition can result from extended exposure to high heat, especially hot humid heat.

In heat exhaustion, blood circulation to the brain and the heart may be disturbed as the body, in its efforts to cool off, pools a lot of blood in the capillaries of the skin.

Symptoms can include damp, cold, ashen skin; profuse sweating; listlessness; fast and weak pulse; rapid, shallow breathing; sometimes, semiconsciousness or unconsciousness.

Often, there are warning symptoms before an attack actually occurs: weakness, dizziness, nausea, headache, mild muscle cramps, blurring or dimming of vision.

The patient should be helped to lie down, preferably in a cool place. If no cool place is available, applying cool, wet cloths may help. All tight clothing should be loosened.

Sips of cool water containing salt should be given as in heat cramps: a half glassful containing half a teaspoonful of salt every fifteen minutes for an hour.

Most often, heat prostration is fleeting. But if there is

profound collapse, medical attention is needed as soon as possible.

HEATSTROKE (SUNSTROKE)

This is a serious emergency.

Caused by excessive exposure to heat or sun, especially when combined with strenuous activity, it involves a severe disturbance of the body's mechanism for regulating heat.

The skin is hot, dry and flushed, and fever is obvious (the temperature often quickly reaches 105 degrees or higher). The pulse may speed up to 160 beats a minute or more. Breathing may be rapid and deep. The pupils of the eyes may first contract and then dilate. Muscle twitching, cramps, convulsions and forceful vomiting may develop.

There may be early warning symptoms: headache, excessive warmth, malaise. When the attack comes, it usually does so abruptly, with sudden loss of consciousness, convulsions, or delirium.

Because heatstroke can be a serious threat to life, medical attention is needed as soon as possible.

Until a physician arrives, body temperature must be reduced to help prevent brain damage or death.

The patient should be undressed and either placed in a tub of cold water, or covered with continuous cold packs such as wet blankets, or sponged with cold water.

It is critically important to check the temperature rectally every ten minutes and to work to bring the temperature down only to 101 degrees but not lower or it may go on falling to dangerous levels. During the cooling, massage the skin to help return of cooled blood to the heated brain and other body areas.

At 101 degrees, stop the cold applications. If possible, place the patient in a bed in a cool room with fan or air conditioner blowing toward the bed. If temperature starts to rise again, the cooling will need to be repeated.

HEEL PAIN

Heel bruising is common among runners and can represent simple overuse injury.

It may occur in other athletes as well. Sometimes, what is involved is a tear, partial or complete, of the fascia covering muscles on the bottom of the foot and extending from the bottom of the heel bone to the five toes.

One possible cause of a tear is a sudden turn which puts great pressure on the fascia. Shoes can be at fault when they have very stiff soles or inadequate support for the arch of the foot.

Rest is an essential part of treatment. As much as possible, putting weight on the heel should be avoided until healing has occurred. A switch to another form of activity such as swimming to stay in shape may be advisable until full recovery.

Warm soaks and massage may help in treatment.

Prevention of recurrences may require change of shoes or use of sponge rubber, metal or plastic arch supports or other corrective devices.

HEMORRHAGE (See BLEEDING)

LACERATIONS (See CUTS)

MOUTH INJURIES

Small wounds of lip, tongue, or cheek usually heal quickly without serious infection.

If there is bleeding, direct pressure with a sterile gauze dressing usually will control it.

Rinsing the mouth well with a solution containing sodium bicarbonate (bicarbonate of soda) several times a day until healed can be helpful.

If there is a large cut or a gaping wound, suturing may

be required and a physician should be seen as soon as possible.

MUSCLE CRAMPS

These are painful, involuntary contractions of muscle fibers that may last from less than a minute to several hours.

They can affect any athlete, young or old, in any sport.

A muscle injury or strain can produce them. But they also can result from salt deficiency, hyperventilation (over-breathing) which can disturb the body's mineral use, or from inadequate levels of such minerals as potassium and magnesium.

According to some sports medicine physicians, perhaps the most common cause is deficiency of potassium and magnesium.

Often, victims of repeated muscle cramps can benefit from an increased intake of fruits and vegetables which help replace the minerals which may be lost in sizable amounts during vigorous activity.

If cramps continue despite this, a physician should be consulted.

MUSCLE PULLS

In a muscle pull, muscle fibers are torn and there is sudden localized pain. Sprinters are especially likely to suffer a tear in the hamstring muscle in back of the thigh, swimmers in a shoulder muscle.

Any sudden sharp pain in a muscle is a probable indication of fiber tearing and calls for immediate cessation of the activity, otherwise there may be added damage to the fibers and longer time for healing.

Rest is essential in treatment. Elevation of the injured area and the application of ice and compression with an elastic bandage can help. Elevation should be continued for as long as there is any swelling; ice and compression need be continued no longer than twenty-four hours.

Two days after the accident, some sports medicine physicians believe, heat often helps by dilating blood vessels, increasing blood flow and nutrient supply to the injured area, and may possibly speed healing.

Usually, a pulled muscle will heal in less than two weeks, sometimes even within a few days. The younger the victim, as a general rule, the quicker healing is likely to be.

Muscle pulls often can be avoided by attention to adequate warm-up to ready muscles for action. Ten minutes of performing in slow, easy fashion the usual motions involved in the sport, gradually increasing the pace, can do the trick. Also important is to restore flexibility to muscles after hard games by stretching.

MUSCLE SORENESS

Muscle soreness is common.

It usually appears within twenty-four hours of vigorous activity, especially when the activity has involved use of previously little-used muscles.

If the soreness is sharply focused in one area, there is some possibility that the muscle may have been injured to some degree.

More often, the soreness will be diffuse and stems from simple swelling of muscle fibers.

Liniments are used by some athletes. These preparations, which are rubbed on the skin, may help to relieve the soreness to some extent, but they do not speed healing.

Very often, all that is needed on a sore muscle day is to exercise or play at an easier, relaxed pace and, by the following day, the soreness is likely to be greatly reduced or gone.

NAIL INJURIES

When a fingernail or toenail is subjected to a severe blow, the nail not only may become black and blue but there may be intense pain as bleeding occurs under the nail and a blood blister, or hematoma, forms.

Cold compresses should be applied immediately.

If the pain from the hematoma becomes increasingly intense, it may be necessary to get the blood out for relief. A physician can do this. Under some circumstances, it may be desired to do it at home, although it is better by far to have it done in a physician's office or hospital emergency room.

The hand or foot should be cleansed with soap and water.

The head of a straight pin or the tip of a pocket knife should be heated in a flame until it glows or dipped in boiling water for several minutes.

If the hot pin or knife tip is then carefully pressed— perhaps with some turning in a kind of drilling motion—into the center of the blood accumulation through the nail, taking care not to penetrate into underlying tissue, the tiny hole will release pressure and allow the blood to ooze out. There is likely to be quick relief of pain.

Apply a sterile dressing over the area.

NECK PAIN

Any injury to the neck sustained in sports should have medical attention.

Neck injuries may occur because of sudden snaps, violent twists, and overexertion.

Most commonly, the neck muscles go into spasm, or involuntary contraction, and movement becomes painful.

But there is a possibility of injury to upper vertebrae in the spinal column which could be serious unless given prompt expert attention.

When the injury is found to involve only strain of neck muscles or sprain of ligaments, ice massage may be used to begin with. And gentle motion during the massage may be advised.

After a few days, heat treatments such as hot packs or baths, may be used, sometimes alternated with cold applications.

With beginning of improvement, the physician may prescribe a program of exercises to restore normal motion. Sometimes, a neck brace may be needed for a time.

With recovery, exercises to strengthen neck muscles as a help in preventing recurrences may be recommended, possibly using a head harness to which weights can be attached to provide resistance to neck movements and help in the muscle strengthening.

NOSEBLEED

This is a common, usually minor, problem that may result not only from getting hit in the nose during play, but in some cases from blowing the nose too vigorously.

For treatment, the patient should be seated leaning forward. If, for any reason, the patient can't lean forward and must lie down, head and shoulders should be raised.

Gently but firmly place thumb and forefinger on each side of the lower end of the nose and press together. The pressure should be maintained for ten minutes or more and repeated if necessary. Cold compresses or ice packs can be applied at the same time to the bridge of the nose or above the nose.

If bleeding persists—or if the blood is bright red and profuse, indicating injury to an artery—maintain pressure until a physician or hospital emergency room can be reached.

PUNCTURE WOUND

A puncture is an open wound that may be caused by any sharp object such as a pin, nail or tack. The opening may be small and often there is little bleeding and the very lack of bleeding may increase the chance of infection.

Press—don't squeeze—around the wound to encourage bleeding to help remove any contamination.

If the wound should bleed on its own, allow it to do so enough to wash out the contamination unless blood gushes out indicating that an artery is injured, in which case, apply pressure to stop the bleeding.

After washing your hands thoroughly, check the wound for any foreign object. If there is one, remove it; otherwise a physician must do so.

Use soap and warm water to clean around the wound, then cover with sterile dressing. Warm water soaks several times a day will help keep the puncture open so microorganisms and debris can drain out.

No matter how minor the wound may seem, consult your physician by phone about possible need for an antibiotic and a tetanus shot.

SHOCK

Shock—the medical kind rather than the electrical—involves depression of vital functions of various body organs because of disturbance in blood circulation.

Sometimes life-threatening shock may follow a severe injury such as crushing of chest or abdomen, fracture of a large bone, or other extensive or very painful injury. It is also associated with loss of large amounts of blood, allergic reactions, infections and many severe illnesses.

The signs and symptoms include: paleness of the skin which also may be cold and sometimes moist; breathing which usually is rapid and shallow but sometimes may be deep and irregular; thirst, nausea and vomiting; weak and rapid pulse (usually over 100); restlessness, excitement and anxiety which may later change to mental dullness and still later to unconsciousness.

Even when shock symptoms are not evident, it is wise for any seriously injured patient to be treated for it to help prevent its possible development.

Treatment may include many or all of the following measures:

Have the injured patient lie down and cover with a blanket only heavy enough to maintain normal body temperature. Too much heat, as it increases surface temperature of the body, may transfer too much blood from vital organs to the skin.

Elevate the patient's legs about twelve inches to help blood flow to heart and head. But do NOT do this if there is a head or chest injury or breathing difficulty. If there is a head injury, the head should be at the same level or higher than the body.

If the patient is unconscious or has facial injuries, place on the side to permit fluids to drain from mouth and nose.

If there is any bleeding, control it with the measures noted under BLEEDING.

Give fluids—but NOT if the patient is unconscious, drowsy, or convulsing, and not if there is a puncture or crush wound in the abdomen or any possible indication of brain injury. Use lukewarm water containing one teaspoonful of salt and half a teaspoonful of baking soda (bicarbonate) to each quart of water. For an adult, half a glass every fifteen minutes may be used; for a child, about two ounces.

Get medical help as soon as possible. It may be necessary for a physician to administer fluids by vein, transfuse blood, and treat the condition which led to shock.

STIFF NECK

Especially in a healthy young athlete, this is likely to be a mild disorder involving a muscle cramp resulting from unusual exercise or activity, a sudden neck twist, a chill, or sleeping in a cramped position.

Hot wet packs, hot showers, and massage, along with aspirin usually suffice. If the stiffness persists, a doctor should be consulted.

SPRAIN

A sprain is an injury to soft tissues around a joint. A ligament holding the joint together is stretched and sometimes may be partially or completely torn. Muscles, tendons and blood vessels may also be affected.

The most common sprains in sports are of ankles and knees in basketball and football, of elbows in tennis, and of knees in high jumping. But sprains can occur in many other sports and may involve fingers and wrists.

With a sprain, there is likely to be swelling, tenderness, pain on motion and, in some cases, skin discoloration over an extensive area because of the rupture of small blood vessels and bleeding under the skin.

Even a physician may have difficulty distinguishing between a sprain and a fracture without an X ray. So if a sprain seems severe—and certainly if you have any reason to suspect there may be a fracture—handle the problem as you would a fracture (see FRACTURE).

If you believe the problem is a sprain and not a severe one, rest and elevate the injured part and apply cold compresses to minimize swelling.

The cold will also help constrict blood vessels and minimize or stop any bleeding.

There should be no walking if an ankle or knee is affected. For a wrist or elbow sprain, place the arm in a sling.

Keep a mildly sprained area at rest and elevated for at least a full day and keep up the cold compresses during much of that time. Even if the sprain seemed mild to begin with, get medical help if swelling and pain persist.

STRAIN

A strain is a muscle injury, usually the result of overexertion. Muscle fibers are stretched and sometimes may be partially torn.

Muscles of the back tend to be strained more often than those of the thigh and leg.

There is likely to be sharp pain or cramp. Other symptoms may include pain on movement and stiffness which tend to increase after several hours. The muscle also may become swollen and there may be some discoloration if vessels have been injured and blood escapes into the tissues.

The injured area should be kept at rest in a position comfortable for the patient. Hot compresses will help to relax the muscle spasms. Gentle massage in the direction of the heart will stimulate circulation and may help to relieve pain and reduce stiffness.

Sometimes, it is difficult to distinguish between a strain and a sprain. In that case, many authorities believe that it is best to treat the injury as a sprain for twenty-four to forty-eight hours.

STITCHES IN THE SIDE

These sudden, sharp pains that occur in the right upper part of the abdomen below the last rib are a form of muscle cramp.

One common cause is distention of the large bowel with gas. It's natural for gas to form in the intestinal tract and for the gas to be pushed along by intestinal contractions to the rectum where in due course it can be released. Because vigorous activity often tends to speed up the intestinal contractions, it is not uncommon for athletes to pass gas during play.

But if a hard stool should block the gas, the large bowel can become distended and a stitch is felt.

A stitch sometimes can be relieved by pushing fingers into the painful area and bending forward and exhaling.

If stitches occur frequently, a change of diet may help prevent them. The change should be in the direction of less starchy foods and more vegetables and fruits.

Stitches also may sometimes result from eating shortly before exercise, or from milk or wheat intolerance. According to some reports, there are athletes who may have milk or wheat intolerance and who develop cramps only with vigorous exercise within twenty-four hours after eating such foods.

Avoidance of eating for several hours before exercise can be tried. If that doesn't help, a trial of avoiding milk for a few days may help. If that fails, a trial of wheat avoidance may be in order.

SWIMMER'S EAR

Anyone who does much swimming is five times as likely as others to get ear canal infections—a problem so common among swimmers that it is often called "swimmer's ear."

The condition is marked by itching and pain. Another indication: tenderness when the ear lobe is pulled or the jaw is rocked from side to side.

Medical attention is needed. Although often considered a minor problem, the infection sometimes may move inward, affecting balance and hearing, and may spread to the brain.

Effective treatment may require use of antibiotics, alcohol to dry the moisture, acetic acid to restore the protective acid mantle in the ear.

The ear infection is preventable.

A critical factor is water, often contaminated, left in the ear canals. To counter that, one or more simple measures can be used:

Dry the canals after diving or swimming. Shaking the head vigorously or jumping with the head tilted to one side can help remove any trapped water, and fanning the ear canal openings will help in the drying. A hair dryer can be especially effective. Do NOT use cotton-tipped applicators either to dry the canals or remove ear wax. They may abrade the canal lining, making it more susceptible to bacteria and may remove the protective wax coating of the canals.

Recently, in *The Physician and Sports Medicine*, Dr. John H. Sampson of Long Beach, California, has reported that a simple, low-cost, readily available ear solution has completely controlled swimmer's ear in his practice.

The solution consists of thirty drops of white vinegar added to one ounce of boiled water. After swimming, Dr. Sampson recommends to his patients, two drops of the cooled solution should be placed in each ear.

TENDONITIS

Tendons are the strong fibrous bands that attach muscles to bones.

In tendonitis, a tendon becomes inflamed. Sometimes, this may occur in connection with diseases such as rheumatoid arthritis, gout and even elevated blood cholesterol levels. But more commonly, especially among healthy athletic youngsters, it results from strain and may be especially likely to occur when muscles are tight and keep pulling on the tendons.

The site of tendonitis varies with different sports. In tennis, the elbow is most often affected; in baseball and swimming, the shoulder; in basketball, soccer, football and other sports involving running, the most common site is the Achilles tendon which attaches the calf muscle to the back of the heel bone.

There is likely to be at least localized tenderness. It may be severe and associated with disabling pain on movement.

Commonly, tendonitis is marked by a peculiarity: pain, which may be intense early in the day, often lessens later in the day and may be especially likely to do so when the tendon is put to use. That can be detrimental if it causes the young athlete to go right back to the activity that led to the tendonitis in the first place.

An important element of treatment for tendonitis is to

stop all vigorous activity involving the affected tendon. A youngster wanting to stay in shape can try a substitute activity—for example, swimming instead of running or tennis.

Cold applications may help. And aspirin may be useful.

After several days when the pain is gone or almost gone, a start can be made toward correcting the muscle tightness which may have paved the way for the tendonitis. For that what is needed is stretching of the muscle—not quick or jerky, but rather slow and gentle, holding the stretched position for half a minute or longer.

It's possible to go another route: get an injection into the tendon of a steroid or cortisone-type drug. That may stop the pain all right. But many sports medicine specialists strongly advise against it because some studies indicate that the injections may weaken the tendon and may later lead to tendon rupture when activity is resumed.

TENDON RUPTURE

A tendon rupture can involve a tear in the tendon itself or a separation from either a bone or muscle.

The immediate cause usually is a sudden, violent contraction. Here, as with tendonitis, the most likely victim is one with excessively tight muscles.

Along with agonizing pain, a rupture often produces an audible popping sound. Pain usually persists for days and a large black-and-blue mark is likely to appear after a day or so because of broken blood vessels and bleeding into the tissues.

Medical attention is needed. Until it is available, apply ice, compression, and elevation.

Often, a tendon reattaches itself within a few weeks as it sends out fibrous filaments. Occasionally, however, the tendon may have withdrawn too far for reattachment to occur naturally and surgery may be required.

TENNIS ELBOW

This painful strain of the wrist-moving muscles of the forearm near where they attach to the humerus, the bone of the upper arm, at the elbow can be disabling.

It's a common problem, particularly among less experienced players.

According to a study by Dr. Robert P. Nirschl, chief of orthopedic surgery at Northern Virginia Doctors Hospital, Arlington, an experienced player usually uses the power source of shoulder muscles as well as body weight force in swinging a racket, thereby reducing strain on the elbow. The inexperienced player, on the other hand, often tends to rely on the power force of the forearm, which transmits considerable strain to the elbow, especially in backhand strokes.

The type of racket used also may be a factor. Metal rackets, particularly stainless steel alloys, Dr. Nirschl reports, tend to apply the least force against the elbow when the racket is swung. He also recommends a stringing tension not greater than fifty pounds.

Another study by Dr. James D. Priest of Stanford University Hospital, Stanford, California, suggests similarly that use of a steel or aluminum racket—and, in addition, of a two-handed rather than one-handed backhand stroke—may make for the best chance of avoiding tennis elbow.

Treatment must include rest. Icing the painful area with cubes or crushed ice in a plastic bag, and wrapping the area with an elastic bandage, may help. The ice can be kept on for about twenty minutes at a time and the procedure can be repeated several times a day to minimize pain and inflammation.

In severe cases, an injection of a local anesthetic such as procaine followed by injection of hydrocortisone may bring relief.

What can be done to avoid recurrences?

These recommendations come from Drs. Nirschl and

Priest and from other orthopedists, all of them tennis players and researchers in the field.

Before going on the court do some brief exercises. Reach with arms high and wide, bend, stretch legs, and jog in place for a few minutes.

Wear a warm-up suit or sweater until the body is warmed. Keep the elbow warm by wearing a Neoprene bandage (which also helps hold the joint firm), or an elastic band or even an old sock.

Use light balls, not any of the pressureless type.

Avoid carrying any heavy objects at any time with palms facing the body. Instead, carry them in the arms whenever possible, with palms up.

Daily exercises to strengthen muscles extending from elbow to hand can be of great help.

One valuable exercise involves placing the forearm on a table or on the knee, hanging the hand over the edge with palm down, then moving the hand up and down, putting the wrist through the greatest possible range of motion. Repeat with palm up.

After three days or so of doing this exercise fifty times, three times a day, do it with a two- or three-pound dumbbell and in due course, as the muscles strengthen, with even heavier weights.

Another useful exercise: with both hands on a broom handle, try to twist in opposing directions.

Certainly, not least of all, for a young novice who develops tennis elbow—and even, for that matter, for an older one—a few tennis lessons with emphasis on proper grip and stroking can help reduce the likelihood of repeated attacks as well as improve the game.

TOOTH, KNOCKED OUT

A permanent tooth which is knocked out often can be reimplanted successfully if prompt action is taken.

There is a period of about six hours during which the

outer periodontal tissue can survive and permit reimplantation. And if reimplantation can be done within half an hour, even the interior pulp may survive.

A dentist should be seen as quickly as possible. If there is any delay, put the tooth back into the socket. If that doesn't work, put it in a container of water or wrap in a well-soaked cloth (add a little salt to the water) and get to the dentist.

Keeping the tooth moist is important.

INDEX

Abrasions (scrapes), treatment
for, 234–35
Acidosis, 116, 119
Acne, effect of steroids on, 139,
146
Adaptation of body to demands
on it, 99
Adult sports, most popular, 85
See also lifetime sports
Aerobic exercises, 22
American Alliance for Health,
Physical Education, and
Recreation (AAHPER), 94–98
Youth Fitness Test, 96–98
American Academy of Pediatrics:
on coed sports, 36–37
on drugs and sports, 143–44
on fitness in the preschool
child, 17–19
on girls and sports, 36–37
on skateboards, 206–07

on sports for children with
heart problems, 21–23
on sports for children with
skeletal abnormalities,
27–29
on sports for mentally
retarded, 29–31
on use of sedatives, 149
on use of steroids, 145
American College of Sports
Medicine, 146, 153
American Medical Association
(AMA):
on asthmatic children,
needless restrictions, 23–24
recommendations on sports
with various illnesses,
31–32
on relationship of physical
activity to obesity, 9–10
on sports for epileptics, 25

Amino acids, 113, 114, 133
Amphetamines, 146–48
    dangers of, 147
    effect on fatigue, 147
    effect on judgment, 147–48
    See also Stimulants
Anabolic steroids. See Steroids
Androgens. See male sex
    hormones
Antibodies, 113
Anti-inflammatory agents, 150
Anxiety, 7–8
Archery, 14
Arteries, 230
Arthritis as result of excessive
    pitching, 3
Association for Intercollegiate
    Athletics for Women, 35
Asthma:
    effect of exercise on, 24
    effect on sports activities,
    23–24
    exercise-induced, 24, 215
    sports for asthmatic children,
    24, 215
Asthma medications, 24
Asthmatic Athlete, The (AMA), 23
Atherosclerosis, 19
Athlete's foot, treatment for,
    235–36
Athletes, professional, medical
    care of, 156
Athletic abilities:
    hereditary factors, 87–92
    girls vs. boys at various ages,
    42–43
Athletic activities/sports
    categories (mild/moderate/
    vigorous), 27
Attitudes and habits taught by
    sports, 69–70

Badminton, 14, 175–76

injuries common to, 176
Balance, differences between
    male and female, 44
Barbiturates, use of, 149
Baseball, 14, 176–79
    equipment for, 177
    history of, 176–77
    injuries common in, 64–65, 67,
    177–79
Baseball Hall of Fame, 176
Basketball, 14
    development of basic skills,
    82–83
    for girls, 179–80
    injuries common in, 67,
    179–80, 212
    size as factor in, 179
Bicycle:
    choosing suitable, 181–83
    maintaining, 183–84
Bicycling, 18, 85, 181–84
    high injury rate of, 181–82
    number of participants, 181
    safety rules for, 181–83
    and weight-loss program, 135
Biomechanics, 157
Black eyes, treatment for, 236
Bleeding, control of, 236–38, 251
    direct pressure, 237, 246
    elevation, 237
    pressure points, 237–38
    tourniquet, 238
Blisters, treatment for, 239
Blood, 229–30
    components, 229
Blood doping (blood transfusion),
    148–49
Blood fat levels, 139
    in children, 5
    effect of vigorous activity on, 6
    as risk factor in heart disease,
    11
Blood pressure, elevated

(hypertension):
effect of exercise on, 22
forbidden activities/sports with, 22
in high school students, 5
as risk factor in heart disease, 11
Blood sugar levels, 11
Blood vessels, types of, 230
Body build, male vs. female, 39–41
difference in height, weight by age group, 41
Body fluid balance, 132, 167
altering, 130
Body heat, dissipation of, 59
Body response to imposed load, 17. See also "SAID principle"
Bone meal tablets, 110
Bones:
broken, 47, 233
composition and structure, 226
growing, 3, 133
Boston marathon, 46
Boxing, 184–85
equipment for, 185
Breakfast, importance of, 125
Breasts, injury to, 49
Breathing/heart pumping response to exercise, 58–59
Breathlessness, 59
Bronchospasm, relief of, 24
Bruises (contusions), treatment of, 239
"Burnout" of young athlete, 76
Bursitis, 239–40
treatment, 240
See also Tennis elbow
Butazolidin (bute), 150
Butkus, Dick, 155
Button, Richard T. (Dick), 200

Byrd, Ronald, 93, 138

Calcium, 110, 112, 138
food sources, 123
Calories, 131–34
for athletes, 110, 124–25
average daily requirements, 10, 128
burning of, 115, 117
for weight reduction, 133–34
Capillaries, 230–31
Carbohydrates, 115–19
body storage of, 117
food sources, 124, 126
metabolism of, 115–16
in pregame meal, 126
as source of immediate energy, 126, 133
Cardiopulmonary efficiency, 19
Cardiovascular disease/problems, effect of sports on, 17, 31
Cardiovascular endurance capacity, girls vs. boys, 42
Cardiovascular fitness, 19, 22, 67
sports which promote, 67
Casts, fiberglass and plastic, 157
Cereals and breads in diet, 124, 133
Chest injury, 240
Chest pain, 13
Childbearing and pregnancy, effect of sports on, 36
Chin-ups, 101
Cholesterol, 5, 11–12, 115, 119, 123
Coaches, 77–81
attitude toward sports officials, 78
intimidation of players by, 78
lack of nutritional knowledge, 109, 112, 127
Coaches, women, 48
Coaching attitudes and

philosophies, 62, 78–79,
81–83, 90–92
for girls, 36, 48
See also Winning,
overemphasis on
Coed sports/teams, 36–37, 46,
82
Cold, when to apply to injury,
233–34
Collision sports, 31, 186
contraindications for, 32
epileptics and, 25–26
girls and, 36
Competitive sports too early,
effect of, 53, 72
Concussion. *See* Head injuries
Conditioning, 89, 93–107, 130,
133, 150, 159
effect on muscle mass and
strength, 129, 139
for girls/women, 36, 48, 180
importance of, 65, 177, 180
principles of, 99–106
progression, reaching a
plateau, 100–01
for specific sports, 101–03
and weight loss, 135
Consumer Products Safety
Commission:
on baseball injuries, 177–78
on football injuries, 186
on hockey eye injuries, 199
on ice skating safety, 201–02
on injury rates in gymnastics,
191
on safety rules for
skateboarding, 207
on selecting, maintaining a
bicycle, 182–83
on skateboard-related injuries,
205
on trampoline safety, 192–93

Contact sports, 31, 66
contraindications for, 64
and epileptics, 26
Convulsive disorders and sports,
32
Cooling down after workout,
importance of, 106, 205
Cooper, Dr. Donald L., 110, 115,
125, 127, 163–64
Cortisone, 150
use in tendonitis, 257–58
Cramps and stiffness, causes of,
106, 116, 127
Cross-country (running), 14, 219
Curve ball throwing, abolishing
for children and adoles-
cents, 64, 74, 176
Cuts (lacerations), treatment for,
241
Cycling. *See* Bicycling
Czonka, Larry, 156

Dairy products in diet, 123
Dehydration, 114, 121, 167
effect of, 130–31
Diabetes, 11, 31
Diarrhea, 108, 114
Diet, 132, 133, 137
effect on performance,
110–11, 171
high-carbohydrate, 117
high-fat, 115, 132, 139
high-protein, 115, 132
low-carbohydrate, 117
Diet, well-balanced, 108, 111–12,
122–24, 133, 139–40
Diet for weight loss, 134
Digestion, 113, 126, 132
Dislocations, treatment for, 241
Diuretic drugs, 130
Drive for achievement, male vs.
female, 44

Drugs as athletic aids, 141–50

Eggs in diet, 123
Elbow, exercises to strengthen,
    102
Endurance, 13, 60, 214
    development of, 8, 67
Enzymes, 113, 117, 120
Epilepsy, effect on sports
        participation, 25–27
    restricted sports, 25–26
Epiphyseal injuries/abnormalities,
    28, 63–65
Ergogenic aids, 143–44
Estrogen, 41, 57
Evert, Chris, 34, 39
Exercise, 58–62
    during dieting, 135
    effect of, 9–10, 22, 145,
        195–96
    and the heart, 10–13
    importance of, 4–5
    and weight control, 8–10, 135
Exercise physiology, 157–58, 162
Exercises, preski, 209–10
Eye injuries, 65, 199, 214

Face protectors/masks, 179, 213
Facial injuries, 65, 197–99, 252
Fad diets, 132–33
Fascia, 228, 246
Fat, percentage of total body
        weight, 50, 118, 129, 130,
        161
Fatigue, 7–8, 17, 19, 116
    effect of amphetamines on,
        146
    effect of B vitamins on, 120
    psychological elements of, 8
Fats:
    amount in diet, 118, 140
    food sources, 118

metabolism of, 115, 118–19
role in heart disease, 119, 123
as source of stored energy,
    118–19, 133
Fear of failure, 91
Fish in diet, 123
Fitness testing, 94–99
Flexed-arm hang, 95
Flexibility, 103–04, 164, 190–91
Fluids:
    loss during exercise, 168–69
    requirements, 110, 127–28
Food fads, 109–12
Food groups, basic, 123–24,
    132–34
Food supplements, 110–11
Foods, high salt, 136–37
Football, 65, 69, 185–89
    deaths due to, 186–87
    injuries common in, 65, 67,
        186–88, 212
Fracture (bone break), 47–48
    treatment for, 242
Fructose, 117, 127
Fruits in diet, 123–24, 127, 133

Garrick, Dr. James G., 46–47
Genitourinary infection, 31
Gillette, Joan V., 47, 49
Girls and sports, 33–52, 66–68
    abilities vs. boys, 37–46
    injuries, 46–50
    number involved in, 34–35
Glucose, 117, 126–27
Glycogen, 103, 117
Golf, 189–90
Grana, Dr. William A., 62, 64, 66,
    179, 180
Growth and development, 56–58,
    133, 138, 161–62
    boy/girl differences, 56–57
    effect of steroids on, 139

growth spurts, 41, 56, 57
  individual variations, 57–58
Gymnastics, 190–95
  high injury rate, 65–66, 191
  injuries common in, 47, 67,
    195, 212

Hammer throwers, 88–89
Handball, 195–97
Handicapped, sports for, 16,
  214–15
Havlicek, John, 84
Head injuries, 25
  breathing difficulties after, 243
  late-developing symptoms,
    243
Head and neck injuries in
  football, 186–87, 189
Heart, athlete's, 12, 165
Heart disease/attacks, 19
  risk factors in, 5–6, 11, 139
  role of diet in, 119
Heart disease in children, effect
  on sports activities, 5–6,
  20–23
Heart surgery, sports after, 31
Heat, when to apply to injury,
  233–34
Heat cramps, 243–44
Heat exhaustion, 131, 244–45
Heatstroke (sunstroke), 131, 147,
  169, 246
Heel pain, 246
Hemophilia, sports activity and,
  32
Hepatitis, 31, 149
Hernia, 32
Hockey, common injuries in, 65,
  199
Hormones, 57, 113
Horsepower capacity of human
  body, 8

Hyperventilating, 216

Ice hockey, 14, 197–99
  common injuries in, 197
Ice skating, 199–201
Infection, 31, 226, 231
Injuries, 4, 13–16, 167–68
  by age groups, 63
  body response to, 231–32
  to male/female genitalia, 47,
    49
  to preadolescents, 62–68
  prevention/reduction, 49, 73,
    160
  professional athletes vs.
    school athletes, 8, 73
  requiring physician, 47–48,
    225–26
  by specific sport, 47–48,
    64–66
  types/rates for girls, boys,
    46–50, 180
Iron, 120–24
  absorption of, 112
  deficiency in girls/women, 121
  food sources, 121, 123–24
Isometric exercises, 22

Jaundice, 31
Jenner, Bruce, 89
Jogging. See Running
Joints, 99, 226–27
Journal of the American Medical
  Association (JAMA), 47–48,
  108, 131, 134, 169–70

Ketosis, 118–19
Kidney disease, 11, 31
Kidney function, 115–16
King, Billie Jean, 39, 49
Klissouras, Dr. Vassilis, 87–88
Korbut, Olga, 34, 190

Kraft, Eve F., 53–55

Lacrosse, 14
Lactose, 116
Leukocytes (white cells), 230–32
Lifetime sports, 85, 166, 176, 203, 214
Ligaments, 227
Lighthouse Boys' Club Baseball Program, 73–75
Liniments, 169, 148
Lipoproteins, 11–12
Little League baseball:
  injuries, 178
    "Little League elbow," 58, 65, 177
    limits on pitching, 64–65
    number of participants, 69
    objectives of, 72
Little League football, 185
  injury rates, 188
Local anesthetic, 149–50, 157, 170, 258
Losing, attitude toward, 71
Low blood sugar, 127, 165
Lymph and lymphatics, 230–31
Lynn, Janet, 24

Magnesium, 110
Making weight, 129–40
Male sex hormones (androgens), 41, 60, 138–39, 144
Malnutrition, 138, 145
Maltose, 116
Manganese, 110
Marathon runners, 42, 53
  diet for, 117
  women, 45–46
Massage, 144, 164
Maturation, sexual, 138
  age for, male/female, 41, 56–57

effect on speed and power, 60, 93–94
effect of steroids on, 145–46
Maximal oxygen uptake, 42, 87–88
Mayer, Dr. Jean, 9, 110–11, 115, 125, 127–28
Meals, 125–27
  pregame, 126–27
Meat in diet, 123, 133
Menstruation, 36, 121
  cessation of, 50
  effect of exercise during, 49–50
  effect on performance, 50
Mentally retarded children and physical fitness, 29–31
Midget football programs, 185, 188
Milk in diet, 110, 113, 123
Minerals, 119, 133
  food sources, 120–21, 123–24
  role of, 120–21
Moretz, Dr. Alfred, 67, 179, 180
Motor skills, 42–43, 60
Mouth injuries, treatment of, 246–47
Muscle cramps, 243–44, 247
Muscle fibers, 102, 226–28, 248, 253
Muscle mass, 36, 134, 139
Muscle pulls/strains, 163–64
  treatment of, 247–48, 253–54
Muscles, 60, 104, 115, 227–28
  development of, 162, 191
  effect of conditioning, 8, 99, 100, 106, 139

Nail injuries, treatment of, 248–49
National Football League (NFL), 150, 156
  injury rate in, 186

Neck pain, 249–50
Neck, stiff, 252
Nerves, motor/sensory, 229
Nervous system, 60, 105
    effect of amphetamines on,
        147
Noncontact sports, 31–32, 191
North Carolina sports medicine
    program, 159–60
Nosebleed, treatment for, 250
Nutrition, 108–28, 159

Obesity, 5, 9, 11, 19, 64
Organized athletics, positive and
    negative values, 69–86
Orthopedic injuries, 67–68
Overexertion, 147
Overloading of body capacity,
    100
Overorganization of sports by
    adults, 61–62
Overtraining, 103, 163
Oxygen, 115, 117, 216
    inhalation of, 143–44
    requirements, 58–59, 87–88

Pain, 147, 157, 170, 233
Pain-killers, use of, 149
Paralysis due to injury, 186–87,
    191
Parents:
    influence of, 62, 80–81
    involvement in sports program,
        82, 84
    pressure from, 79–81, 84
    youngster's anxiety to please,
        54
Peewee football, 188–89
Pentathlon, 14, 142
Performance analysis, 157–59
Phosporus, 110, 112, 133
Physical examination for sports,
    106–07

Physical fitness values of
    individual sports, 85–86
Physician and Sportsmedicine,
    The (Hale), 61, 178, 180,
        189, 256
Physique types, 57–58
Pitching:
    injuries due to excessive, 3,
        73–75
    recommended limitations, 65,
        74, 177
Potassium, 103, 110, 121
    food sources, 120–21
Poultry in diet, 123
Practice, 96
    excessive, 76–77, 177
    injuries during, 180, 187
Preadolescents, 53–68, 72
    and football, 188–89
    suitable sports for, 66–68
Pregame meal, 115–16, 126–27
Preschool child and sports,
    17–19
President's Council on Physical
    Fitness and Sports, 9, 10,
        85, 181, 201–02, 207, 213,
        215
Pressure points to control
    bleeding, 237–38
Pressure to win, 15, 72, 75–77,
    79
Princeton Community Tennis
    Program, 54–55
Protective head gear, 186–88,
    199
Protein, 108, 112–16, 123, 133
    digestion and metabolism of,
        115–16, 127
    excessive, 108, 114
    food sources, 113–14, 117,
        123–24
    requirements, 114–15
Protein supplements, 108, 114

Puberty. *See* Maturation, sexual
Pull-ups, 95
Pulse rates, 12–13
Puncture wound, treatment for, 250–51
Push-ups, 95, 101
    for girls, 95

Racquetball, 102
Reaction times, male vs. female, 44
Rehabilitation after injury, 155–57, 159–60, 167
Reinforcement, importance of, 92
Respiratory infection, 31
Restrictions on sports activity, valid reasons for, 21–22
Rheumatic fever, 26, 31
Rheumatoid arthritis, 28
Roller skating, 201–03
    injuries common in, 202–03
Rubberized warm-up suit, 130, 167
Runners, 89, 158
    programs for beginners, 204–05
Running, 7, 85, 203–05
    common injuries in, 205
    conditioning for, 102
    importance of warm-up/cool-down with, 106, 205
    shoes, clothing for, 204–05
Running high jump, 95–96

"SAID principle," 17
Salt:
    effect of loss, 244
    food sources, 127, 136–37
Salt tablets, 121, 127
Scholarships, athletic, 34–35, 185
Sedatives (downers), 144, 149
Sedentary life style, effect of, 11, 51

Seizures, epileptic, 25–26
Self-confidence, 89, 91
    developed through sports, 5, 34, 52
Self-discipline, 5, 70
Sex hormones, 41, 57
Shin splints, 164–65
Shock, 251–52
    treatment, 252
Shot put, 219
    men's, 43, 142
    women's, 38, 43
Shuttle run, 96
Sit-ups, 44, 94
Skateboarding, 205–07
    injuries, high rate of, 205–07
    safety rules for, 206–07
Skeletal abnormalities, effect on sports participation, 27–29
Skiing, 18, 207–11
    common injuries in, 158, 209, 211
Skin, 115, 228–29
Skin-fat fold measurements, 129, 140
Smoking, 11
Snacks, calorie count of, 134–35
Soccer, 211–12
    low injury rate of, 65, 67, 170–71, 212
    plays involving the head, 170–71
Sodium, 119, 120–21
Softball, 212–13
    injuries common in, 177–78, 213
Special Olympics, The, 30–31
Splinters, removal of, 234–35
Splints, 242
Sports, 13–15
    categories of, 31
    function/purpose, 45, 61, 72
    most popular, 166

positive values of, 4–13
Sportsmanship, 69, 71, 77,
    82–83, 144
Sports medicine, 32, 63, 142,
    151–60
    application/functions of, 15–17,
    159–60
    history of, 151–53
    Soviet/Eastern Europe,
    152–54
    United States, 154–56
Sports officials, attitude toward,
    78, 82, 84
Sports physicians, 71, 151
    finding one, 172
    training of, 152–53, 159
Spotter, role of in gymnastics,
    192, 194
Sprain, treatment of, 253
Sprints/sprinting, 95, 101, 102,
    177
Squash, 213–14
Standing broad jump, 44
Standing long jump, 95
Starches, 110, 116–17
    food sources, 116
Steroids, 138–39, 142–146
    dangers/side effects, 139, 144,
    146
    disqualifications due to, 142
    effect on girls/women, 139
    medical uses for, 145, 257–58
Stimulants, use of, 142, 144–46
Stitch in side, 254–55
Strength, 18, 102
    male vs. female, 40–42
Stretching, 104, 164
Stretching exercises, 104–06,
    163–64, 205, 216
Sucrose, 116
Sugars, 116
Sweating, 59, 122, 127, 130, 167
Swimmer's ear, 255–56

Swimming, 14, 18, 38, 214–16
    conditioning for, 102
    effect on growth and
    development, 161
    low injury rate of, 65, 67–68,
    216
Swimming, competitive, 37–38
    endurance (long-distance), 38,
    43, 215
    women vs. men, 43, 45,
    215–16
Synovial fluid/membrane, 227

Table tennis, 14
Tackling, dangers of, 188
Team sports vs. individual sports,
    15, 67
Teeth, loss of, 198
    reimplantation, care of tooth
    for, 259–60
Tendonitis, 256–57
Tendon rupture, 257
Tendons, 228
Tennis, 9, 14, 39, 85
    age to start, 54
    conditioning for, 101–02, 217,
    259
    warm-up for, 105–06
Tennis elbow, 217, 258–59
Tetanus shot, 235, 251
Thirst, 122, 168
Title IX of Education
    Amendments Act, 35
"Tomboys," 35, 47
Torg, Dr. Joseph S., 61, 73–74,
    155–56, 186–87
Tourniquet, 238
Track and field, 14, 38, 217–19
Trampoline, 66, 191–95
    injuries common with, 191–92
    safety check list for, 193
Tranquilizers, 7, 149
Tuberculosis, 25, 31

Tutko, Dr. Thomas, 71–72, 79
Twins, athletic accomplishments
        compared, 87–88

Ultrasonic devices, 144, 157
Urine, 119–22

Vegetables in diet, 123–24, 133
Vitamins, 120, 122–23, 133
    absorption of, 118, 133
    amounts needed, 120
    excretion of, 119–20
    food sources, 117, 123–24
Vitamin supplements, 110, 120
Volleyball, 9, 219–20
Vomiting, induced, 130

Wall push-ups, 104, 164–65
Warm-up periods, 96, 105–06,
        216
    importance of, 24, 205
Water, 121–22, 136
    drinking during sports
        activities, 122, 168
Water retention, avoiding, 136–37
Weigh-in, the, 130, 135–38
Weight, gaining, 138–40
Weight lifters, 144–45
Weight lifting, 14, 40, 42, 66, 102,
        177

contraindications, 22
    for women, 162
Weight loss:
    during vigorous activity, 13,
        196
    harmful methods, 130–31, 221
    sound methods, 10, 131–35
Weight loss diet, 134
Wilkens, Lenny, 77–78
Wind knocked out, 166
Winning, overemphasis on,
        15–16, 70–78, 111
    effect on children, 15
    as factor in injuries, 73–75
    proper perspective on, 81–84
Women athletes, attitudes toward
        competing with men, 45–46
Workouts, 90, 204
    progression of strenuousness
        in, 100–01, 103
Wrestling, 14, 221
    common injuries in, 65, 221
    making weight, 129–30, 135

YMCA sports programs, 65,
        82–84, 94, 196
Youth Basketball Association
        (YBA), 82–84

Zinc, 110, 112